MW00331365

Heartbeats:
The Insider's Guide to Israel

A Nonconventional Anthology
by Leading Tour Educators

Ya'acov Fried

Gilad Peled

Yishay Shavit

Editor
Amnon Jackont

Cover illustration: Erez Aharon

English version Editor: Sorelle Weinstein

Cover Design: Leah Ben Avraham/Noonim Graphics

ISBN: 978-965-7023-77-8

1 3 5 7 9 8 6 4 2

Gefen Publishing House Ltd.   **Gefen Books**
6 Hatzvi Street   c/o Baker & Taylor Publisher Services
Jerusalem 9438614,   30 Amberwood Parkway
Israel   Ashland, Ohio 44805
972-2-538-0247   516-593-1234
orders@gefenpublishing.com   orders@gefenpublishing.com

www.gefenpublishing.com

Printed in Israel

Library of Congress Control Number: 2021909743

Contents

Geopolitics

Communities

Jews and Judaism

Vision and Reality

THE PRESIDENT

Jerusalem, July 6, 2021

To: Gilad Peled,
Ya'acov Fried,
Yishay Shavit

Dear Gilad, Ya'acov, and Yishay,

I was pleased to receive your collaborative book, *Heartbeats: The Insider's Guide to Israel*, which tells the story of Israeli society in the State of Israel. Indeed, this is not a standard guide book, rather an in-depth work that strives to understand Israel's citizens and people. The collection of essays provides the tourist with a new, refreshing perspective and insight into the heart of Israeli society. The journey that the reader undergoes enriches not only the tourist coming to visit, but even the native-born Israeli who has lived and breathed this society for generations.

Today, there is no longer a majority and a minority in Israeli society, but rather four sectors or tribes that are growing to equal sizes. Each tribe has its own educational system, sectoral media channels, and even its own cities and towns. But we must not view the Israeli mosaic as carved in stone; rather, it is an amazing opportunity to create a very special type of harmony. When genuine, sincere partnership is forged between the sectors, out of mutual trust and attentiveness, without forfeiting the fundamental values of each tribe, we will be privileged to see a new Israeli era.

It is my profound hope that this book will strengthen our connection with the fifth tribe – the Jews abroad, who may be far from sight but are definitely not far from our heart. I wish you continued success in your educational endeavors.

*"Bless us, our Father, all of us **as one**, in the light of Your countenance,"* because it is our destiny to live together.

Sincerely,

R. Rivli

Reuven (Ruvi) Rivlin

State and Religion, 2016
Oil on canvas
mounted on wood
50X50

Introduction

When a Trip Becomes a Journey

Ya'acov Fried

Israel's Independence Day 2020 – A Personal Journey

It's nine o'clock at night as I drive on Highway 1 from Jerusalem to Tel Aviv. Today was Yom Hazikaron, Israel's day of national remembrance to commemorate those who lost their lives while defending the State of Israel. I was in Jerusalem today to participate in a discussion on the tourism crisis that has emerged in the wake of COVID-19.

The driving begins to take its toll on me, and I decide to stay with my brother, who lives in the Jerusalem mountains, so I can watch on TV the concluding ceremony of Yom Hazikaron and then the ushering in of Yom Ha'atzmaut, Israel's Independence Day. It's a moving ceremony that always fills me with Israeli solidarity and Jewish unity, perhaps more than any other date on the Hebrew or general calendar.

Israel is usually packed with tourists during this week of Yom Hashoah (Holocaust Remembrance Day), Yom Hazikaron, and Yom Ha'atzmaut. But not this year. This year, time stands still. The streets are barren of locals and tourists. In contrast to every other Yom Hazikaron, today bereaved families were prohibited from visiting the graves of their loved ones. As of 6 p.m., a full lockdown was imposed in Israel, as part of an attempt to curb the spread of COVID-19, and out of a fear that Yom Ha'atzmaut celebrations would spiral out of control and lead to a spike in infection rates.

The realization that we are in the midst of a huge global crisis hits me tonight with an intensity that is different from anything I have ever experienced before. Like many others, I have spent the past months feeling overwhelmed and emotionally turbulent. The familiar and known have been supplanted by feelings of uncertainty, a lack of control, and a fear of being infected by – or infecting others with – the virus. I am enveloped by a feeling of dissonance between the silence around me and the internal storm brewing inside me at this new and foreign reality.

One of the busiest highways in the country, on what should be one of the busiest nights of the year, is completely empty. Not a car driving by my side on the way to Tel Aviv, or opposite me on the road ascending to Jerusalem. I drive alone, seeing on the way just a few ambulances and two police cars parked at the side of the road at central junctions.

A tremor of fear courses through my body as I worry about getting caught by the police for violating the curfew.

"What's upsetting you?" I ask myself. "Is it the big fine that you might receive?"

"It's not the fine that frightens me," I answer myself. "Perhaps it's the fear that my fate is not in my own hands. Perhaps it's because a cursed virus is changing everything that is familiar, right before my eyes. Perhaps it's the fear that the government has declared a curfew as a way of scaring me and controlling my mind. What is the point of this curfew and lockdown anyway? Perhaps it's the fear that from now on, the situation will only get worse economically, and the lockdown is a sign that the economy will plummet to its lowest level. Perhaps it's the loneliness that

I feel tonight – that specifically on Yom Ha'atzmaut, I don't feel part of a big family, part of a community, or even part of a nation."

I now hear the sound of twittering birds, of whose presence I used to be unaware. The silence of skies empty of planes accompanies me throughout the day, countered by a tempest of emotions at a new life where we are forced to function in an altogether unfamiliar way. Tourism, which was such a pivotal part of my world, has vanished and been replaced by infinite surfing between television channels and social media sites.

Usually, on Yom Ha'atzmaut, we have dozens of tourist groups in Israel. They visit historical sites, discover the complexity of establishing and maintaining the Jewish state, grapple with the delicate relationship between Israel and the Diaspora, and celebrate Yom Ha'atzmaut. These journeys throughout Israel, especially on Yom Ha'atzmaut, are filled with countless encounters with locals that give visitors a chance to experience the beating heart of the Israeli people and the country as a whole. There's nothing like Yom Ha'atzmaut to give you that feeling.

Yom Ha'atzmaut, as a Jewish holiday, always seemed to me the clearest expression of the common destiny shared by Israel and all Jews, wherever they may be. On this evening, I always feel such happiness and pride that I am one of those people who gets to facilitate the Israeli story, as part of the Jewish experience, being told to American Jews. This evening emphasizes how important it is to me that Israel be a central component of Jewish identity in the Diaspora.

The curfew, complete lockdown, and accompanying fear make me think of the curfews that my parents endured. My mother told me about her experience escaping a British soldier during curfew when she was just a high school student living in Meah Shearim in Jerusalem. Fast-forward a few years later to another curfew: my mother presented her nurse's badge to the British soldiers when asked why she was violating the curfew. In actual fact, she was on her way to a friend.

Perhaps, I think to myself, I should prepare a convincing excuse in case a police officer stops me.

I pass by the Latrun Police Station, one of the many that the British built throughout the country, and remember my father's journey. He arrived in Israel immediately after he was liberated from Auschwitz, enlisted in the army, fought in the battles in the Jerusalem region, and – unlike most of his refugee friends who participated in the battle at Latrun – survived. I remember hearing how, as a fifteen-year-old boy, he violated the curfew in the shtetl as the Nazi soldiers, aided by local residents, gathered all the Jewish residents into an enclosed space. I recall one particular story about him violating the curfew and leaving the ghetto to bring food to his young nephews. My father's remarks fill the car as I drive: "*After the Holocaust, I didn't go back to the shtetl. I didn't go to the United States. I came to Israel, so that I would be a master of my own fate. I knew that I would only have personal and national liberty in a Jewish state.*"

Tonight, my personal liberty has been taken from me, as well as the possibility of celebrating our national freedom.

I pass by the Ramle-Lod interchange, two cities that embrace Ben-Gurion Airport, the main gateway to Israel. Suddenly, I think about the story of Operation Danny, the battle to liberate the cities of Ramle and Lod during the War of Independence. Today, these cities have mixed Jewish and Arab populations, but during the British Mandate period, prior to the establishment of the State of Israel, they were Arab cities. The battle in Ramle and Lod is one of the central junctions in the establishment of the state.

Two diametrically different narratives exist of the war in the cities of Ramle and Lod. The Jewish majority views it as a legitimate operation to liberate the Arab cities, which were part of the State of Israel, when the Arab population refused to recognize the 1947 Partition Plan announced by the United Nations and fought against the Jewish state. The Palestinian side views the war as the cause of the Nakba, an Arabic word meaning "the catastrophe" or "the expulsion" of the Palestinian people from their home in Palestine, the result of which was the Palestinian refugee issue.

On Yom Ha'atzmaut, decades after the establishment of the State of Israel, various populations feel such polar opposite emotions, from joy to disaster, from partnership to disconnection, and even from the feeling that this is the most important Jewish holiday to the feeling that it symbolizes a national crisis.

I suddenly hear my father's voice in my head: *"What's going on here? Curfew? Lockdown? On the night of Yom Ha'atzmaut? Have we lost our minds?"* I hear him continue, *"Let's separate between the panic aroused by our attempt to deal with COVID-19 and the need for common sense and a commitment to independent, free thinking. Even if the current situation dictates a curfew, we still have a commitment to celebrate our independence. Nothing should be allowed to stop the joy on this day."*

I park at the side of the road; the quiet music plays in the background as I ask myself, what lesson can I learn from the quiet around me? Which new insight can I gain at this moment?

Throughout the journeys of my life, I am usually driven by goals. If I don't have a goal, I sometimes feel that I am drifting, unsatisfied, not living to the fullest, and sometimes failing to absorb the full experience. A goal, I say to myself, has its eyes set on the future. How can that be balanced with the experiences of the present?

Over the years, I have felt that the journey of my life carries both an external goal and an internal goal. The external goal is to fulfill what I have set out to do, and of course, look toward the future. The experience, which is the internal goal, is the feeling that I am successfully creating something within myself in the present – a connection to the moment. This is the reality in which I live, and it influences everything that I absorb and feel. Concentrating on a goal grabs my attention, to the extent that it becomes more important than my experiences in the present. Often these two goals are in a state of tension as they struggle to align.

I have often suspected that thinking and planning ahead prevent me from living deeply in the moment. Tonight, I discover that the silence around me teaches me a new lesson about inner peace. I feel present in a way I never have before. I feel that my external goal and my internal goals are harmonious, blending into each other.

Instead of absorbing the connection to my people, Israeli identity, and Jewish heritage, which flow through my veins, from external sources such as ceremonies and celebrations, tonight my connection comes from the deafening silence around me. It strikes me that I feel even more Israeli sitting here in silence than I would sitting in a ceremony surrounded by fellow Israelis. I feel connected and even united to my fellow Israelis sitting in their homes tonight. This feeling begins to arouse within me an inner sense of awakening.

Perhaps, I wonder, this is the difference between a trip and a journey.

Intense silence envelops me. I am having an internal dialogue: my personal and internal journey tonight from Jerusalem to Tel Aviv is an elevated and upgraded version of the experience that I would like to plan for tourists in the future. *I understand that crises push us to think outside the box. In our routines, we eternalize the familiar. This time is a gateway to new opportunities. Perhaps it is an opportunity to think of ways to enable tourists to have a deeper and fuller experience during their visit.*

Here, on this night, along with the magic of my internal discoveries, I reflect on the need to create opportunities and tools for tourists – beyond touring and intellectual experiences – that will arouse their own internal discoveries.

On the journeys that we plan and lead, along with the cultural experience and the opportunity to appreciate breathtaking views, participants also can enjoy the possibilities of introspection, which will deepen and intensify the experience far more than a visit to yet another site. *Being present in the experience* is what is important.

Throughout my life, I emphasized building educational journeys in Israel as a tool for developing and exploring one's inner world. I did this, in various capacities, as manager of Melitz in Jerusalem, as a research associate at the Van Leer Institute, as a community *shaliach* (emissary) in the United States, and in leading Da'at, a pioneering company in the field of educational tourism, founded out of a belief that journeys, not trips, are what facilitate a different type of experience. During the weeks following Yom Ha'atzmaut, I replay this drive an infinite number of times in my mind, and I view the experience as a journey. It solidified my decision to write this book, together with my fellow educators who participated in its compilation and helped turn the dream into a reality.

The Secrets of the Contributors

What do all these contributors have in common? There's not a trace of yellow journalism or anything sensational in what they write. On the contrary.

Tour educators are a group of people who are dedicated to their mission. They are teachers who lead with their words and actions, characterized by fine character traits, a respect for knowledge, discretion, and morality.

Aside from having formal, multifaceted educations, they are gifted with independent, critical thinking. Educators or guides refuse to serve as an external authority or representative of the majority opinion.

Although they are leaders, they do not behave like superiors, and do not adopt an opinion without logical grounds and factual evidence.

More important than the intellectual qualities of the tour educators are the ethical nature and moral backbone that each of them brings to the experience. They are not motivated by power, money, or prestige. They are characterized by self-control and respect for others. They fulfill their mission out of respect for every opinion and belief, taking care to facilitate free discourse.

A tour educator notices the red lines and stops on time. An educator is motivated by integrity, truth, and loyalty to the position. "Serving" the tourists is not perceived as something negative. Service means sensitivity and openness to the people you work with. Service in the human sense, not just in the functional sense. As Koren, one of the contributors, said: "Service is listening to an eighty-year-old grandmother and paying attention to the jittery child. Showing an interest in the father's professional life as he juggles between his family and his business during the trip. Being pleasant is human and makes a much stronger impression than anything else." A tour educator feels and implements decision making and modes of operation during the course of the journey that allow the tourists to feel that the focus is on them.

A tour educator is the primary facilitator of the experience. He is the teacher, the instructor, the director, and the motivator. He is not a classic tour guide who provides information that is accessible without him. Throughout the journey, he raises questions and dilemmas that are connected both to history and to the complex realities in Israel today. He encourages dialogue that helps tourists process the experience, and he creates infinite opportunities for multi-sensory, unprovoked, liberated, and captivating experiences, without making the trip any less enjoyable.

As I write, I feel that our members lead a unique moral journey, and when dealing with morals, we should turn to examples of leadership.

One is from the prophet Isaiah, who said that we must be wary of those that "decree unrighteous decrees," leaders whose ways are foolishness and fraud. The second is from the Chinese philosopher Mencius, who said, "Never has a man who has bent himself been able to make others straight."

The Secret Behind the Art

Five years ago, I had a conversation with a very good friend of mine about leading a life of wonderment and how central art is in that respect. As we were talking, my friend suggested that we walk over to his next-door neighbor, who is a painter. As I entered Erez Aharon's studio, I immediately understood why my friend took me to this wonderland. Throughout the years, I fell in love with Erez's work – especially because of how his paintings depicted a variety of issues, dilemmas, and myths that relate to life in Israel. While writing *Heartbeats*, I felt that Erez's art beautifully mirrors and captures what we are trying to accomplish in our anthology – and therefore would be a perfect addition to the book.

The Guide to a Journey to Israel

This book, written and compiled by educators and tour guides who have shared their experiences and are motivated by a multi-dimensional inner understanding, uncovers a wide range of complex topics, dilemmas, and stories to which a tourist is not usually exposed. The book is a gateway into the inner worlds of the educators, through their personal journeys in Israel.

Our hope is that reading this book before your journey to Israel will give you an opportunity to delve deeper, not just into the country but into yourselves.

Exploring these Israeli journeys will give you, the reader, a chance to experience, feel, learn, and appreciate your visit to Israel on levels that are hidden from the eye. We hope that this guide will be a tool to arouse, invigorate, motivate, pique your curiosity, and will provide you with an opportunity for a different type of journey.

The tour educators are not attempting to expose the reader to any absolute truth. Rather, they desire to share their personal journeys with you as a way of allowing you to experience the country on another level. None of the articles are meant to be "copied and pasted." They are an opportunity to explore the crevices of the souls of each of the authors.

The journeys in the book touch upon complicated, intricate subjects. We step off of the well-worn tourist paths to unfamiliar places, occurrences, and topics.

The tour educator is driven by enthusiasm, and presents thoughts, approaches, and angles that are the results of many years of work. These give way to a fresh, unconventional approach that is based on the experiences of thousands of tours in both classic and new sites, conversations with organization directors, rabbis, priests and ministers, public figures and many tourists, which produce new paradigms and different ways of thinking.

As educators, we all share the strong desire that curiosity will be your inner guide as you visit and experience Israel. My wish to you is that this book will serve as a map through which your curiosity will be able to run free and become your sixth sense, before, during, and after your visit to Israel.

Context

1

Biography Is Also
a Matter of Geography

How Israel Is Shaped by Its Location

Gilad Peled

Sometimes a man's gotta do what a man's gotta do – and propose marriage to that special someone. Since I love a bit of drama mixed into my romance, I decided to try my luck at the top of the highest mountain in Israel.

Mount Hermon is an alpine peak between Syria and Lebanon and the only ski resort in Israel. On a good year, the resort offers ski enthusiasts about three months of moderate-level skiing. It was a hot summer in 2004, and the cover story I told my future wife was that we would be spending a romantic weekend in a tent on the banks of the Jordan River, at the foot of the mountain that is void of skiers and visitors in the summertime.

Standing hand in hand at the top of the Hermon, we could see the country beneath us in all of its glory: to the south, in front of us, the green, fertile valley through which the Jordan River gently winds; to the east – the fringe of the vast Arabian Desert that stretches all the way to the shores of the Persian Gulf; to the west – the peaks of the Galilee Mountains, and beyond them, the dazzling blue of the Mediterranean Sea. From the top of the mountain, it's easy to see the flourishing, narrow corridor in which we live, and to understand how the land of Israel became an important international crossroad. Even the excitement of the upcoming moment didn't diminish from the beauty of the landscape beneath us. There's no better place to begin the rest of my life, I mused, than this perfect overlook of the land where, hopefully, we will build our home.

I kneeled down on one knee and asked for her hand in marriage.

Most of us rarely think about the influence that geography has on culture, society, and human relationships. Did the fact that Rome is situated upon fertile soil, on the banks of a river that flows to the Mediterranean Sea, play a part in its growth into an empire? Did the Himalayas impact the unique culture of the Indian subcontinent? How did the fact that England is an island influence its relationship with the European continent? These questions are essential to understanding a place. To paraphrase Sakini's famous line from the play *The Teahouse of the August Moon*, one can say that biography is also a question of geography, especially if it's the biography of a geographical region.

The same is true of the land of Israel, whose geographic location shaped its biography and the reality that exists here today. Like a large pot, Father Time and Mother Nature added various ingredients, mixed and stirred, cooked, and spiced. Gradually, nature evolved over thousands of years until it became what it is today: two primary geographic facts dictated the biography of the land of Israel.

The first is the fact that Israel has always been nestled between two significant regional powers: Egypt in the south and Mesopotamia, with its changing mighty empires, in the northeast. Between them – the land of Israel, east of which stretches the Arabian Desert, while the

Mediterranean Sea is on its western side, both of which were impassable in ancient times. Thus, the land of Israel is a narrow continental corridor that provided a thoroughfare, water, and food to nomads, merchants, and armies, marching in pursuit of conquest and glory from Egypt to Mesopotamia and vice versa. In the absence of any significant natural resources, the land was only ever historically important due to the fact that it was an essential passageway. Whoever controlled it possessed a significant advantage over their enemies.

Over the past millennia, dozens of military campaigns passed through the land of Israel, leaving their mark in tangible, or less tangible, ways: construction styles, art techniques and crafting skills, philosophical and theological ideas, mythology, stone monuments, victory inscriptions, genes, and a lot of destruction and ruin. The forces that fought here are part of the history, culture, and landscape of Israel, and in many cases, the story of the land of Israel remained a central part of their own history. Israelis calmly accept the fact that they share their home with people who lived here thousands of years ago and who represent a diverse range of cultures. Past and present exist here side by side, which is expressed in daily life. For example, in Israel, you cannot start building a home before you receive approval from the Antiquities Authority that there are no important archaeological artifacts at the site.

A prominent example in this context is Megiddo, one of the most ancient, important cities in the entire region. Megiddo controlled a central junction on the longitude axis between Egypt and Mesopotamia. It was situated in a spot where a constricted mountain pass opened up to the expansive Jezreel Valley, before the terrain continued to wind between the Galilee Mountains and along the length of the narrow Jordan Valley. For this reason, some of the most important battles in the history of the region, over the past thirty-five hundred years, took place in the Jezreel Valley and its environs.

The Jezreel Valley is also one of the first areas in the land of Israel where Jewish immigrants settled down during the modern period, and Kibbutz Megiddo is now adjacent to ancient Megiddo. Settlement in Megiddo began about six thousand years ago, and archaeologists have excavated through more than twenty layers of settlement (and destruction!). As early as the fifteenth century BCE, Pharaoh Thutmose III secured his reign in Egypt here, after his victory over a broad coalition of rebellious Canaanite kings, in what was later known as the first Battle of Megiddo. About eight hundred years later, in 609 BCE, Pharaoh Necho II crossed through the territory of the Judean kingdom on his way to a decisive battle with the rising Neo-Babylonian empire. When Josiah, king of Judea, refused to allow the Egyptian army to pass through his land, the second Battle of Megiddo was sparked, ending in a crushing victory for Egypt.

In the twentieth century as well, Megiddo played an important part in regional politics. During World War I, this was the site where the Allied forces met the Turkish army for a final, decisive battle. Their victory ended four hundred years of Ottoman rule. General Allenby, commander of the battle, received the title First Viscount of Megiddo after the war, commemorating his victory in the third Battle of Megiddo. The final battle of Megiddo has not yet occurred. It is expected to happen, according to Christian theology, at the end of times, at Armageddon, which is derived from the Hebrew *Har Megiddo* (Mount Megiddo). Islamic prophecy also mentions Armageddon as the place of the final war at the end of times.

The second geographical fact that dictates the biography of the land of Israel – aside from it being a continental corridor – is its location at the junction between three different continents: Asia, Africa, and Europe. Although it is possible to drive from Israel's southernmost tip to the north in just seven hours, and to cross from east to west in twenty minutes, its location at an intercontinental junction creates a diverse, rich natural habitat. The land of Israel is not just a continental corridor between two powerful regional powers; it is also a junction that creates unique climatic, human, and botanical phenomena.

When we descended, in that summer of 2004, from the mountain adorned with alpine, windswept summer blossoms, growing between exposed hillside rocks, we found ourselves, within just thirty minutes, standing among dense Mediterranean aquatic vegetation on the banks of the Jordan River. Temperatures rose by about seventy degrees Fahrenheit, humidity jumped by 70 percent, and the density of the population grew unreasonably. Heading home the next day, it took us forty-five minutes to reach the Sea of Galilee, the only freshwater lake in Israel, and another hour later, we had reached the arid Judean Desert. Less than an hour of driving brought us to the lowest place on earth – the Dead Sea, which was hot as an oven. Thirty minutes later, and about three thousand feet higher in altitude, we breathed in relief the chilly air of Jerusalem. In three and a half hours, we had crossed half of the length of the State of Israel.

The geographic and climatic diversity of the land tells a biographical story of accessibility and separation simultaneously. The small Judean Desert, situated at the outskirts of important cities such as Jerusalem, Bethlehem, and Hebron, offers access to isolated sites that are just a few miles away from the settled land. It provided a quick escape for young David as he fled from King Saul, for Elijah as he ran from Ahab's anger, and for John the Baptist and Jesus, who searched for a place where they could be in solitude.

Eight hundred years ago, the land was divided between the Muslims of Saladin and his heirs, who resided in the mountains, and the Crusaders, their bitter enemies, who lived just a few miles away, on the coast of the Mediterranean Sea. For about a hundred years, they lived alongside each other, just a stone's throw away, but separate from one another thanks to the diverse geography of the land. The Muslims enjoyed support of a homeland, stretching through Asia and Africa; the Crusaders enjoyed the benefit of access to supply routes from Europe. Both groups fortified the land and married its residents.

Yet geography does not only impact the human biography of the land of Israel, but also its zoological and botanical biography. The land was always a meeting point for species from all three continents. When we were on Mount Hermon, a small black and white songbird chirped next to us. It was a Sombre Tit, and this is its southernmost distribution limit in the world. On the other side, the Doum palm, Moringa peregrina, the Acacia albida, and other African species find their northernmost habitat in Israel, while various Asian species have their westernmost limit here.

Botanically, Israel is at a crossroads between four phytogeographical regions (a term that refers to the geographic distribution of plant species), out of just six such regions that exist in the entire world! These are the Irano-Turanian region, the Mediterranean region, the Saharo-Arabian region, and the Sudanese region. Israel is blessed with 47,069 biological species, which constitute three percent of the total number of biological species in the world. Compared to countries of similar size, located at the same geographic latitude, this is an exceptionally high number. In Israel, there are also about twenty-six hundred species of wild plants that belong to 130 families. Numbers like these usually exist in countries that are significantly larger than Israel, such as England or Germany. Being a bottleneck between Europe-Asia and Africa, about half a billion (!) birds fly over Israel on one of the busiest migration routes in the world, on their way from northern countries to Africa and back. The 511 bird species that can be spotted in Israel make it a virtual paradise for birdwatchers.

Israel's unique geography created its special biography. It facilitates visiting an exceptional range of sites related to various areas of interest that are just a short distance from each other. It offers experiences of different types even on a short visit. It invites encounters with a wide range of social groups, beliefs, religions, and lifestyles, all sharing life in Israel but still retaining their singularity. Armies, travelers, merchants, animals, birds, and plant species have been wandering through the land of Israel for thousands of years. They come bearing aromas of distant lands and then continue on their way, leaving signs of life protruding from all sides when you visit. From snowcapped Mount Hermon in the north, to the coral reefs of the Red Sea in the south, from the hilltops of the Jerusalem mountains, seeped in history, to the natural wonder of the Dead Sea, in Israel, everything is within reach. Even the future. And what do you know – she said yes!

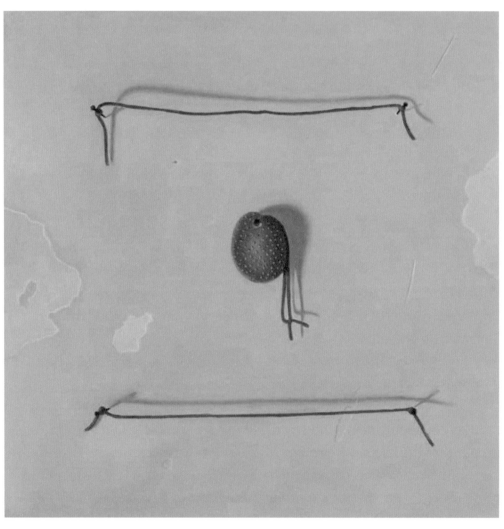

Flag, 2020
Oil on canvas
mounted on wood
43X43

2

Inside the Israeli Mind

Gilad Peled

When I was twenty-five, I went on a long trip to Canada. It was my second time traveling abroad, and the first time that I was on a trip, alone, in a foreign country. I chose to travel specifically to Canada after I saw on a map the large lakes in the northern part of the country; the region looked captivating to me. I also had a Canadian girlfriend at the time. When I arrived in Canada, I discovered an opposite reality to everything I had known my whole life in Israel – huge expanses, thick forests, clean, fresh water flowing everywhere, and a friendly laid-back population spread out comfortably in private homes in the heart of nature. I never made it to the lakes because they were so far away that they could only be reached by plane (on an expensive flight). It turned out that the lakes were roughly the size of the entire State of Israel.

The year was 1995, and on that trip, I understood for the first time that my conception of countries that I had never visited was very different from the reality. I also felt during my visit as if I were "floating" above the surface rather than experiencing what it feels like to actually live there. This frustrated me, because as much as I was astounded by the landscapes and natural wonders, I wanted to know what life in this country was like. What did people do in the evenings and on week-ends? What kind of music did they like to listen to? Where did they go to meet a potential spouse? Where did they like to hike? What did they talk about around the dinner table? What were their worries? How did they pick a place to live?

I had tons of questions to ask, so I made every effort to meet peo-ple. I hitchhiked from coast to coast, I was a guest at people's homes, I connected with people I met along the way, and in general, I tried to chat with everyone I encountered. It was a thrilling experience, and yet – I knew that there were things that they weren't talking to me about, probably because they were so obvious and deeply ingrained that they had never consciously thought about them.

This is exactly what I'd like to write about here – what you need to know when you meet Israelis, what you should pay attention to, what Israelis will never talk to you about, simply because it's part of their lives and they've probably never even thought about it. The following are three perspectives on life in Israel that you won't hear from Israelis themselves, about the geography, the demographics, and the history.

I'd like to start with a story about tea. We all have that legendary tea (fine, sometimes it's coffee, and in especially pathological cases, it's Coca Cola), that perfect tea we tasted once and remember for the rest of our lives. We remember the burning sensation on our tongue, the intoxicating aroma, the way we inhaled deeply between each sip, the feeling of satisfaction, the serenity that spread across our body as the liquid slid down our throat, and all we could hope for was that the experience would go on and on. It is usually an experience outside one's comfort zone, probably with a dear, loved one, often in a special location, after making an exceptional effort.

I drank my legendary tea at the age of ten on an isolated beach at the northern end of the Sinai Desert, with my father, after an exhaust-ing and bumpy twelve-hour drive in a truck. It was the furthest I had ever traveled in my life, and I never drank such tasty tea again. The sandy beach, where we slept during star-studded nights, was just over 140 miles from the small kibbutz where I lived at the time, but we felt like we were in a different world. Twelve years earlier, Israel conquered the Sinai Desert from Egypt which was twice as big as the size of the country. Three years after that trip, however, Israel returned it as part of the peace agreements between our countries.

For a country whose entire length can be crossed in just a seven-hour drive, and whose width is just nine miles at its narrowest, Sinai was a wonderland. The expanses that opened up before the residents of our little country were exhilarating; the enormous mountains attracted hikers and adventurers; the enchanting beaches were covered with carefree young people, and families packed up their tents and children and went to experience the magic of driving for an entire day without reaching any borders. The spell lasted for just fifteen years, before Israel stepped back to its previous borders, the price tag of a quiet border in the south being one broken heart. The "big country" experience provided by Sinai's expanses opened up our eyes to a geographic perspective that we had never known, and that we hurried to forget.

There is a price to living in a small, isolated country – a price that its residents rarely ever think about. Israel is roughly the size of New Jersey or Wales. It could fit into the area of the United States about 473 times, and into the area of Britain about twelve times. Someone who lives in North or South America, Europe, Australia, or most of Asia, can get into the car in the morning and drive in almost any direction for days on end. Try to do that in Israel, and within thirty minutes, you'll run into a border, most likely a hostile one, protected by a fence, guard towers, and armed soldiers on both sides. The high birth rate in Israel results in constant population growth, and every year, the country becomes more crowded.

When the state was established in 1948, there were about 800,000 residents. When we drove to Sinai thirty years later, there were already 3.8 million, and today, there are over nine million residents in Israel. The population density is higher than any state in the United States; in Europe only the Netherlands, Malta, and the Vatican are more crowded (but without free access to the neighboring countries). Think about the effect that this has on the mental well-being of the residents. On an everyday level, this means increased congestion on the highways and less open natural area to escape to on weekends. If we add the fact that 60 percent of Israel's area is desert, we receive a country that is filled to the brim, suffocated, and stressed.

On an existential level, this means that many Israelis feel trapped in their small home and see it as a "villa in the jungle." It's not something that we think about on a daily basis, because it's the reality of our lives. Most of us don't take this into account when we go about our daily lives, and we don't talk to tourists about it, because it's part of who we are. However, the mental well-being of a nation trapped in a small, crowded country, constantly threatened by its neighbors, could put our decisions, our actions, and our reactions into perspective.

The demographic perspective is a reflection of Israel's small population and geopolitical situation. Out of slightly more than nine million Israelis, about 75 percent are Jews and the rest are Muslims, Christians, Druze, and other small minorities. This means that the Jewish population, which experienced seven wars and an infinite number of violent incidents since the state's establishment, accounts for only seven million. That's a trivial number in comparison with the hundreds of millions of residents in the hostile countries adjacent to us. Living in a small country means that enemy soldiers are just around the corner, literally. This is not a fact that facilitates sane everyday life, and therefore, most Israelis tend to ignore this reality. However, deep inside of us, we all live in a sense of constant threat. Add to that hundreds of years of anti-Semitic persecution, which are etched into our collective national consciousness, and one Holocaust, and you get a country with a persecution complex, living in constant fear of destruction. Try to look at national policies and personal decisions through this prism, and you'll understand Israel better.

On the other hand, living as part of a small population means a very intimate, family-style society with very few degrees of separation between Israelis. In Israel, every random encounter is a springboard for an animated conversation in an attempt to uncover mutual friends from school, the army, university, or work. This fact of life creates a sense of mutual responsibility during times of external threat, and a high level of national resilience during times of crises. All of these are part of the fundamental components of our life here. Most Israelis see them as a given, don't invest too much thought in them, and probably won't talk to you about them.

The third perspective, which perhaps most impacts our lives here, is our history. It's also the perspective that Israelis are the least aware of, although it shapes our lives no less than the first two. In 1936, Reinhardt Lay left a large home and successful business in Germany, in exchange for a windy tent, malaria-carrying mosquitoes, and difficult physical labor in Palestine. He changed the name his parents had given him to a Hebrew name, Mordecai Lahav, and volunteered to join the British army in fighting the Nazis. Chana, his eldest daughter, my mother, was born during his military service.

My grandfather risked his life and sailed to a distant, impoverished land for one reason – he believed that he should build his future where the roots of his past were planted. We all live in Israel with a deep sense of historical continuity. Although the vast majority of Israelis are the first, second, or third generation of immigrants, we all live with three thousand years of history on our backs. Compared to most countries, that's a heavy burden to carry.

A few years ago, I visited Germany during the summer months, when there are many medieval knights festivals that recreate life in the Middle Ages and celebrate Germany's culture and heritage. Strolling through these colorful, vibrant festivals, I was amazed at the way the Germans are careful to preserve traditions that are hundreds of years old, and I felt a pang of sorrow that we, in Israel, do not have such a history that we can celebrate. Then I remembered that when the mighty Temple in Jerusalem was destroyed, and the last Jewish kingdom was conquered two thousand years ago, pagan Germanic tribes were living in Germany. That was after over a thousand years of diverse history of the Jewish people in the land of Israel.

Benjamin Disraeli, the British statesman of Jewish descent, had a good reason to retort to Irish nationalist Daniel O'Connell, who had insulted him for being Jewish: "Yes, I am a Jew, and while the ancestors of the right honorable gentleman were brutal savages in an unknown island, mine were priests in the temple of Solomon."

The archaeological sites all over Israel are some of the most ancient in the world. Most Israelis are not cognizant of the extent of the impact of our history on our lives in Israel, an influence which has the Bible at its foundation. Although there are lively, passionate discussions about the degree of historical accuracy of the Bible, most of the Jewish holidays commemorate biblical events and we are surrounded by biblical sites. Moreover, the founders of modern Israel, as secular as they were, drew their inspiration from the Bible as a historical-national source. They invested great effort in identifying biblical sites, utilizing history, archeology, philology, geography, biblical criticism, and linguistics. They restored Hebrew names to the sites and thus created a reality in which the biblical narrative is woven into the modern geography of our country. All of us, even in the secular public schools, study the Bible in class, though the perspective is historical-cultural and not religious.

Let's take the urban region of Tel Aviv as an example – the secular, liberal, economic, and cultural center of modern Israel. Tourists often tend to think that Tel Aviv is larger than Jerusalem, and there are even those who think that Tel Aviv is Israel's capital. The truth is that Tel Aviv is significantly smaller than Jerusalem – about half its size. However, Tel Aviv is surrounded by about a dozen cities located right next to each other, creating an urban continuum known as the Dan Block. This is indeed the big metropolitan area of Israel. It is home to over four million residents, which is about 45 percent of the country's population (2019).

In modern Israel, there's nothing contradictory about the fact that the high-tech hub of Israel is named after the biblical tribe of Dan, to which God promised the region where Tel Aviv is located today (Joshua 19). Another example is the Israeli parliament, which is called the Knesset. The name commemorates the Knesset Hagedolah, the assembly of the nation's elders that was active here about twenty-four hundred years ago. No less interesting is the fact that there are 120 Knesset members, corresponding to the number of members of the historical Knesset Hagedolah. Reaching a majority decision with an even number of members could be the source of great difficulties, of course, but that fact didn't bother the country's founders, who preferred the historical connection over modern practicality.

The feeling that we are but a link in a long historical chain is deeply embedded into the Israeli consciousness, but most of us take this for granted and don't put too much thought into it. The Israeli motivation to fight for this small strip of land stems, to a great degree, from the historical feeling that this is where our roots are planted. In a cyclical pattern that feeds itself, the public sphere that we create reflects this perspective and reinforces it simultaneously. Many Israelis will talk to you about our right to the land without considering the ramifications of a present that so heavily relies on the past.

On the one hand, this perspective constitutes a firm foundation for the Jewish presence in modern Israel – a willingness to deal with numerous challenges, existential uncertainty, physical threats, and mental tensions, which stem to a great degree from a feeling of a historical right to the land. On the other hand, this perspective also leads to a high level of psychological closedness toward critical approaches to Jewish history, and an unwillingness to consider the rights of another nation to the land.

Yet in 2019, Israel ranked thirteenth place on the United Nations' World Happiness Index, out of 156 countries. Are Israelis happy because they don't know anything else? Is it the result of a sense of historical mission? Or perhaps dealing with challenges makes people appreciate what they have? The answer lies in your encounter with Israelis on your trip. In all likelihood, they won't talk to you about geography, demographics, or history, but in Israel, any question is legitimate. Choosing what to ask is in your hands.

3

The Heavenly and the Earthly

Israel's Spiritual Allure

Yishay Shavit

I love the city of Jerusalem. When I was twenty-five, I made Jerusalem my home, and it became home to my children who were born there. To this day, I still feel a spiritual buzz when I think about where I live. Anyone who knows me will probably say that this doesn't really sound like me. After all, I consider myself a rational person. Why does the city's holiness have such an effect on me when I am not even such an observant Jew? Why is it that every time I enter one of the gates of the Old City, I feel a different energy flow inside me? The answer to this seeming contradiction between intellect and emotion is complicated but crucial in order to understand the State of Israel today.

Take a look at the map on the next page. The Bünting Clover Leaf Map, also known as the World in a Cloverleaf, was drawn by German theologian and cartographer Heinrich Bünting in 1581, and it shows the world as this Protestant scholar knew it. The three continents – Europe, Asia, and Africa – create somewhat of a clover shape. The continent of America is in the bottom corner of the map (no one in Germany was taking America seriously in 1581...). Now look at the center. You can probably see a city there. Bünting wanted to make sure that his intention was crystal clear, so he also noted the name of the city – Jerusalem. According to Bünting, Jerusalem is the center of the world!

I can promise you that if you try to hike or travel using Bünting's map, you're not going to get very far. The map is obviously not precise and teaches us almost nothing about geography. But I can assure you that understanding the message of this map is crucial to understanding Jerusalem and the State of Israel today. Essentially, there are two Jerusalems: heavenly Jerusalem and earthly Jerusalem. One city is a physical, rational city. A city where the garbage must be collected and where you pay property taxes. Parallel to this, there is another city, an emotional one – Jerusalem of the heavens. This is a spiritual city that is in the hearts of countless people across the globe. Could there be a contradiction between these two cities?

When you stand before the walls of the Old City, I recommend that you stop for a moment and think – when was the first time you heard the name Jerusalem? You were probably about three or four, like I was. What did the city look like in your imagination? Without a doubt, the traditions that shaped our upbringing impact the way that we understand the physical city that we visit or that is our home.

Consider the Tower of David, one of Jerusalem's most iconic symbols which is located neared the Jaffa Gate entrance to the Old City. The name "Tower of David" alludes to one of the city's past residents, King David. Many Israelis will tell you that he was the king who built the tower. But that's not true at all. The Tower of David is essentially a minaret of a mosque, and King David certainly didn't build it! The first mosque in the world was built by the prophet Mohammed in the seventh century, about sixteen hundred years after King David's era. If that's the case, how did that famous tower on the walls of Jerusalem receive the name Tower of David? This is the very point that I'd like to explore.

For hundreds of years, Muslim, Christian, and Jewish pilgrims visited Jerusalem, traveling via the port city of Jaffa. After an exhausting sea voyage, they would begin their walk toward the holy city. Two or three days of walking brought them to Jaffa Gate, where they set eyes for the very first time on the city that had occupied their dreams. They saw the walls and noticed the most prominent tower in sight. If this is the most prominent tower, they thought, the greatest king must have built it. Who was that king? No doubt about it. In the eyes of those pilgrims, Jews, Christians, and Muslims alike, it was King David, one of the greatest kings of the Bible, if not the greatest of all.

What can we learn from the story of the Tower of David? The most important lesson is that it demonstrates the power of the emotional perception of Jerusalem and the land of Israel. I like to tell visitors that if they want to understand Jerusalem's Old City, they need to "turn off" their rational thinking that accompanies them in their everyday lives. Dry facts are less important and powerful than the traditions which are a part of Jerusalem's reality. Jerusalem's spiritual allure has everything to do with the traditions which are the beating heart of the city.

Another great example of the power of heavenly Jerusalem is the Western Wall. The Western Wall is an external retaining wall of the Temple Mount. Its purpose during the Second Temple period was completely physical – to support the huge Herodian structure and create a platform on which the Temple itself and the Holy of Holies were built. The wall was not holy. Yet today, it is difficult to imagine a visit to Jerusalem without a visit to the Western Wall. Not only that, but for many Jews visiting the city for the first time in their lives, it is the highlight of their visit. I have often guided tourists who define themselves as completely rational people – physicians, architects, scientists. Throughout the entire tour, they challenge me with wonderful questions about earthly Jerusalem, but when they reach the Western Wall, everything changes. There are those who walk away from the experience with tears in their eyes, totally surprised by their reaction. Many note that standing opposite the stones of the Western Wall, they thought of their parents, or their parents' parents. (Of course, there are also those who say that the visit to the site didn't leave a spiritual impression on them at all.)

As many of you know, there is a Jewish tradition to write your prayers on a note and insert them into the cracks of the Wall, in the hope that God will be more likely to answer your prayers. This custom has no basis in Jewish law. It's a tradition that has endured throughout time and touches people's hearts; even those who aren't visiting the Wall themselves still ask friends and family to place their notes between the stones of the Wall on their behalf.

The lesson is simple – thinking rationally does not facilitate an understanding of Jerusalem. The different traditions here have the power to change reality. A person who is incapable of understanding that people are willing to sacrifice their lives for these traditions cannot understand what his eyes are seeing at the Western Wall, or in Jerusalem in general.

What holds true for Jerusalem's Old City is correct for the entire State of Israel as well. The Israeli story cannot be understood on a purely rational level. The different traditions – Jewish, Christian, and Muslim – have immense power in this country. In 1897, the year when the first Zionist Congress was held, was Herzl's vision rational? Is the discussion regarding the political future of the West Bank conducted on a purely political-diplomatic level? Is Al-Aqsa Mosque merely a place where Muslims go to pray? Of course not. These are highly emotional issues. If you want to understand this country in depth, learn the different traditions and try to think from your heart, not from your head. The reality here, to a great degree, is the result of this type of thinking.

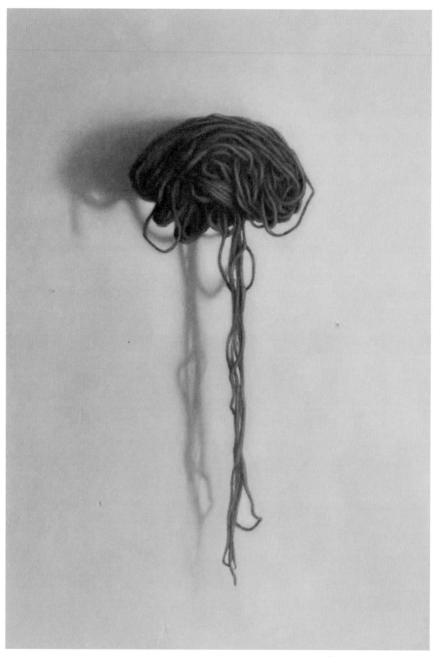

Rationale, 2016
Oil on canvas
mounted on wood
70X50

4

Jewish Time and Jewish Space

A Country That Runs on a Jewish Calendar

Muki Jankelowitz

From the moment you step onto an El Al plane or arrive at Ben-Gurion Airport, you are stepping into Jewish space and moving within Jewish time. Some may immediately notice the differences; for others it might take longer to articulate what they are.

In many ways, this different time and space is a fulfillment of the Zionist aspirations of the founders of the state who sought to create a Jewish majority. Each sovereign nation controls its time by determining which calendar to use and which days of national importance and religious tradition to commemorate. Israel is the only country in the world where the sovereign majority is Jewish. As a result, the calendar is also Jewish.

In Israel, the school and work week begins on a Sunday, based on what is written in Genesis, where the first day is Sunday and the seventh day is the Sabbath, which begins at sunset on Friday. The weekend here is Friday-Saturday rather than Saturday-Sunday.

I still remember the thrill I experienced some thirty years ago upon my aliyah, immigration to Israel, when I tuned in to hear the news on the radio on a Friday evening and it began with a greeting of "Shabbat Shalom." It was a wow moment for me because "even" on the radio they knew it was Shabbat. The radio was in sync with Jewish time! I still get a kick out of that today!

Similarly, Jewish holidays like Passover or Rosh Hashanah, whether observed as religious days or just as holidays, are public holidays. You won't find Christian holidays such as Easter or New Year's on the public calendar. Instead, the events that are commemorated in the Hebrew calendar are of significance to the Jewish people, such as Israel's Independence Day (Yom Ha'atzmaut) or Holocaust Remembrance Day (Yom Hashoah).

As in other countries, the ebb and flow of time that plays out in space reflects the majority culture, and once again Israel is unique in being the only nation with a Jewish public space. This is seen in both the most trivial and dramatic of ways.

Just like outside of Israel, where the dominant culture reminds shoppers that there are only twenty shopping days left till Christmas, here you will find candle and oil products on sale before Hanukkah, fancy-dress costumes and three-cornered hamantashen before Purim, and kosher for Passover foods, new plates, and cleaning products before Passover. Similarly walking down a hotel hallway where the door to every room has a mezuzah (a piece of parchment called a *klaf* contained in a decorative case and inscribed with specific Hebrew verses from the Torah), or the myriad possibilities of Judaica available for purchase, reflects Jewish space.

At first glance, the fact that we speak Hebrew in Israel doesn't seem to be especially reflective of being in Jewish space until we remember that Hebrew was not a living language 150 years ago. Its rebirth as a modern language – for everyday use rather than just for prayer – draws idioms and figures of speech from the Bible and the works of the Sages into our poetry, prose, and speech. In Jewish space we even argue using Jewish idioms.

And just as other sovereign majorities, we determine our "holy" sites. As an independent people, we determine which parts of our history, both ancient and recent, we wish to emphasize. Jewish space reflects the Kotel (Western Wall), a last remnant of the holy Temple complex, and Mount Herzl, burial site of the visionary leaders of Israel. Open a map of Israel and look at the list of our towns and villages; many of them are named in honor of significant personalities in Jewish history. In Jewish space, Jewish history is recounted in our geography. Even the flag of Israel reflects Jewish space; unlike the flags of so many nations that carry Christian or Muslim symbols, Israel's flag carries the Star of David.

Of course, there are Jewish spaces that function on Jewish time outside of Israel: temples, JCCs, Jewish summer camps, and day schools are all examples of Jewish spaces, but none of them are public Jewish spaces. One enters the facility and enters Jewish space. One leaves the facility and returns to the public space of that country.

Outside of Israel, there are always those who are out of sync with the time and space in which they live: the Muslim in Denmark who is uncomfortable with the cross on their national flag; the Jew in the US who is forced to reschedule an exam or class because it falls on Yom Kippur. Of course, there are also the Jewish doctors taking the Christmas shift so their colleagues can get to celebrate with their families.

This is also true in Israel. The time and space may be Jewish, but not all the people in the space are necessarily Jewish. Here, the familiar majority and the minority have been flipped. My son's Muslim Arab cab driver wishes me "Shabbat Shalom" when he says goodbye at the end of the week. The doctors taking the Shabbat shift in my Jewish town on Shabbat are overwhelmingly Arabs, both Muslim and Christians.

Whether you are a Jewish or Christian tourist, pay attention to the difference in time and space; for those used to being part of a majority it is a chance to experience what it's like to be part of the minority, and for those used to being part of the minority, it's now your opportunity to be part of the majority.

Mind and Matter

Wealth, 2019
Oil on canvas
mounted on wood
40X50

5

Israeli Culture as a Strategic Asset

Ya'acov Fried

Summer of 1983. I'm sitting on the grass in New York's Central Park, in an audience of about 100,000 people, listening to the heavenly music of the New York Philharmonic, conducted by maestro Zubin Mehta. It's my first time visiting the most beautiful urban park in the world, enjoying a free concert by one of the best orchestras in the world. The experience moved me. I loved the relaxed atmosphere in the park and felt proud, as an Israeli, that Zubin Mehta, one of the greatest conductors in the world, is also the conductor of the Israeli Philharmonic Orchestra. During the concert, I stretched out on the grass, closed my eyes, and continued listening to the serene music.

About thirty minutes after the concert had started, I suddenly heard a familiar melody that sounded like an Israeli song. It took me a few seconds before I recognized the music and thought, *They're playing "Hatikvah"...* Could it be that the conductor felt so connected to Israel that he decided to include the Israeli national anthem in the concert? During the break, still excited by the discovery, I chatted with my Israeli friends who had arrived at the park together. None of them could explain why the Israeli melody had randomly been played, in a different musical arrangement.

In front of us, on a blanket spread out on the grass, sat a pleasant, smiling man who introduced himself as Dan. I had noticed him before the concert started because, unlike us, he had come equipped with a blanket to sit on with a thermos of hot coffee in hand. I assumed that he was no newcomer to concerts in the park, which explains why he knew exactly what to bring. He told us that he was a lecturer and researcher at NYU who taught sociology. He had obviously heard us speak Hebrew because he added with a smile, "We're from the same tribe."

We mentioned to him the strange musical phenomenon that we had noticed. My Israeli friend mused that maybe the Israeli national anthem had been stolen. Our new American friend Dan replied that the piece we had heard was called "Vltava," named after the river that passes through Prague, and was composed by the Czech composer Bedřich Smetana. He pulled out a New York newspaper, *The Village Voice*, and showed us the ad for the concert. The piece we were discussing included six symphonic poems. Dan explained that the piece was originally intended to glorify the heritage of Czechia, and that the composers of the Israeli national anthem had apparently "stolen" or adapted the words written by the author of "Hatikvah," Naftali Herz Imber, to part of Smetana's composition.

The concert ended. We invited our friendly neighbor to join us for a glass of wine at a nearby café on the west side of the park. He told us that he had visited Israel a few times, and even spent a sabbatical year at Hebrew University. The conversation that developed between us in the local café centered around Israeli culture. Our new friend remarked that he was a scholar of culture and was very curious about the complexity of Israeli culture. I remember it as a magical evening, flowing with conversation, mostly focused on the question of whether Israel has its own original, unique culture.

Dan referred to himself as a cultural Jew. With great enthusiasm, he added, "There is a unique phenomenon in Israel that is unmatched anywhere in the world, and Israel is at risk of losing this special asset if it does not protect and cultivate it. You are a country that absorbed immigrants from seventy different cultures. There is no other place in the world, not even the United States, where there are so many different cultures all under one roof. I fear that you are trying to create cultural uniformity and running too quickly toward the American model of a melting pot, and toward imitations of American culture." He added, "I visited Israel in the sixties and in the seventies. I think that creation of a shared lifestyle is justified, for people from all of the different cultures. But you must not try to completely erase the original cultures."

I remember what I answered him. "Our goal of unifying and creating a shared Israeli culture between all of the tribes was and still is strong, but if you come to Israel today, you will discover that every culture that was brought to the country is still alive and well." In retrospect, I understand that the early eighties apparently marked the beginning of a more diverse Israeli culture, which started to display greater sensitivity in respecting the traditions of immigrants from different countries. It succeeded in drawing from them while building something new.

A month after the concert in New York, I hosted one of the most famous theater actors in Israel, Shlomo Bar Shavit, as part of my role as a community emissary and director of emissaries in the Midwest. He was a member of the leading theater group in Israel. I invited him to give a series of lectures and workshops at universities and in Jewish communities. This was in 1983, a very complicated year in the life of the State of Israel. The Lebanon War was complex and Israel's international image was tainted. Criticism in the United States, where I lived for several years, became increasingly venomous. In my position, I could continue to organize seminars on political subjects but instead decided to bring Bar Shavit to shift the focus from politics to culture. I spent two captivating weeks with Shlomo Bar Shavit all over Ohio, Kentucky, and Indiana. Bar Shavit, a dramatic theater actor, opened each lecture or event by reading in his baritone voice from a text by Konstantin Stanislavski, founder of Habima Theater.

"I have had the privilege of playing a role in the creation of Hebrew theater, and I am deeply happy for this, because by doing so, I have fulfilled one of the great vocations of an artist. Art is a field where human beings gather on behalf of the beauty and joy of creativity." He continued and explained that after the 1917 Russian Revolution, as the Zionist movement began to flourish, a group of Jewish theater actors requested from the authorities that a theater be opened in a language of the past [Hebrew – Y.F.], to be called "Habima." The group put on its first play in Moscow, entitled *Neshef Bereshit* (Genesis Ball). Stanislavski was at the play, and was moved by the unbelievable sight: a Hebrew theater – real, alive, and kicking. The theater was not just an artistic performance; it symbolized the revival of Hebrew and of Zionism.

In 1926, Habima left Moscow and made a round of performances throughout Europe, eventually reaching New York. In June of 1927, most of the actors left New York and moved to Israel. They were dedicated to excellence and derived inspiration from international cultures, while still basing their foundation on Jewish culture and original Israeli works. Bar Shavit added, "Throughout the years, Habima put on some of the most famous plays written by renowned playwrights worldwide, right alongside the works of Nobel Prize laureate S. Y. Agnon or Bialik, Israel's national poet, and local modern Israeli playwrights such as Sobol, Kishon, and others."

For two weeks, I enjoyed listening to Bar Shavit and watching clips from some of the 260 plays and characters that he played throughout the years in classical, Jewish, and original modern Israeli plays. The snippets of the plays in which Bar Shavit acted included many personal dramas as well as political issues related to Israel. But the discussion that he led with the audiences was an intimate conversation – a conversation on culture.

I met Dan on a few other occasions, in New York and in Israel, and we discussed Israeli culture and art, as well as watching various cultural performances together. We even watched a few plays with translations at Habima Theater. In our conversations, the main point that we agreed upon was that the "People of the Book" isn't an empty nickname; it's a singular phenomenon in history. The People of the Book means a culture of study, a culture of respect for the Bible and for the values it includes. It is a culture of holidays and festivals, of leisure, of family life, of lofty moral values and abstract faith in an infinite spiritual entity. It was clear to us that authentic Israeli culture and art do not need to be based solely on the past, but also reflect what is alive and brewing in this developing state.

My friendship with Dan strengthened over time. During his visits in Israel, I introduced him to the modern dance troupe Batsheva. We went on a trip in northern Israel and got to see the Batsheva Dance Company perform at the ancient synagogue in Katzrin, in the Golan Heights. I told him how I fell in love with the troupe many years earlier, when a relative of mine in the United States was invited by the founder, the legendary choreographer Martha Graham, to join the dance company as one of the original members.

We were on our way to watch the modern ballet performance Anaphaza, which the group performed according to choreography by Ohad Naharin. Like before every show, we wondered out loud whether it would be authentic. Would it show progress? Would the artist indeed have a message, and would he succeed in relaying it to the audience? Would a connection be created between the people watching the show together, and would we be able to see with greater clarity and sharpness who and what we are through this expression of art? At the end of the performance, on our way home, we felt that all of our questions had been answered. Anaphaza, and its main dance, "Who Knows One," were the group's winning ticket to international stages. Many art critics in New York deemed Batsheva the leading creative troupe in the modern dance world.

In 2008, Dan visited Israel again, in time for the country's celebration of sixty years of independence. As part of my work as the director of Da'at, we hosted American friends of the Technion, booking them seats at the gala concert of the Israeli Philharmonic Orchestra, conducted by Zubin Mehta, as well as a personal meeting with the maestro before the concert. I invited Dan to the event.

In the eyes of the members of the group, Zubin Mehta was an electrifying personality. He has been the musical manager and conductor of the orchestra since 1961 and was responsible for making it one of the best orchestras in the world. Mehta told us how the philharmonic orchestra of the land of Israel was established in 1936 thanks to the Jewish violinist and musician Bronisław Huberman, who was born in Poland. He saw the Holocaust approaching and managed to convince about seventy-five Jewish musicians who played in some of the most famous orchestras in Europe to immigrate to Israel. On the sandy shores of Tel Aviv, they founded what Huberman called "the realization of Zionist culture in the land of the forefathers."

Huberman invited the greatest conductor of the generation, Arturo Toscanini, who left his own orchestra for a few months in order to "provide fatherly care to the new baby." Toscanini, who had escaped Italy earlier due to the rise of fascism, said, "We are taking part in this endeavor on behalf of humankind." Mehta emphasized the fact that from the establishment of the orchestra to this day, it has been committed to two central principles: first, musical excellence and openness to international musical worlds, including by inviting the finest conductors in the world; two, cultivating Israeli artists and creators who will become partners in the development of new art. The orchestra is dedicated to playing for the Israeli population while also attempting to integrate into the Mediterranean and international arenas.

Mehta said that although he was born in India and is not a Jew, he feels like a member of the Jewish tribe and is very proud of the musical excellence of the orchestra, as displayed by its musicians, such as the violinist Pinchas Zukerman and the pianist Daniel Barenboim, as well as the local and international recognition that the orchestra received. This is in addition to the fact that excellent immigrant musicians from a range of countries have successfully joined the orchestra.

Mehta explained that the philharmonic orchestra plays a significant role in inspiring the renewal of Israeli culture. This is achieved by incorporating the melodies of Israeli composers into the orchestra's repertoire and into special concerts dedicated to leading local musicians, such as Moshe Vilenski, Sasha Argov, Naomi Shemer, and Yoni Rechter. The orchestra is also dedicated to influencing values such as cooperation and coexistence between different populations in Israel, in the context of relationships between Israeli and Palestinian children as well. To that end, it developed a program called Mafteach (KeyNote), with about twenty thousand participants involved every year. When Mehta stepped down as maestro in 2019 and was succeeded by the young musical manager Lahav Shani, the orchestra became even more Israeli.

The term "Israeli music" is composed of two entities: music and Israel. So says Michal Zmora-Cohen, one of the most important scholars on the subject of Israeli culture. "The two are interdependent and influence each other. Israelism is the source of Israeli music's existence, and makes it different than any other type of music."

The philharmonic orchestra, aside from playing classical music at a level that is among the highest in the world, also plays music that was composed in Israel by Israeli artists. The world of associations of its composers is Israeli, influenced by the East, the West, and by Jewish culture. The orchestra serves as a personal example of quality Israeli culture. The orchestra imparts cultural values as part of the world of developing Israeli culture.

Looking at Israel from the outside, people are liable to think that there is nothing but problems here. True, Israeli society does face serious social, security, and political problems, but this reality gives its culture a range of roles. It connects individuals to a special aesthetic and cultural experience, but also connects those individuals to each other and reflects life in Israel back to the Israelis. Even a tourist can get a glimpse of Israeli drama by becoming familiar with the artists or works of Israeli culture.

It is important to remember that Hebrew is only spoken by about ten million people, which makes a small market for verbal cultural performances. The geographic and political situation also made Israel somewhat of a cultural island which is hardly influenced by, or has an influence on, its close surroundings (the Arab countries). Perhaps it is for this very reason that there is so much motivation to create two-way influences with the Western world.

I believe that Israel is not just a start-up nation. It's an art-up nation too. A start-up nation is based on innovation and creativity, the same components that drive Israeli culture today to create original cultural and artistic works in the fields of theater, painting, fashion, and music that are unique and far-reaching.

I personally invite you to watch a musical performance by an Israeli singer or group, such as Idan Raichel or the Balkan Beat Box, who take world music and integrate Israeli and Jewish culture.

There's nothing like sitting in the Cameri Theater and watching a translated play. There's nothing like visiting Nissan Nativ's acting studio. There's nothing like experiencing an Israeli Philharmonic concert at the Heichal HaTarbut auditorium. There's nothing like going to a fringe theater, not only in Tel Aviv, but in Jerusalem too. There's nothing like visiting a studio in the western Galilee of the Kibbutz Contemporary Dance Company, and there's nothing like visiting the final exhibitions of the art and design schools in the summer.

To conclude – let's return to our conversation about the source of the Israeli national anthem, "Hatikvah." The tune to "Hatikvah" was actually stolen from us, and not vice versa. I learned this two years ago, when I met the concert pianist and musicologist Dr. Astrith Baltsan. She performed before our groups in Israel in the seventieth year of Israel's independence. "Like many of us, for years I was told that our 'Hatikvah' derived from the work of the Czech composer Bedřich Smetana, who wrote it in 1874. When I started researching the subject, I discovered that the source of our anthem is much older than the Czech poem and comes from an old Spanish prayer called the 'Prayer for Dew,' composed back in the fourteenth century in Toledo, Spain, by a liturgist named Rabbi Yitzchak Barsheshet. After the Jews were expelled from Spain, the tune spread throughout Europe. It even found its way into one of Mozart's works, and it also reached Smetana, who wrote that it was a tune identified with 'wandering tunes in Eastern Europe.'"

Given that "Hatikvah" was inspired by a Jewish melody, it's no wonder that the national anthem aroused intense national unity. "Hatikvah" became a Jewish and Zionist prayer, the spearhead of Israeli culture.

The Czech writer Milan Kundera clearly defined what culture is made of: "Culture is the memory of a nation, its common conscience, the continuation of history, and the way that the country thinks and lives."

Culture is a strategic asset and constitutes a central element of a nation's resilience. It creates a sense of pride in who we are, gives us faith in our path, moves us and calms us, and creates connections between most of Israeli society.

Culture influences the orientation of the nation, our personal and public behavior, and the attitude toward those who are different. The national anthem, "Hatikvah," had and still has a central role in shaping and establishing Israeli culture.

6

The Soundtrack of Israel

A Personal Music Journey

Ya'acov Fried

Stretched out on the couch in the guest room in my childhood home on a Saturday afternoon, I listened to the music playing in a fixed sequence. My father put records on, and as I listened to the music, I experienced the calmest moments of my childhood. I felt the music coursing through my veins, like a generator pumping power into my entire body, especially my heart. Over the years, especially on trips, I learned that sounds and music can uplift my soul instantly and arouse within me a spirit of prayer and love. Listening to music chases away gloomy feelings and elicits, like a magic wand, memories of lost loves or friends who passed away. Music lets me play, pray, believe, jump, dance, and overcome obstacles.

The journey in the footsteps of Israeli music – since the State of Israel's establishment over seventy years ago, and during the years before – is a long, tempestuous love story. Love for the place, the friends, the family, the couples, and the love of music itself. Today, Israeli music is a mixture of styles woven together into one tapestry. Its sources, like its creators, come from many different places. But it especially stands out for its polarity between East and West. Even 120 years ago, we sang in Israel and listened to music anywhere and everywhere: at work, on trips, on the street, at home, and in the shower. In good times and in bad times. Hundreds of songs accompanied the Zionist endeavor, which was characterized, at least at the beginning, by pioneer texts about loving the land, its breathtaking landscapes, ideals, war, revival, realization, and Zionism.

In 1948, the young state fought for its physical existence and explored the question: Who are we? Music artists at that time also grappled with the question: What is an Israeli song? Arab music? Melodies from Eastern Europe? Russian folk songs? French chansons? Classical music? North African music? Pop? Rock? Maybe we need to create a new Israeli melody, one that doesn't speak Yiddish, Arabic, or English, but rather the new Hebrew, with a melody that has not yet been born? Another question that they dealt with was whether the role of Hebrew music is educational. Is it meant to give meaning to the challenging lifestyle in Israel? To encourage and comfort in times of war? To convince people that it is worth living in Israel? Or perhaps its main purpose is to entertain. Is it necessary to sing about "us" in the plural, or is there room for personal, private musings? These questions regarding the correct way to develop Israeli music have followed Israel throughout all of the different periods – from the songs of the old Yishuv to military bands and folk dancing, and until the arrival of rock, pop, Mizrahi (eastern/oriental), and Mediterranean music. What is Israeli music?

Michal Zmora-Cohen, one of the most important scholars of Israeli music, said, "We must be aware of the singularity and uniqueness of Israel. Israel is the only modern country whose residents did not live on their land many years prior to its independence. Therefore, Israeli music lacks a uniform tradition. It includes numerous traditions and is painted in the shades of the immigrants' countries of origin. It is very possible that this obstacle is the basis of the uniqueness, creativity, and depth of the Israeli music that we have created."

Moshe Zorman, an important Israeli composer, explains: "Israeli music draws from the sounds of the Hebrew language, from its pronunciations and from its internal music. All of these are the deeper levels, the infrastructure, with which the Israeli composer begins working, and atop which he builds his modern world. It is a world that is open to sounds from the four corners of the earth – American jazz, world pop and rock, European avant-garde, melodies from Arab countries, the Far East, and the sounds of the computer and synthesizer."

Musicologist Edwin Seroussi and sociologist Motti Regev claim that "popular Israeli music reflects power struggles, economic and political changes, and status wars, while contending for the definition of Israeliness."

For years, I have been studying the essence of the connection between songs and the places where I heard them. When traveling, I feel that music becomes a sublime atrium where I can experience the glory of existence. Music can drive away dark thoughts with the beat of a drum, to sing the praise of the holy, and to call out for God's help. Driving next to the Dead Sea and the Judean Desert, I feel that the music and notes are the voices of the soil and the sky, the ebbing and flowing, the storms. Driving through the expanses of the Negev, I experience music as the first breath of creation itself and the stuff that my dreams and emotions are made of.

On trips throughout the world, I have experienced similar feelings and discovered that becoming familiar with local music is a powerful way to intimately learn the local culture and gain the experience of a multisensory trip. When I listen to a song at a specific location while on a trip, the experience is twofold. First, there is the experience of listening and the internal reaction, which are not related to the location, and second, there is the experience of the location. When I listen to the song again in a different place, under different circumstances, my memory transports me back to my original experience hearing the song in the context of the location where I heard it. The listening experience in a specific location on a trip left an emotional imprint on me. Therefore, I have chosen to present the central components of the mosaic of styles that make up Israeli music at various junctions I have crossed throughout Israel.

On the slope descending from Jerusalem toward the coastal plain, between forests of cypress, pine, carob, and almond trees, lies the military cemetery of Kibbutz Kiryat Anavim. As a twelve-year-old boy, I visited the site for the first time with my fellow members of the Tzofim (Israeli Scouts) youth movement. We held a memorial ceremony for the fallen soldiers of the Harel Brigade, who fell near the kibbutz during the War of Independence. During the ceremony, we sang the song "Hare'ut" (which means "friendship"), a Hebrew poem written by Haim Gouri and set to music by Sasha Argov, one of the most important composers in the Israeli music world. I will never forget the feeling of friendship and Israeli solidarity that enveloped me, as expressed in the concern for soldiers, for a neighbor in need, for a new immigrant who does not speak the language, and many other situations. "Hare'ut" celebrates the values of bravery and friendship, and the memories of the fallen. All of these made the song a classic part of the formation of Israeli fraternity and solidary.

About a week after the Six-Day War in 1967, I walked with my family from my home in western Jerusalem toward the Western Wall in the eastern part of the city. The Six-Day War, during which eastern Jerusalem and the territories of the west bank of the Jordan were conquered/liberated by Israel, completely changed the borders of the country and the face of Israeli society. About three weeks before the war broke out, the song "Jerusalem of Gold" was released, written by

Naomi Shemer and sung by Shuli Natan. It aroused memories and an intense yearning for the Old City of Jerusalem.

I remember the excitement we felt when the song was played on the radio as part of a musical event on Independence Day. Three weeks later, when the Western Wall was liberated, the paratroopers who fought there sang the song as soon as they reached the area of the wall. Tears welled up in my eyes when I heard them singing on the live broadcast from the site. I will never forget that walk to the Western Wall about a week after the war. The aromas of the spices and incense from the shops, the awkward expressions on the faces of the shop-keepers, Arabs from East Jerusalem, and the sights in the alleyways of the Old City.

When we reached the Western Wall plaza, there were already hun-dreds of groups of people. My father and mother shook with emotion. My father held my hand with one hand and my brother's hand with his other hand and encouraged us to approach the huge wall. He had two requests: one, that we kiss the stones of the Western Wall, and two, that we write a note of prayer, according to the custom with which I was of course unfamiliar. I only obliged his second request. We met family friends, whom we hugged and kissed as if it was a wedding, and together, we all recited the shehecheyanu blessing (common Jewish prayer said to celebrate special occasions) and enthusiastically began to sing the song "Jerusalem of Gold."

An entirely different type of event on my musical journey occurred one summer afternoon in 1977. I got off a bus from Jerusalem at the old central bus station in Tel Aviv. I was greeted with heavy heat and humid-ity, to which I was unaccustomed as a born-and-bred Jerusalemite. We crossed the huge bazaar that surrounded the station like a wide belt. Stalls bearing fruit, vegetables, various small items, and new and old clothing were everywhere, including many stalls with tape cassettes, a product that no longer exists and is considered a relic today. Unfamiliar tunes filled the air – Mizrahi music in Hebrew, blasting from various stalls. To my ears, it sounded like Arab music. I looked at the names of the singers and discovered names that I never knew existed.

A few years earlier, I had started randomly listening to Israeli Mizrahi music, which I considered inferior songs that weren't really part of the Israeli music world. Mizrahi music during those years was broadcasted on the radio during certain hours and on programs that were defined as sect-specific. At that time, there was only public radio and television in Israel, and they confined Mizrahi music to its own cultural ghetto. Three years earlier, at parties at the university where I studied, Mizrahi music was very rarely played, and we treated it as something inferior that didn't belong to us. I will never forget the embarrassed looks on the faces of my friends who grew up in homes where Arab music was played, whose parents had immigrated from Arab countries.

Walking through this music fest, I heard Zohar Argov singing "Flower in My Garden," written and composed by Avihu Medina, which had won at the Mizrahi Music Festival two months earlier. The intensity of the singing that burst forth from the heart and the Yemenite trills, combined with elements of Western pop, caused me to genuinely listen to the music for the first time. Zohar later paved the way, for himself and for other artists, to entering the heart of the Israeli consensus. Gradually, the superficial obstacles fell to the wayside.

Over the years, I connected to Mizrahi music, which includes three elements: joy, singing from the depths of the heart, and rare vocal capabilities. When I'm feeling down and look for a "musical medicine" to boost my spirits, I put on headphones and listen to Mizrahi music, such as Itay Levi, Sarit Hadad, or Omer Adam. The "medicine" usually works. When my two children got married, the most important thing to them was for the wedding to be joyous. The soundtrack prepared for the wedding included plenty of Mizrahi music that makes people jump and dance. To understand the extent of this drastic change of the integration of Mizrahi music in Israel, it is worth noting that the only performance before an audience of thirty thousand that sold out completely within two hours of opening the ticket boxes was the concert at Park HaYarkon in Tel Aviv in the summer of 2019 – a concert by Omer Adam, a Mizrahi singer who is the most popular singer in Israel today.

Who isn't familiar with that drive home in the evening after a stressful, exhausting day of work? Who isn't familiar with the feeling that we have a long night ahead dealing with parental responsibilities and other work tasks to be completed? A few years ago, I discovered a trick that I am willing to share without a copyright. It is an exercise in awareness. After getting into my car, I ask myself: What upbeat music should I listen to? Which music should I choose to listen to during the drive that will bring a smile to my face and maybe even make me laugh? Which music will help change my mood from heavy to light?

I have a few options, but the winning answer is Kaveret, a band that appeared in the middle of the seventies and succeeded in creating funny parody songs that were Israeli rock and pop style. It was innovative, not only in its lyrics, but in the fact that it was the first to bring guitars to center stage. In the band's reunion concert, as I lay sprawled on the grass, I broke out into uncontrollable laughter at the song "Baruch's Boots." It's the story of a man named Baruch who bought a pair of boots when he was seventeen. He was very connected to them and showered them with warmth and love. One day, his boots disappeared from the closet. He was very depressed and embarked on a journey to find his boots, until he found them in the arms of another man. He whipped out his gun, shot the man holding the boots, and put them back on his feet.

Kaveret fulfilled music's role of entertaining, making people laugh, raising their spirits, and even being nonsensical, in contrast with the role of instilling national values – the role that music had fulfilled until that time. Kaveret was one of the pioneers in the creation of Israeli pop and rock and a genre that became a central component of Israeli music.

In the Carmel forests, opposite the Mediterranean Sea and the fish ponds of Kibbutz Maagan Michael, lies the educational institution Yemin Orde. Dr. Chaim Peri led Yemin Orde for years as the school and dormitory principal. There are few people who deserve the credit and esteem that he does for his leadership in absorbing immigrants, which is one of the biggest challenges in the State of Israel. Yemin Orde houses students from broken homes, many of whom are high school students from families of Ethiopian immigrants.

As we listened to the school choir during one of my visits, Chaim Peri shared his thoughts with me. "If you let immigrant children sing in their mother tongue, you teach them that they can walk upright, without being ashamed of their country of origin and the culture from which they came. If you teach them Hebrew, you open the door to immigration and integration. If you create a choir where they can sing in both languages, Hebrew and Amharic, you've truly healed their souls."

As part of the performance, the choir sang the song "Out of the Depths," written by Idan Raichel, a composer and artist who has had a far-reaching impact on Israeli music. He served in the military at a dormitory for Ethiopian children, was exposed to Ethiopian folk music, and integrated it with pop music. Modestly and with restraint, he began his project and opened up the door for Israeli artists at the beginning of their careers. He creates Israeli music that integrates music from around the world. Chaim Peri's comment about cultural integration through music echoes in my mind every time I listen to Idan Raichel, who became the most successful Israeli artist in the world today. In my opinion, Idan Raichel represents and leads the Israeli music scene that combines world music. Attending an Idan Raichel concert during your visit to Israel is one of the best gifts you can give yourself.

Over the past few years, unnoticed, a genre of Israeli music has developed that is anchored in Jewish culture and tradition, and is becoming a prominent part of the Israeli music scene. What caused us to suddenly fall in love with Jewish texts again? For years, Israelis were ashamed of their Jewish roots and tried to hide Jewish music, as if it were part of the culture of the Diaspora. Over the past decade, a huge change has taken place. There are even those who would call it a revolution. Many leading artists in the Israeli music world, some of whom do not conduct religious lifestyles, started to write and sing songs depicting a renewed Jewish-Israeli identity. Materials inspired by Jewish sources, including ancient liturgy that is hundreds of years old, suddenly experienced an updated, modern musical rejuvenation.

An example of this phenomenon is the song by Ovadia Hamama "Ana B'Koach," and the works of artists such as Eviatar Banai, Ehud Banai, Kobi Aflalo, Berry Sakharof, Shlomo Gronich, Ishay Ribo, and others. Based on my encounters with them, I sense that for many of these artists, this is not because they have become more religious. Rather, they feel a renewed connection with their Jewish-Israeli identities, as part of a process of curiosity and a desire to know more about its treasures. Jewish-Israeli music touches upon the language of the heart. It expresses emotions in an unmediated way. Some songs express the longing for a connection to the heart, consciousness, or spirituality. It represents curiosity, the search for a way of life, and it plucks at the hidden soul strings that we didn't know existed. It's like music from a different dimension.

Israeli music is like a slow-cooked stew. At any given moment, the flavor of the stew is different. In Israel today, music is no longer responsible for the national ethos. It is also almost never written from a place of oppression. It is not obligated to a specific style, but there is an increasing commitment to authenticity and to personal compositions. In Israel, there is an unfathomable abundance of nonstop creativity and vitality. The Israeli music scene is full of artists who create and perform with a wide range of messages. What is happening today is a type of fusion-style that has no rules, free creativity that is captivating, moving, and revolutionary.

A soundtrack of Israeli music can transform your trip to Israel. There is a chance that by listening to Israeli music before and during your trip, you will ignite a powerful experience, feeling the music's presence and absorbing the experiences of your trip like a sponge. Songs never disappoint. Music is always above all communication and language, and can spark a romance of the heart during your trip.

7

The Israeli Kitchen

From Survival to Freedom

Ya'acov Fried

The Jaffa flea market is buzzing with shoppers. Tourists and locals sit in the cafés, located in a restored building from the Ottoman period, when the Turks controlled the land of Israel. They eat French croissants, identical in their taste and quality to those served in a Parisian café. In the courtyard opposite them is the empire of Dr. Shakshuka, where Tunisian, Libyan, and Moroccan cuisine is served on huge plates. Nearby, next to the clock tower, there is a long line at Abulafia's bakery empire. On the pedestrian street mall leading into the alleyways of the market, there are Arab and Italian restaurants, Greek taverns, and Mediterranean bars, with international menus, as well as a long row of Asian restaurants.

When you ask a cultural anthropologist, such as Professor Nir Avieli, to define Israeli food, he answers: "Israeli food is the product of immigrant kitchens." Meaning, kosher versions of peasant foods from Poland, Morocco, or Iraq that coalesce with the local weather, local produce, and Arab cuisine. Everything gets mixed together, and you have shakshuka.

Is it possible that the trauma of the Holocaust, the generous Mediterranean heart, the kibbutz kitchen experiences, and the military mess hall also contributed to the development of the Israeli kitchen? Is it possible that certain scholars are right in their claims that over the last seventy years of the country's existence, or the 130 years of Jewish settlement in the land of Israel, we haven't created a local cuisine? If so, will an authentic local cuisine ever be created? Perhaps the biggest question of all: How is the Israeli character related to the style and essence of the creation of an Israeli cuisine?

The year of the Six-Day War, 1967, was a revolutionary year in the history of the State of Israel. Israel changed unrecognizably, and the borders were opened to entry, encounter, and exposure to the Palestinian population. That year I had the privilege of being a student of science teacher Batya Shalev. Batya moved to Jerusalem from Nahalal with her husband, the legendary poet and Bible teacher Yitzchak Shalev. For the first time, I learned to smell the soil, collect, and taste plants, and understand what a kitchen based on foraging means. For the first time, I felt that learning can also involve scents, colors, and tastes. Her husband joined for one of the classes, and they guided us together on a field trip on the subject of "Israeli food during biblical times."

During the trip, Yitzchak Shalev asked us: "Do you know what food was on King David's table, and how early shepherds made cheese in the fields? Was hummus the national food during biblical times?" We climbed up a hill covered in wild plants, which is the location of the Supreme Court in Jerusalem today, and he continued to ask: "Did children in those times eat popcorn too?" He led us on a journey through a time tunnel, to the days when the ancient Israelite kitchen was created, days when the pace of life was slow. In the shade of a fruit tree orchard, between blushing pomegranates and figs not yet ripe, they demonstrated to us together how shepherds turned milk into cheese. The teacher and her husband poured milk into a metal pot, squeezed some white sap from the nearby fig tree, and within a few minutes, the milk curdled.

Recalling that trip, I remember how we foraged and tasted edible wild plants, and how the teacher and her husband roasted wheat berries in a pan. Yitzchak Shalev told us about toasted grain, mentioned several times in the Bible, which was prepared as a snack over a fire in the field, or at home to be served to guests. The couple gave us the grain to taste, nicknaming it "biblical popcorn." It was crunchy and crackled in your mouth, and I felt as if I was a guest in King David's palace. Later, when I began to work in the field of educational tourism, I remembered Yitzchak Shalev's immortal statement, quoting his teacher, Arye Alkalai: "A trip backpack that has provisions but no Bible is like sacrifices of the dead."

In the early seventies, I had the opportunity to meet the author and poet Haim Gouri, one of the most important writers to describe the pre-state settlement period in the land of Israel and the early days of statehood. He read us the poem "Ichlu Yeladim Lechem Totzeret" (Eat, children, "homemade" bread) by Aharon Ze'ev, set to music by Sara Levi-Tnai.

Eat, children, "homemade" bread!
The wheat grew next to the Sea of Galilee.

The people of Degania worked by the sweat of their brow.
There, the light of the sun is seven times stronger.

There, the guard does not slumber, the plowman does not sleep.
There, even a child in kindergarten knows how to sow.

Eat, children, "homemade" bread!
The wheat grew next to the Sea of Galilee.

Gouri claimed that farmers had always tried to emphasize the healthy attributes of their wares. In the new Jewish Yishuv in the land of Israel, at the end of the nineteenth century and beginning of the twentieth century, this element took on new, unique dimensions. Concern for healthy, correct nutrition won significant attention from public institutions, organizations, and movements. It was a national goal as part of the effort to create a "new Jew" in the land of Israel. Food became a tool for inculcating national values of responsibility for security, independence, national pride, and the creation of an Israeli culture.

The central role of agriculture in the new Jewish economy of the land of Israel was a strong expression of the public emphasis placed on food – its production, marketing, and consumption. The fledgling Israeli society attempted to create a significant status for those who worked the land. Production of food by a Hebrew farmer was a genuine ideological goal. It is important to remember the centralist approach that was prevalent at the time and the need for control over agricultural production.

When the austerity policy was implemented after the state's establishment, nutrition became a broad public issue. The state developed control mechanisms over the distribution of food, because food sources were limited. This was done by distributing food stamps. As a result of the scarcity, a black market for food developed. The shortage made the consumption habits and ingredients in the Israeli kitchen even more extreme. During those years, the Israeli kitchen was in survival mode, on the one hand, and was still a direct continuation of the ethnic foods according to country of origin, on the other. The focus of the food cooked in those years was calculated in terms of not being hungry. It was basic and unvaried. The restaurants that operated were mainly workers' restaurants, which strived to fulfill the need for healthy nutrition while using poor quality, unvaried products. Yet most people were satisfied with their lot. As a child, I remember hearing the phrase at home, "We have everything."

Before the political upheaval of 1977, there were two separate kitchens that existed in Israel – the Ashkenazi kitchen and the Mizrahi kitchen. They remained intact, in separate bubbles, each in their own homes. The Ashkenazi, Eastern European kitchen seems like a sad one to me. It gives off a pessimistic air that utilizes the humoristic element of despair. Fish filled with fish. Kishke – intestines filled with a mixture of fat and flour – and other stuffed foods using the same ingredients represent foods of suffering to me. The Eastern European cooking methods turn everything into the same pale shade of gray.

It is no wonder that the author Shai Agnon, when depicting the Jewish meal in *A Simple Story*, describes it as "carcasses of chickens and fish." Comparing the European kitchen to the Mizrahi kitchen is not meant to degrade the European one, in my opinion. Some of the Eastern European Jewish foods, such as the kugel, can be culinary masterpieces. But the pessimism that wafts from their inner voice is the voice of constant tragedy. As a child who experienced only the European kitchen until the age of fourteen, I remember my first encounters with the Mizrahi foods of Jews who immigrated from Arab countries. I remember the elderly grandmother of my friends in the apartment across from us who stuffed zucchini or onions or made kubbeh. I remember the holy feeling that accompanied the neighbor's cooking process – the amazing aromas, the delicate steps, the enjoyment.

The sixties, seventies, and eighties were characterized by the trauma of the Holocaust and the hunger, which were passed down to the second and third generations too. Jews from Arab countries, who didn't undergo the Holocaust, are characterized by "fattening" up the diners. The understanding of Jews from Muslim countries is that a gracious host welcomes their guests to a laden table. In the Middle East, an unspoken competition takes place between the guest and the host. The guest says: I can't eat any more, and the host says: We haven't even started eating; there are five more courses! There is a feeling that if you, as the host, don't load the table with food, your honor has been tainted. On one occasion, after a meal with friends of Moroccan descent, I asked the hosts' daughter, after we had left the house, "Why did they serve so much food?" Her answer was, "In Moroccan, there's no word for 'a little bit.'"

To understand the exaggerated portions of the Israeli kitchen, we must also look at the origins of the Israeli breakfast served at hotels, created from the seventies and onward, which is one of the symbols of Israeli cuisine. This meal includes a never-ending series of bowls and trays that aren't really connected to each other. These are sometimes arranged in various different shapes and patterns, a geometric row of salads, soft and hard cheeses, pastries, quiches, sweet puddings, different types of herring, an assortment of olives and pickles, tahini and spreads, mountains of loaves and rolls, piles of laffah, and we haven't even reached the desserts. How can you eat all that in the morning? I wonder. It turns out, though, that the tourists love it. There are other nationalities that "eat with their eyes."

For as long as I can remember, the creation of an authentic Israeli kitchen has always been a relevant topic. It is a longing to be like all of the other nations. We deserve to have our own kitchen too, a culinary tradition, foods that were born and cooked up here in this wonderful melting pot of an ingathering of exiles.

Until 1977, I think that people were closed off in their ethnic kitchens because of the sense of Ashkenazi elitism in the State of Israel. The political revolution and the change of the Ashkenazi hegemony sparked a process of openness and a desire to become familiar with the colorful kitchens that the Jews from Arab countries had brought with them. I remember the food of the eighties, at the modern Israeli restaurants, and the feeling that an independent food culture might finally be developing here. The dishes that were created at the Tzrif restaurant in Jerusalem, for example – who remembers them today?

Quite a few dishes were developed and disappeared during the process. I will mention, for example, an original Israeli dish that was conceived here about ten years ago: roasted eggplant in tahini. We felt that here, we had finally invented something that was our own. A unique recipe that characterizes us and Israel. Not a decade had gone by before it became impossible to find this dish in any respectable culinary establishment. Israelis feel that they have had enough pretty quickly. What was considered special last year is no longer trendy or appropriate this year.

Many trends in the local Israeli culinary world are related to the Israeli personality, which is always searching for something new. I don't want more of the same. I want new, I want different, I want someone to surprise me, to touch me. I want to try something I've never had before, I want to be where they invented the wheel, and maybe invent it myself. My sense is that especially among the population that goes to the fanciest restaurants in Tel Aviv, this personality, which is constantly looking for something new, causes people to skip that excellent restaurant, because they already tried it a few months ago.

When a new restaurant opens, they'll hurry there to experience the new, not to miss out, to keep current, to be among the first. The result is that a top chef restaurant that was constantly packed in its first year is empty in its second, because the buzz has worn off. This reality is part of the reason that restaurants close all over the country. The restaurant can be very good, but after a while, customers will look for new experiences and prefer them over the "old but good." This is very different from the reality in France or Italy, where restaurant menus remain identical for years, with light changes, and customers loyally return for the familiar cuisine. There is a sense of inner quiet and security in these countries which facilitates the existence of a culinary tradition and identical foods for years.

The unsatisfied desire for renewal, for surprises, and for the unfamiliar creates a situation in which dishes created in Israel don't last over time. Restaurants, like the foods, lose their attractiveness, as good and beloved as they may be.

It is important to note that this restless personality exists among Israeli chefs as well. From the same nation, in the same culture, a generation of chefs has emerged that are constantly inventing and creating new things. It has reached the point where Israeli culinary news captivates the culinary world. A kitchen has developed here that is unlike other places in the world. The best international chefs have made the pilgrimage here to taste and experience new Israeli culinary trends. Dozens of creative Israeli restaurants have opened branches in some of the leading cities in the world.

Is there a revolution underway here, and has something central changed? Yes – it's the flipside of the same coin, the same personality that caused the development of new things here. It's the same personality that caused Israel to become a world leader in the field of high tech and the same personality that thinks differently than everyone else and is constantly searching for what hasn't been done yet.

Over the past ten years, a captivating process has been underway of the creation of a unique Israeli kitchen. In order to understand it in greater depth, I spoke with three of the leading Israeli chefs who represented the transition from a survival-oriented kitchen to a free kitchen and led a genuine revolution in the Israeli kitchen.

Meir Adoni explains, "You need to cook yourself; you need to explore who you are. My kitchen became a biographical kitchen and a geographical one. I have cooked gefilte fish made of shrimp. It was part of a developmental process for me. If you aren't authentic to your biography and your geography, while still remaining open, you don't create genuine food at all, especially not Israeli food."

Another leading chef, Eyal Shani, represents the formation of the authentic Israeli kitchen, in my opinion. He started his journey in an Israeli kitchen that was transplanted from the French kitchen in the eighties. "I realized," he admits, "that I was restless and arrogant. Until I realized that I needed to listen to the local traditions, including the Jewish traditions, I didn't successfully develop a real kitchen. When I understood that Israeli food needs to be happy, to raise the spirits and be a holistic experience, that was when the precision kicked in. I feel a sense of mission in creating an Israeli kitchen, in Israel and in the world."

Erez Komarovsky established and managed several luxury restaurants in central Israel, as well as leading a revolution in the quality of Israeli breadmaking. Ten years ago, he left central Israel and moved to Mitzpe Mattat in the upper Galilee. He studies and researches the essence of Israeli food in ancient periods. He views recreating the ancient dishes as an important step in developing the Israeli kitchen and determining its character. Komarovsky claims that the Israeli kitchen is growing today and becoming a leading kitchen in the world because we have finally started familiarizing ourselves with the roots of the ancient Israeli kitchen. Through them, we can connect to the original values of the essence and characteristics of the foods. We are returning to the local ingredients and to seasonal cooking.

A life of survival, scarcity, withdrawal, seclusion, a lack of respect for the different parts of the population, and living in the shadow of traumas, did not allow Israeli creativity to break free during the fifties, sixties, and seventies and build a quality, happy, authentic Israeli kitchen. We needed about three decades to loosen the chains. To do so, we enlisted the Israeli ability to think outside the box, and found alternatives for everything. All that's left is to hope that this ability will lead us to new heights.

Predator
Oil on canvas
mounted on wood
75X55

8

From Paving the Roads to Waze

Transformation of the Israeli Economy

Yona Leshets

In the summer of 2011, after an intense and successful career in high tech, at the beginning of the sixth decade of my life, I took my first steps in my newly chosen profession as a tour guide. At Ben-Gurion International Airport, I welcomed a delegation of businesspeople that included the mayor of one of the largest cities in the United States. The purpose of the visit was to learn about Israel in general, and specifically about its business-economic world.

As befitting of an important delegation, they were staying at the famous King David Hotel in Jerusalem. The welcoming dinner of the trip took place in the Ambassadors Hall, overlooking the Old City Walls. The group members introduced themselves and their knowledge of Israel. They mentioned terms such as: immigrant society, lack of resources, military service, small local market, chutzpah. Many of them mentioned what was a new term at the time – "startup nation." As the introductory discussion continued, I realized that a book by that name had just recently been published. As the final person to speak, I said,

"This is my first time hearing about the book, but from what I heard here, I lived and experienced everything mentioned in it."

I was the firstborn son to my parents, Holocaust survivors who were both born in Poland. Each of them reached Israel independently immediately after the state was founded in 1948. During the first decade of the country's establishment, its population tripled and reached the two million mark. At the end of the decade, most of the country's Jewish citizens were immigrants: Holocaust survivors from Europe like my parents, Jews from neighboring Arab countries, Jews from North Africa, and other countries. When those involved in immigrant absorption turned to Prime Minister David Ben-Gurion and asked that the flow of immigrants be slowed down, because there weren't enough economic resources (housing, food, employment) to provide for all of them, his answer was: "Three thousand three hundred years ago, when Moses took the large nation out of Egypt, he didn't wait for houses and infrastructures to be ready. In the Promised Land – we take everyone."

I was born and raised in Kiryat Haim, in the Bay Area. I'm referring to the Haifa Bay, the only bay along the western coastline. Kiryat Haim was established in 1933 east of the Haifa-Acco train tracks as housing for the railway workers. After the state was established, transit camps, called *ma'abarot*, were built for the immigrants between the train tracks and the sea. Later, housing projects containing rows of buildings were built in the same area. My family lived in one such apartment. My childhood friends were named Messinger, Steinberger, and Eisenband, and their parents were from Europe. Maman, Sabag, and Deri's parents all immigrated from North Africa. We also had friends with the last names Magen and Navon, whose parents were already second- and third-generation residents in the country. In today's terms, the western Kiryat Haim was on the periphery, if not geographically, then definitely socially. One friend's father worked for the electric company, another at the refineries, and the third at the port.

My father worked outside of Haifa. Soon after his immigration and until his retirement thirty-five years later, he worked at Soylel-Boyneh, which is Yiddish for Solel Boneh – or in English, Pave and Build. As a teenager, I often accompanied my father to construction sites. In the fifties and sixties, housing projects were built hastily and in a fixed format in over twenty towns, which were referred to as development towns. These were populated by many of the immigrants who arrived during those years, sometimes against their will. If you travel outside of the holy and ancient Jerusalem, and outside of the new, trendy Tel Aviv, you will notice these towns, which have already become cities by now.

The United States was built by private initiatives. The Zionist movement that was established during the transition from the nineteenth century to the twentieth century was primarily influenced by socialism. The same spirit was the driving force behind the establishment of kibbutzim as a way of life and a way of establishing the borders of the future state. Professional unions were founded under the umbrella organization of the General Histadrut, and most of the service and industrial companies were subordinate to it. Solel Boneh is an example of one of them. Those who managed to secure themselves a place in these companies were considered lucky. The job was usually for life, and often the children and relatives of employees inherited the privilege. Thanks to their connections, of course. In those days, Israelis referred to it as "protexia." A bus driver in the public cooperative Egged had a prestigious status like today's airline pilots, because he was a shareholder in the cooperative, received a fair salary, and was protected from dismissal too.

To this day, I am surprised that my hometown, Haifa, is not very well known and does not have a prominent spot on the tourism map.

The city was developed at an accelerated speed in the twenties. The British, who controlled the land of Israel and other regions in the Middle East at the time, established the central imperial seaport in the eastern Mediterranean Sea. Jews from Salonika, Greece, dockworkers by profession, immigrated to Israel at that time, settled in Haifa, and worked at the port. Nearby, the refinery industry was established, processing crude oil that came from north Iraq by pipe. Petrochemical plants, a power plant, and a regional train center were built. All of these can still be seen today from the gorgeous overlook at the Bahai Gardens at the top of the Carmel. If you have a sharp eye, you will also be able to see the region where I grew up, right on the other side of the oil storage tanks.

During the British Mandate period, Haifa was also called Umm al-Amal (in Arabic: Mother of Work), and it attracted Arab immigrants from Syria and Lebanon, as well as Jewish immigration, primarily from Europe. Later, it was referred to as Red Haifa, the color representing the workers' movement. All of this took place just a few decades after the visionary of the Jewish state, Theodor Herzl, published his utopic book *Altneuland*. In the book, Haifa is described as the city of the future, an electric-technological city where peoples of different religions and cultures live together in peace. It seems that Herzl's vision is quickly becoming reality. The need for constant labor in this large industrial area made operating public transportation necessary seven days a week. To this day, Haifa is the only area in Israel where there is a Jewish majority but public transportation still runs on Shabbat. The fact that Jews, Christians, and Muslims all live side by side in Haifa was also influential in this decision.

Haifa is home to the Technion, the academic institution that is still fighting with history and with Hebrew University over which was the first one established, somewhere between 1924 and 1925. At the Technion, they studied engineering; at Hebrew University, they emphasized philosophy. Both received the blessing and merited the involvement of Albert Einstein, who was at the height of his international fame. From my parents' home we could see the Technion complex soaring above the cooling towers of the refineries.

In the early eighties, I completed my BSc studies in electrical engineering, prior to my military service. The IDF needed increasing technological capabilities and founded a special military track that allowed excellent high school graduates to defer their military service, earn a degree, and then be recruited for professional military service in their area of expertise – engineering, medical, law, etc. Five years of technological service in a secret intelligence unit taught me how to deal with unique challenges, which came with a lot of responsibility but also the freedom to dare and to create. This knowledge base significantly helped me later on.

I was pretty surprised when many of the members of the delegation mentioned "8200" during that meal in the Ambassadors Hall of the King David Hotel. In Hebrew, we call it *"shmone matayim."* This is the military unit that I served in, and we weren't allowed to say its name. Two decades later, after the book was published, it became famous around the world. By the way, there are other IDF units that are just as sophisticated, which still operate far from the public eye.

The eighties were also years of rapid transition for Israel's economy. Until then, the many decades that the Mapai Party and the Labor Party were in power were characterized by a socialist approach and centralized economy. The electoral upheaval that took place at the end of the seventies, when the right-wing Likud Party won the election and presented a national-capitalist agenda, led to the privatization of companies and services, as well as liberalization of the currency. The quick change caused a counterreaction, which led to a financial loss of control and hyperinflation, soaring to 400 percent in 1985. The currency changed its name from the shekel to the new shekel, erasing four zeroes. Only a national unity government and close cooperation between the Likud and Labor parties succeeded in establishing economic stability.

In the early nineties, when I finished my MSc studies in Electrical Engineering at the Technion, I joined a small company established by graduates of my military unit and former Tadiran employees, which was one of the large electronics companies controlled by the Histadrut, and whose primary customer was the Defense Ministry. The job market in Israel was showing signs of something new and preliminary. Entrepreneurs who had worked in companies affiliated with government or defense-related companies dared to establish startups, with the goal of reaching the big world – selling commercial electronics to the Japanese, medical devices to the Germans, software to the Americans. In short, they wanted to sell ice to the Eskimos. The beginning was hesitant, and only the "nerds" pursued it, but over time, startups attracted the right level of government involvement, and were also boosted by the arrival of engineers from the Former Soviet Union in another huge wave of immigration. Venture capital funding started flowing in, issuances on the Nasdaq increased, followed by mergers and acquisitions – M&As.

DSPC, the company where I was one of the first employees, was the leading company developing chipsets for innovative cellular phones for the Japanese market, right when it started to ramp up. The combination of academic knowledge, military experience, and the chutzpah to submit development proposals based on technical specifications written in Japanese led to technological successes that were quickly translated into business successes. The company's stock market launch took place in the mid-nineties; before the decade was over, it was purchased by Intel for an amount that was sixteen times its issue value. This was the beginning of a wave that continued to grow.

The worldwide dot-com crisis and the bloody Israeli-Palestinian conflict of the second Intifada in the early 2000s didn't stop the trend. Israelis turned to the world to do business, and businesspeople around the world came to Israel in search of technological solutions and investment opportunities. Anyone who visits Israel and travels between the various sites will notice the high tech parks that have sprouted at the edges of the big cities. Matam in south Haifa, Atidim in east Tel Aviv, Har Hotzvim in north Jerusalem, and the high tech park in west Herzliya are the largest parks in Israel. It is hard to miss the logos of international corporations – such as Intel, Microsoft, and IBM, at the tops of buildings and campuses for thousands of employees. There's also the long-time companies, Checkpoint and Amdocs, or the younger Wix and Fiverr, which were established and continued to develop as Israeli companies.

In the second decade of the twenty-first century, there are already serial entrepreneurs and lessons to learn from successes and failures. The quantity and quality of the new companies increased quickly. Young companies grow very quickly, and the "unicorns" (private companies worth over a billion dollars) can already be counted by the dozens. High tech parks are also springing up in those same development towns where my father had built housing projects. Like many other places in the world, companies are entering the large city centers. As tourists taking a taxi in Israel, you can expect that the driver will strike up a conversation with you. In the past, conversations usually revolved around politics and the security situation, but today, you'll probably hear about an amazing idea that the driver has, because in Israel, "I have an idea" is synonymous with "I have a startup." Driving in the heart of Tel Aviv on the Ayalon Highway, there are many high tech company towers. Many of the heritage buildings of the White City, built in the eclectic and Bauhaus styles, as well as the new towers that have popped up between them, are now populated by startups, international companies, venture capital firms, and coworking spaces. Anyone who roamed Rothschild Boulevard in the not-so-distant past and returns there today will notice that the suited lawyers and bankers have been replaced by young people wearing t-shirts and sandals, with an employee tag from one of the high tech companies.

I finished high school in the summer of 1979 and had two months to kill before I started studying at the Technion. My mother's brother got me a job at a large Histadrut plant that manufactured glass containers. It was called Phoenicia, as a gesture to the Phoenicians, our historical neighbors from the Lebanese coast, who brought glass to the world. Most of the employees were blue-collar workers. They enjoyed the employment stability, referred to as "tenure," but on the other hand, there was little variation and their pay was not related to their performance. All of these elements led to low motivation and low output, which left time for many employees to spend a significant amount of their shift napping – to the dismay of the young, energetic teenager that I was. During those months, I promised myself that even if my engineering studies were difficult, demanding, and frustrating, I would succeed at them so that I could choose a challenging, interesting occupation, and not find myself in the same situation as the employees I had seen there. Indeed, I was drawn toward a career in high tech, which was definitely rewarding and captivating, but also demanding and often exhausting. As a manager, I learned the price of doing away with "tenure" when the company headquarters imposed significant HR cuts even when the company was very profitable, but less than in the past.

In 2009, I decided to reroute my life, leave the world of high tech, and become a tour guide. Many people ask me what caused me to do it. My answer is that it was a combination of a couple of factors. High tech was demanding and high-pressured; I became exhausted and burnt out over time. I also loved guiding. Those who know me remember that as a young engineer, and later on as a manager, I would volunteer to take company guests to the heritage sites in Israel, as well as showing my colleagues and employees the sites in Japan while working hard with our clients there. The enjoyment of the encounter between people and places attracted me to what I do today.

That dinner at the King David Hotel almost a decade ago helped me realize that I lived through and felt the quick, sharp change in Israel's economy, which led it to its impressive achievements, definitely until COVID-19 hit. About nine percent of the Israeli workforce is directly employed in the field of high tech, which obviously has further circles of influence. During this period, many basic values changed in Israel, which impacts the entire population. The pace of life became much quicker, and at the same time, the economic safety net has become significantly smaller and mutual responsibility has declined. The Israel that I knew when I entered the job market is not today's Israel.

As a tour guide guiding individuals, families, and delegations from all over the world, I have often presented the glitz of Israeli high tech, but also the other facets of society and the economy. As a father to four children between the ages of twenty and thirty, I wonder what their journey will look like. Would it be naïve to seek a balance between entrepreneurship, risk-taking, innovation, and efficiency, and a little more stability, help, and mutual responsibility?

Generations, 2012
Oil on canvas
mounted on wood
40X40

9

Naturally Speaking

An Environmental Perspective

Koren Eisner

Born in the mid-seventies and growing up in Jerusalem, I had a soundtrack to my childhood filled with the chirping of crickets, the cry of the jackal and the hyena, the rustling of the feet of the tortoise, the lizard, and the gazelle on the dry leaves – all murmurs of the natural world. Intoxicating carpets of flowers in the middle of winter. The scent of pine forests on summer nights. Jerusalem of those days was a collection of neighborhoods scattered across hilltops, separated by virginal valleys stretching out like fingers from the Mediterranean climate in the west or the wild desert in the east. Leaving the city, even by Highway 1, the main route to Tel Aviv, was an adventure, a drive on narrow, dark roads between towns far away from each other, perfumed by orange blossoms. The beaches were long and empty. The Galilee mountains were cloaked with wild splendor. The mountains of Eilat and Sinai were inspiring, and the Sea of Galilee pristine and quiet.

Much has been said about Israel's importance as a narrow land corridor between Africa, Europe, and Asia, and about the botanical and biological diversity that comes with it. Hiking through the country, it is impossible to ignore the stark diversity of its landscapes, the extreme climate changes, and the abundance of habitats. All of these exist within very short distances of each other. As a tour guide, I always enjoy experiencing the country through the eyes of tourists. I am especially fond of the reaction of Californians: "It feels like at home, but everything is so close together!"

Yet Israel's landscapes are not just its geography – it is holy geography. Historical and cultural geography. Countless people experience its flora and fauna, hills and valleys through holy books and ancient writings. What is the Sea of Galilee that Jesus walked on, and what is the mustard seed that he mentioned in his parables? Where did the Jewish people cross the sea, and what is that gazelle that King David sang about in his lamentation of the deaths of Saul and Jonathan? In Israel, nature is present not only on the surface of the land, but also deep in the hearts of many millions of people, here and all over the world.

Speaking of millions of people, when I was born, there were just over three million people in Israel. As I write these lines, forty-five years later, Israel's population is about ten million. Over three times more! This trend has been continuing since the establishment of the state in 1948, when there were just 600,000 residents. Two years later, when my father reached the country as a Holocaust refugee, there were over a million residents. Twenty-five years later, I was born. I doubt that there is another country, especially in the Western world, that has witnessed such a dramatic population growth. By the way, this data refers to the State of Israel alone, without taking into account the Palestinian population in Judea and Samaria and the Gaza Strip. There are in fact about fifteen million people living between the Jordan River and the sea, in an area of about 14,580 square miles, half of which is desert. Israel is already one of the most densely populated countries in the world, and all indicators suggest that due to rapid natural growth and immigration from abroad, this trend will continue.

The valleys have been paved and covered by artificial lighting. The cities have grown and become crowded, to the extent that the entire coastal plain has become a broad urban center. It will not take long until it falls under the category of a megalopolis. Industry, energy infrastructures, wastewater treatment, seawater desalination, natural gas production, and so forth. Is there any room left in the country, and in the hearts of its residents, for open, virginal expanses? If you have already traveled in Israel, you know that the answer, perhaps to your surprise, is yes.

In northern Israel, there is a wonderful site that encapsulates the dilemmas and processes that come with nature preservation. In the Galilee Panhandle, the northern continuation of the Syrian-African Rift Valley whose borders are defined in the east by the Golan Heights and Mount Hermon, and in the west by the Galilee mountains, there is a unique birdwatching site – Hula Lake. A former marshland which was revived, and today, it is possible to rent bicycles or an electric vehicle and encounter close-up an enormous range of local and migrating birds. Twice a year, close to half a billion migrating birds cross over the area: cormorants, cranes, pelicans, storks, flamingos, and more.

Until the early fifties, the southern half of the small valley, 15.5 miles in length and about four miles in width, was covered by a shallow lake and swamps, which were home to a wide range of aquatic plants and characteristic creatures. However, after the borders were outlined at the end of the War of Independence, Israel was left with a small area of the valley and a strategic disadvantage, above which Syria commanded the east and Lebanon commanded the west and north sides.

The process of drying the biggest swamp in the Middle East was perceived as a modern act of pioneering, a victory of science over desolation. In the eyes of the leaders of the young state, it was critical to make the land available for agriculture and settlement, in order to protect its borders from hostile invasion. In addition, Israel needed the water, and it seemed logical to take advantage of the abundance of water sources, including the Jordan River sources, to feed the increasing numbers of immigrants and refugees. Canals were dug and water directed toward the Sea of Galilee, and the rich peat soil was transformed into agricultural fields and orchards. During the draining process, a small group of nature lovers stood up and expressed their concern regarding the environmental consequences and the fate of the animals and plants, some of which were endemic. Thanks to their efforts, the first nature reserve in the country was founded, and a small part of the lake was preserved.

Over the years, the peat soil lost its quality, and unexpected environmental phenomena began to emerge: the quality of the water flowing into the Sea of Galilee was damaged, the temperature range in the valley became more extreme, and peat dust storms began to bother the residents. Following the Six-Day War, the Syrians were pushed back about twelve miles to the east, while Lebanon sunk into political instability and civil wars, so the security concerns for settling the area diminished. In addition, in the early eighties, a heightened awareness of the importance of preserving Israel's natural elements developed among Israelis, including the wonder of the huge bird migration from Europe to Africa during the autumn months and back again in the spring. The economic importance of this unique phenomenon as a tourist attraction was also recognized. Thus, after ongoing negotiations with the local farmers, areas in the center of the dry marshlands were selected and reflooded. Paths were paved, and recently a new and impressive visitor center was even inaugurated.

It is fascinating to consider the relationship that the farmers have with the site and with the birds that visit it. After all, the birds are a real nuisance to people who grow their bread from that same small area of land. Pelicans touch down on the fish ponds in the tens of thousands. Hundreds of thousands of cranes can clean out an entire season of crops in just a few days. On the other hand, anyone who has met the farmers of this valley knows that they are people who dearly love the landscapes of the valley and its birds. Indeed, the sight of thousands of storks flying in the sky is a gorgeous sight. Local farmers will often have *tzimmers* (guest houses) in their backyards that they rent out to birdwatchers during peak seasons. The combination of the emotional connection to the valley landscapes and the economic advantages of the region encourage the farmers to cooperate and find creative ways to create a golden path between man's needs and the needs of the natural world. For example, a certain percentage of the agricultural produce is essentially donated by the farmers for feeding the birds, in designated fields.

It is captivating to read the trip journals of tourists, such as Mark Twain and Theodor Herzl, who visited the country in the nineteenth century. They paint a dreary picture of a desolate, destroyed land, ridden with disease, almost empty of residents, and very primitive. The dramatic transformation, beginning from the middle of the twentieth century, into an inhabited country with modern infrastructures and flourishing agriculture is unmistakable. The basic ethos of the pioneers at the beginning of the last century was based on terms such as "conquering the desolation" and "we will dress you [the country] in a dress of concrete and mortar," in the words of a famous pioneer song.

But the challenge of this century seems to be no less complex: How do we develop the country for the benefit of its residents while still preserving its natural assets for the benefit of the plants, animals, and the souls of those who appreciate them? How do we preserve the land of the Bible in the era of advancement? Is it possible to find an economic arrangement that enables both the human world and the natural world to mutually flourish, without one succeeding at the expense of the other? This issue has been part of Israel's reality since its founding. Generations of nature lovers worked hard in a range of different areas. The road was, and still is, replete with great successes and terrible failures. There are examples everywhere you step in this country. It is possible to say that the subject of nature preservation in small, crowded Israel can be viewed as a captivating, relevant case study for other countries who are facing similar dilemmas in the twenty-first century.

10

I Swear

The Cry of Generations

Uri Feinberg

In February 2019, I stood in front of the Western Wall in Jerusalem and was shivering. Trying to find warmth however I could, I hopped back and forth, paced this way and that, and did my best to huddle in as close as possible under the umbrella that my wife was holding. My umbrella had already succumbed to the wind, and my parents were standing stoically, clearly uncomfortable but also obviously happy to be there. My sister, who was there as well, had taken my youngest daughter to the women's section of the Western Wall, and they were already out of sight beyond several barriers. To ensure that we had a good spot (it was standing room only), we arrived hours before the ceremony was to begin. We weren't the only ones to get there early. Well-seasoned in these kinds of experiences, we found ourselves shoulder to shoulder (and cooler to cooler with home-cooked food) with endless layers of Israeli society.

As diverse as the growing crowd might have been, the image of huddled clusters of families, all layered up in the same way, did not reveal any differences. We were all there for the same reason. Shortly, the official swearing-in ceremony of our children into the Iron Dome unit of the Air Force would begin. The rehearsal had already started, and as the sun broke through the clouds, I found myself repositioning for the perfect shot. My daughter Meitav, and the young women and men who trained alongside her, had completed their combat basic training, and there was no way I was going to miss the perfect picture of her and her buddies.

My natural height, which isn't that tall, along with a dash of transplanted Israeli chutzpah, which had evolved over quite some time, having immigrated as a child, gave me the close-ups I was looking for. The ebb and flow of the families and the barking orders of the master sergeant to "forward march until you get it right!" forced me to lower the camera and briefly pause my efforts.

As I looked around, waiting for the crowd to open up, just as the clouds had been kind enough to do, I was startled as I realized that my eyes had settled upon the layers of ancient stone in front of me for the first time that afternoon. Having stood in this spot countless times before with groups I was guiding, it was strange not having to explain the history or frame the moment. It might have been the February chill in the air, but it seemed as though my consciousness was taking a break and my subconscious was happy to play host to the familiar mantra that I usually reserved for the tourists I guide: "There are those who see these stones and feel... who stand here and think... who remember and are proud... who are overwhelmed and curious observers."

The multiple layers of carefully placed ancient Herodian stones form the wall toward which the hearts, minds, and gaze of the Jewish world are directed. As the participants in my groups prepare to descend to the Wall, written notes in hand, the layers of emotion are often as stacked as the stones themselves. It seems as if the excitement of being in this sacred space can live hand in hand with discontent, as the

Orthodox prayer space that this has become regulates which types of Jewish prayer are allowed and which are not.

At times it really baffles the mind. A single space that can be such a landmark of longevity in the land of Israel, a beacon of shared memory and an embodiment of heart, mind, and soul can simultaneously be a site that dares to sprout disunity. Just to the south, beyond the security metal detectors and below the egalitarian prayer space, Ezrat Yisrael, we can find the extension of this very Western Wall. At the foot of the remaining upright supporting wall, built two thousand years prior by King Herod, is a pile of large limestone blocks, which lie where they fell in the year 70 CE. There they remain as symbols of destruction, according to the subsequent rabbinic literature, not caused by the Romans, but by Jewish discontent with each other, defined in the Talmud as *causeless hate.*

With the slightest of movements, one's eyes can fall upon ancient graffiti, carved into the stone, a quote from chapter 66 in the book of Isaiah in the Bible, depicting the rebirth of the Jewish people after the destruction of the First Temple. The first image always provides me with an opening to discuss the powerful topic of why Jerusalem was destroyed, and the barely noticeable chiseled quote, why we survived. Separated by only a few meters, each of these relics tells a very different story, not dissimilar to this modern country. At times, the protest in the street against each other is palpable. And yet, there have always been moments that identify a shared vision of a better tomorrow, which all rest upon the very stones that have been the building blocks of our people. Destroyed supporting walls then, and at times, a disunified society now, alongside a unified message of a better tomorrow, then *and* now.

Hearing the final soundcheck, and noticing final inspections of the troops, I realize it's time to get back to our preferred and now several-hours-old vantage point on the other side of the roped-off parade grounds. Perhaps strangely, even as I line up with the other families, complete with the appropriate jostling and slight pushing for position, I can't shake the feeling I always have in hoping that the tourists who are with me when I guide realize that the layers of question, emotion, pride, and challenge that they may have are not lost on me. The fact that I have stood in this very spot countless times before does not disengage me from the very experience that those who are here for the first time are going through.

There is, however, a barrier, and not just the one identifying this as an Orthodox prayer space. It is a barrier which at times *does* separate me from the travelers who are with me. It places me within the frame of a very personal connection to this wall and this space. On its face value, it has little do with the past. Rather, it has to do with a very Israeli experience. Mandatory conscription into the Israel Defense Forces has been a part of the consciousness of Israelis since the War of Independence. The period of time served has fluctuated, and currently has settled on a minimum of thirty-two months for men and for women in combat roles, and twenty-eight months for women in non-combat positions.

Just a mere couple of months after my own induction into the IDF, many, many years ago, as a young, wide-eyed, somewhat bewildered paratrooper, I stood in this very plaza. I stood here as part of the process of basic training. We were not there to reenact the battles of the paratroopers of 1967; rather, we were there to be sworn in to the IDF. It was here, on the inside of the roped-off center of the plaza holding our family and friends at bay, that we would stand at attention, and as we heard the words of our commanders, we would cry out in unison: "I SWEAR!"

So much more impressive when one considers the myriad of tone, dialects, and accents indicative of our diversity in backgrounds. These tones, dialects, and backgrounds did not always see eye to eye in the world beyond the ropes. Then we ceremoniously received our personal weapon and the Bible, New Testament, or Koran. The truth is that with the passage of time, there is much of that cool Jerusalem evening that I do not remember. However, I *do* remember *not* being able to concentrate on the words spoken by our commanders (let alone remember them), to which we responded, therefore, somewhat blindly (if not with much gusto and rightfully placed dedication and pride), in a loud, testosterone-heavy chorus.

The first time I actually *listened* to those very words would occur on that momentous February evening, thirty years later – this time however, standing in the plaza, on the other side of the barrier, looking inward and watching my daughter stand at attention with her comrades and commanders. The rain was back but was ignored (aside from the chattering teeth, of course) as we watched the smiles and determination and gaze leveled forward of the young soldiers and of course, of our firstborn.

"I swear and commit to maintain allegiance to the State of Israel, its laws, and its authorities, to accept upon myself unconditionally the discipline of the Israel Defense Forces, to obey all the orders and instructions given by authorized commanders, and to devote all my energies, and even sacrifice my life, for the protection of the homeland and the liberty of Israel."

"… And devote all my energies, and even sacrifice my life.…" Pain and pride reached a turbulent crescendo that was quite overwhelming, I have to admit. If that wasn't enough, as I stole my fixed gaze from my child, it fell upon my parents and I watched them shift their gaze from Meitav to me and back again. The enormity of being caught in a pendulum swinging between their memories of me, my own memories, and those of Meitav (which were most likely as courageous and confused as mine had been), was as powerful as one might imagine. Each of the families around us had their own stolen glances and their own swinging pendulum. Disagreements, disunity, disillusion seem to dissolve as one either stands within the rope or gazes inward. We all have skin in the game.

Causeless hate can sadly still be found among us. Here in Israel, we find ourselves as diverse, and at times as dislodged, as the very stones in whose shadow we stand. While we have a voice, as loud and proud as the "words of the prophet that were written on the ancient wall," it is often far from a unified voice, or a unified vote, for that matter. Yet it is the declaration made by generations who came before us, through those who are coming up right behind us, that provides the confidence to both challenge ourselves and also to be proud of who we are and what we have achieved.

As the senior commanders leave their mark on their recruits, words that will most likely not be remembered, it is the words of our national anthem, "Hatikvah" (The Hope), sung loud and proud by all, that unifies us, even if only momentarily. While not everyone serves in the IDF, and not everyone agrees with each other, this unified voice is not relegated to a single brief moment in time. Rather the voice is a bridge through time, that allows us to move forward, together, with a shared vision, focusing not on the *causeless hate* of the past but rather on the *causeless love* that paves the way for a unified future.

Geopolitics

Angel, 2015
Oil on canvas
mounted on wood
40X50

11

A People That Shall Dwell Alone?

Yishay Shavit

The exodus from Egypt. The Jewish nation makes its way through the deserts of Moab, east of the Jordan River, and King Balak of Moab is distressed. He summons his prophet, Bilam, and asks him to curse the nation that is crossing his land. God intervenes and Bilam ends up blessing the Israelites instead of cursing them. Bilam's blessing includes the verse "It is a people that shall dwell alone, and shall not be reckoned among the nations" (Numbers 23:9). I must admit that, as someone who likes reading and learning the Bible, I was always confused by this verse. Is this really a blessing, or is it a curse? Must the Jewish nation isolate itself from the nations around it, or should it strive to connect with them? It turns out that I'm not the only one bothered by this. It has been a part of Jewish history from the very beginning and to this day. My favorite place to discuss this issue as a tour guide with tourists is at the top of Masada.

Masada is a must for anyone visiting Israel. It is a unique combination of an archaeological site preserved in excellent condition and a story that is larger than life, set in a breathtaking desert landscape. Those who succeed in climbing up the Snake Path that winds up

Masada, a challenging forty-five-minute hike in the beating desert sun, feel a sense of achievement upon reaching the top of this tall mountain. During the first century CE, one of the founding stories in the history of the Jewish nation took place here, a story whose results impact Israeli society to this day.

In the year 66 CE, the Jews rebelled against the Romans. The rebellion began in the cosmopolitan port city of Caesarea, the bureaucratic and economic center of the province of Judah, which was ruled by Roman governors. This city represented, more than anything else, the desire of certain groups in Judea to live as an integral part of the Roman Empire. And yet, the zealots succeeded in pulling the entire Jewish population into its ranks, even the residents of Caesarea. At first, things looked good for Rome's opponents, supporters of the "people that dwell alone" philosophy. A number of impressive victories on the battlefield caused the Romans to retreat from Judea, and the rebels began to control significant areas of the country. One of the places where the zealots took control was the fortress at the top of Mount Masada.

Masada is on a tall mountain surrounded by deep chasms on all sides. The paths leading to the top of the mountain are few and winding, and the defendants of the mountain were able to control them with fire and sentries. The Hasmoneans were the first to build a small fortress here, but it was King Herod who took full advantage of the inherent potential of the site. At Masada's peak, he built a huge complex that included palaces, walls, storehouses, and cisterns. He even built himself a small, impressive bathhouse in the middle of the desert. When I visit the site with tourists, I like to point out the opus sectile (inlaid patterned) flooring that proves like a thousand witnesses that King Herod was up to date with the popular architectural trends from Rome in the days of Caesar Augustus. King Herod loved Roman culture, adopted it, and flaunted the fact that Roman culture was his culture too. A people that shall dwell alone? Not in the bathhouse of the king of Judea!

This worldview was foreign to the zealots who resided on Masada seventy years after Herod's death, when the Great Revolt erupted. They wholeheartedly believed that true Jewish life (as they understood the concept of Judaism) was impossible under Roman rule. They looked at the flooring in King Herod's bathhouse and saw heresy written all over it. The Jewish nation must not care about the latest Roman fashion, nor rely on its weapons. The zealots had no interest at all in the lavish Herodian buildings. They lived in rooms that they built for themselves inside the modest walls of Masada. This is where a thousand men, women, and children lived out the four years of the rebellion. This is apparently where they received the news of Jerusalem's destruction in the year 70 and realized that the rebellion had failed.

Three years later, the X Legion arrived at Masada. The legion's commander, Lucius Flavius Silva, decided to besiege the residents at the top of the mountain. But when he realized that the quantities of water and food stored at the site could last the rebels a long time, he adopted a different strategy. He commanded his soldiers to build a huge assault ramp that would lead up to the top of the mountain. This impressive engineering project was not at all simple. The rebels at Masada tried everything in their power to stop the Romans. They shot arrows at them and threw huge boulders at them, but to no avail. At the end of a fierce struggle under the arid desert skies, the Romans succeeded in pushing their siege tower with its battering ram up to the top of the assault ramp that they built. The rebels tried to burn the tower, but when the wind changed direction, the flames threatened to harm them instead, essentially helping the Romans break through the walls of Masada.

After breaching the walls, the Romans returned to their base at the foot of the mountain. They were sure that the next day, Masada would fall into their hands. It was clear to everyone that the rebels on Masada did not have the power to stop the legion soldiers. The rebels on Masada themselves didn't have any illusions either. Their leader, a Jew named Elazar Ben Yair, called a meeting in order to decide what to do when the Roman army broke into their complex at the top of the mountain. The speech that Elazar made (which appears in Flavius Josephus's book *The Jewish War*) became one of the most important speeches in Jewish history. He essentially admitted military defeat but stated that this did not mean that the rebels had to surrender to the Romans and become slaves. Death as free men would be better than a life of slavery. The result of this speech was the suicide of the people of Masada and the fall of the fortress into the hands of the Romans.

Many years after the fall of Masada, Elazar Ben Yair's speech became a symbol in the thirties and forties. It is impossible to create a national culture without heroes, and the Zionist movement adopted not only King David and Judah the Maccabee, but the Masada story as well. Zionist youth, many of whom were members of the various youth movements, have read Elazar's speech and set out on difficult treks from Jerusalem to the top of the mountain. They ascended the Snake Path or the ramp, stood on the walls of Masada, and cried aloud, "Masada shall not fall again!" The message was clear to all: we Jews have returned to the land of our forefathers for good. We will strengthen ourselves and make sure that the story of the fall of Masada will never happen again. It all depends on us, the Jews, and not on the whims of other nations. It is a people that shall dwell alone and shall not be reckoned among the nations!

This spirit was dominant among the leaders of modern Israel in its early days. David Ben-Gurion, the first prime minister of Israel, has been quoted as underestimating the importance of the United Nations, and he led the State of Israel in the spirit of the values of Zionism. This was continued by the many Israelis who have visited Masada to admire the sacrifice of the rebels, who preferred to die as free people over slavery and exile. Soldiers have sworn their allegiance on this mountain, and school students have been taught this message.

The Masada story is still an important story in the Israeli ethos. Students still climb up to the top of the mountain, and we, their guides, tell them the heroic story of its defenders. But today, most of the guides also tell another story. It's the story of Rabban Yochanan Ben Zakai, a moderate rabbi who lived in Jerusalem at the time of the Roman siege in the year 70 CE. He was smuggled out of the city by his students in a coffin, and he had the opportunity to meet the Roman general Vespasian. It was at this meeting that Rabban Yochanan Ben Zakai essentially accepted the fact that Jerusalem was going to fall, and he asked the Roman leadership for the city of Yavneh. Not many had heard of Yavneh before the fall of Jerusalem, and not enough people had heard about it afterward, but in Yavneh, Rabban Yochanan Ben Zakai changed Judaism and adapted it to the reality of life without a Temple in Jerusalem, under a foreign sovereignty. By recognizing the Roman rule and the need for compromise, he displayed an impressive level of pragmatism which gave the Jewish nation the tools to survive for two thousand years without political sovereignty, often under regimes that were not known for their religious tolerance of minorities.

The ability to adapt to different, changing conditions and to accept the law of the land (with certain limitations) was characteristic, and is still characteristic, of Jewish communities in the Diaspora. I personally believe that Rabban Yochanan Ben Zakai's pragmatic worldview significantly contributed to shaping the face of Judaism. But what about Bilam's blessing? The idea of "and shall not be reckoned among the nations," of separatism and seclusion, is not expressed in the political and rabbinical worldview after the destruction of the Second Temple. In fact, Rabban Yochanan and his students worked hard to create a religious format for Jewish life without sovereignty. The relationship between Jews and non-Jews had its ups and downs throughout the years, but on a political level, the Jewish leadership understood that it wasn't operating in a vacuum. There is a local government, and if the Jews want to live, they must abandon the worldview of a people dwelling alone and cooperate with the government.

"If you were alive during that period, who would you follow?" we guides ask the tourists and students as we stand at the top of Masada. "Those who chose to die as a free people in an act that echoes heroism, or those who displayed flexibility and pragmatism, enabling Jewish life to continue?" This is not an easy question, and I am not even sure that it has a clear answer. What is clear, though, is that the dilemma of "a people that shall dwell alone" is encapsulated in this question.

Must we, as Israelis in the twenty-first century, rely solely on our strength, isolate ourselves as much as possible, and live our lives separate from the nations around us so that we can preserve our freedom? Or should we be pragmatic and extend our hand in peace to other nations, even to our bitter foes, in order to prevent our downfall? Is the State of Israel like a Masada on the top of a mountain, alone, or should it strive to be a Yavneh – a spiritual center that is not disconnected from those who surround it?

In many ways, the tension that arises from the question of whether the biblical verse "a people that shall dwell alone, and shall not be reckoned among the nations" is a blessing or a curse defines the worldview of many Jews today. Both in Israel and abroad, there are a range of approaches on this subject. There are those who believe in separatism, and those who call for Israel to become a country that resembles other countries. I invite you to use this dilemma as another filter through which you can look at Israeli society and understand it in greater depth.

12

On the Edge

My Home by the Gaza Strip

Raz Shmilovich

It's nine in the morning on a regular, routine day. My eight-year-old son and I get into my new car, on the way to another animal therapy session that helps him deal with the stress.

Coffee, radio playing in the background, and we're about to exit the gate of the moshav. Suddenly, the familiar cry blares through the loudspeaker system – "Red alert, red alert," warning us of missile fire. Instinctively, I stop the car and run to take my son out of the back seat. I know that we have just seconds before the missile falls, but the door won't open! My son is anxious; I see the fear and helplessness in his eyes as he unsuccessfully struggles with the handle, which refuses to open. We hear a weak explosion that sounds distant, and he calms down instantly. This time, it fell far away – five hundred meters from us. But why didn't the door open? It is a new car with all of the safety systems and an electronic door. I didn't know that I had to shift the transmission to Park. Today, two years later, he still remembers the experience, and every time we drive through the gate, I'm reminded too.

My name is Raz Shmilovich. I live in a moshav (an Israeli village) called Netiv Ha'asara, which is where I grew up and have lived most of my life, together with my wife and our four sons. My parents also live in this moshav, as does my brother and his family. As usual in Israel, nothing is simple. My moshav was established in the Sinai Peninsula, in the Yamit bloc of settlements. I was born in Netiv Ha'asara when it was still located in Sinai, close to the city of Yamit. I lived there until I was six years old, which was when it was evacuated.

After the peace agreement was signed with Egypt in 1979, Israel retreated from Sinai and all of the Israeli communities there were evacuated. My moshav, with its name and most of its residents, including my family, moved to its current location in southwestern Israel. Today, this moshav is located in the region referred to as the Gaza envelope. The moshav is considered "adjacent to the fence," which means that physically, the edge of the moshav is essentially the border of the Gaza Strip.

It is common knowledge that the Gaza Strip is currently under the control of Hamas, which refuses to recognize Israel's existence as a Jewish and democratic state. Although Israel retreated from the Gaza Strip unilaterally in 2005, and currently only guards the borders, Hamas still does not recognize our right to exist. Hamas, which is defined as a terror organization, plays by its own rules. It did, and continues to do, everything in its power to harm Israel and try to destroy it. Since it does not have enough power to endanger Israel's existence, it tries with all its might to disrupt civilian life in the country, whether by shooting missiles, launching incendiary and explosive balloons, or digging terror tunnels to penetrate Israel's borders. Living next to the border is the modern Israeli version of living in the crater of a volcano.

What does this kind of life look like, you may wonder? It means that our entire lives revolve around the knowledge that at any given moment, there could be a red alert siren, which gives us between five and seven seconds to find shelter, preferably in a bomb-proof space. The southwestern region of Israel is currently divided, according to the Home Front Command's instructions, into regions with different alert times according to their distance from the Gaza Strip. The map is divided into strips, with every ten kilometers equal to fifteen seconds of warning – the time it takes for a Qassam rocket fired from the Gaza Strip to reach this distance. Since I live at the edge of the first ten-kilometer strip, I don't even have those fifteen precious seconds to run. I have five to seven seconds before I hear the rocket fall and explode. This is my personal volcano.

The frequency of the rocket fire is connected to the overall state of security in Israel. The security situation has a direct impact on the number of times that our children will need to run to the safe room, which is built of reinforced concrete and has a heavy steel door. As the level of alert increases, so do our stress levels. Imagine a reality in which, every day, at any moment, a siren could suddenly go off and you need to run to a shelter. That means that anywhere you go, there will be a shelter, whether it's a house with a safe room, a public space, next to a playground, a sports field, or even anywhere on the street. There are public shelters everywhere. It also means that all schools, from kindergarten to high school, are rocket-proofed. It means that my children always, and I mean always, know where the closest shelter is. Before they know where to turn on the light. Whether they're outside playing soccer, or at a friend's house. These are children who are scared of balloons, because here, a stray balloon could mean an incendiary balloon, or worse, an explosive, booby-trapped balloon.

It's even more difficult when we, as parents, are outside of the moshav at work, and our children need to deal with a red alert siren or alert that someone touched the fence. They must run to the safe room alone.

Often, during periods of tension or hostility, we also need to leave our home, sometimes for several weeks. This happened during Operation Protective Edge in 2014, during the most significant and longest round of fighting between Israel and Hamas in the Gaza Strip, over fifty days of conflict, with the largest number of casualties and wounded since Israel retreated from the area in 2005. We left our home for fifty-two days and wandered like refugees in our own country, in the middle of the summer vacation. One of the places we stayed was with my family in the Jerusalem area. I encouraged my children to go out a bit to play at the nearby playground, but despite my attempts to convince them, they refused. In the end, they explained to me why. Here, in Jerusalem, far from home and from the Gaza Strip, there was no shelter next to the playground. Now try explaining to a kid that "it's safe here."

If we do have to leave home, we make sure that the entire family isn't driving in the same car, and of course, we don't buckle our seatbelts until we are far enough away, so that we can get out as fast as possible if there's a siren on the way.

In Netiv Ha'asara and the surrounding towns located within the ten-kilometer range from the Gaza Strip, we have fifteen seconds to run in the event of a missile attack. As the circle widens and the distance from Gaza increases, the alert time increases as well – but more and more Israelis are exposed to the threat. Since many Israeli citizens live in the range between Tel Aviv-Jerusalem and the Gaza Strip, this means that many Israelis have heard the shrill sirens with their own ears. While residents of Tel Aviv have 105 seconds to run due to the increased distance from Gaza, this isn't a great comfort to anyone who has to undergo this unpleasant experience.

Hamas cannot actually annihilate Israel but what it can do is try to incessantly harm the civilian home front and make life miserable and unbearable for residents. Just like Hamas cannot contend with an army, no army in history has successfully fought against guerilla organizations either. Armies know how to fight armies. While Israel may lack natural resources, it was blessed with an absence of active volcanoes and is not threatened by natural disasters, with the exception of rare, light earthquakes. Therefore, the existential threat that is most similar to living in the crater of a volcano is living next to the border – and we have plenty of places like that. Essentially, from the moment we declared independence and established the State of Israel, we have barely had any quiet. Throughout all of the years of the country's existence, there has always been some sort of violent conflict, hostilities, or a war, on one of the country's borders.

So why would anyone want to live here, you ask?

There are many answers. First of all, this is my home. This is where I lived most of my life, where I got married, and where I built my home. This is where my four children were born and raised, and they don't even think of it as a question. This is home and we're not going anywhere, even when it's hard. My home, and my moshav, are not located in a disputed region according to international law. The only reason that we are under attack, as I mentioned, is because we live physically close to the border with the Gaza Strip.

Perhaps I cling to my home because, after all, what is terror if not adult-style bullying, and leaving would mean submission to terror, letting the bully win?

Maybe it's because, as a friend once said in calm times, we live in paradise. A small, safe, well-kept community, where children can walk around alone, carefree and happy. But when something happens, in a split-second, it becomes hell. There's no in-between.

Maybe it's because of the amazing, supportive community with a rich social life that we essentially built and cultivated here?

Perhaps, at the end of the day, it's the hope, as weak as it may be, that maybe one day, we'll wake up in the morning and it'll all seem like a distant dream? Balloons won't arouse concern that they are connected to incendiary or explosive devices; they'll make us happy. Shelters will disappear from our lives; red will go back to being just a color. Maybe we'll live normal lives again? Humans are adaptive and resilient creatures. We forget negative experiences very quickly, concentrate on the positive and look ahead with optimism. We dream that both sides will realize one day that all of us are here to stay, and we'd be best learning how to live next to each other.

And perhaps, as we already know, it's because *every* place in Israel has been through challenging times, whether that means wars on the borders or terror attacks in the heart of cities deep in the country.

At the end of the day, you can run, but you can't hide.

13

Home Is Where the Heart Is

In the Footsteps of Abraham

Ronen Malik

There is a place, far beyond the sea

There, the sand is white, the home is warm

There, the sun shines above

The market, the street, and the port

Home is there, beyond the sea

– Amos Ettinger

The song "There Is a Place" was originally written for *Kazablan*, one of the most successful films in the history of Israeli cinema. The film describes the life of Yosef Siman-Tov, known to all by the nickname Kazablan, a Jew born in Casablanca, Morocco who immigrated to Israel. It depicts the feelings of the Moroccan Jews who lived in their country of origin for thousands of years but when they said "home," they were referring to two places across the sea from each other. The land of Israel and Morocco.

This feeling that the home of all Jews can be also in the land of Israel and not necessarily in the place where they live is not unique to the Jews of Morocco. Essentially, this perception can be found in most Jewish communities, if not all of them. Many Jewish families living in Israel today can tell the story of their family's immigration and the accompanying yearning for the land of Israel in general, and for Jerusalem specifically. My family is no different.

In the mid-nineteenth century, my grandmother's grandfather lived in the town of Bunheim, Hungary. He spent his entire life there, knew most of the local residents, and was respected. All in all, he lived a comfortable, good life. Then, in 1850, he decided to leave everything behind and travel to the land of Israel. What caused him to do that? To abandon everything that he had and immigrate to an impoverished country that he had never seen, at the edge of the waning Ottoman Empire?

In our family, we say that the cause was his heart, which didn't leave him alone. He wanted to reach the home over "there," in the land of Israel! The journey was not easy, but after a few weeks of traveling, he reached his destination – the city of Jerusalem, the holy city. Ever since, for seven generations, my family has proudly called it our home.

I was born in Jerusalem. I spent my childhood, adolescence, and early adulthood there. Jerusalem is the source of my joy. But when I fell in love, my spouse and I decided to follow our hearts. Like my grandmother's grandfather back then, we apprehensively left our city in 2002 and established our home with a new, dynamic community in Netiv Ha'avot (Route of the Patriarchs), located in Gush Etzion. Netiv Ha'avot is about 7.5 miles south of Jerusalem, in Judea and Samaria, where there are thornbushes, rocky terrain, and harsh, difficult winters. We still live there today.

Moving to Netiv Ha'avot and Gush Etzion wasn't easy for me. As someone who grew up his entire life in the big city and loved the urban lifestyle, I had a hard time suddenly finding myself in a community of just ten families, without an asphalt access road and a mini-market nearby, and with snow every winter. But today, a long time after my adjustment period has passed, I am happy to say that while my first love will always be Jerusalem, there is room in my heart for another beloved home – my home in Netiv Ha'avot.

The name Netiv Ha'avot was not selected randomly. The community is located exactly on the ancient route through the mountains that connected the cities of Be'er Sheva and Jerusalem. This route was one of the most important thoroughfares in the land of Israel in biblical times. If you open the book of Genesis to chapter 22, you can read about our forefather Abraham, who walked on this route on his way to Mount Moriah, where he faced an immense test and eventually did not sacrifice his son, Isaac. Essentially, all of the biblical patriarchs and matriarchs used this route. Abraham, Isaac, and Jacob. Sarah, Rebecca, Leah, and Rachel. To me, this fact is very significant. Just as our biological parents are the ones who shaped our personalities, educated us, and imparted values to us, the Jewish nation's matriarchs and patriarchs also served as parental figures who raised and taught the entire Jewish nation. We grew up looking at their characters, and Jews mention their names in prayer every day. Is it possible that the stories of the patriarchs and matriarchs were what caused my grandmother's grandfather to view the distant land of Israel as his home?

A short walk from my home, on the route through the mountains, it is possible to see a milestone. Engineers from the Roman Empire also understood the importance of this route and paved a path whose remnants are still visible today. The Roman numeral XI is still visible on this milestone today. This is the precise number of Roman miles that separate between Jerusalem and my home in Netiv Ha'avot. The stone bearing the Roman numeral I was found by archaeologists at the foot of the Temple Mount, the site where the Temple once stood. I like to think that the fact that these two milestones were discovered is a testimony to the connection between my two loves – Netiv Ha'avot and Jerusalem.

Not far from the site where the Roman milestone is situated, it is possible to see a Jewish ritual bath dating back to the second century BCE. The ritual bath is impressively beautiful, completely excavated in the firm limestone, and the partition wall that separated between those descending into it and those ascending from it was perfectly preserved. I can't help thinking of the Jewish pilgrims who used this route on their way to the Temple in Jerusalem. In my imagination, I can see them immersing themselves in this ritual bath and purifying themselves just a few hours before the end of their journey. Entering the holy city, the city of their hearts, they would already be pure. It can be assumed that among those pilgrims from thousands of years ago, there were also people who had never visited Jerusalem before. People who traveled a long, dangerous journey because they believed with all of their hearts that the land of Israel is their home, even if they chose not to live there of their own free will.

Netiv Ha'avot is built on one of the highest mountains on the central mountain ridge of the land of Israel. It soars at about 3,190 feet above sea level. On a clear day – and in the winter, there are quite a few such days – I can see the Mediterranean Sea to the west and the Edom Mountains located in Jordan to the east, all from my house. This is the entire breadth of the biblical land of Israel. In a country like Israel, where civilian settlement and security policies are intertwined, the location of Netiv Ha'avot has strategic significance that greatly surpasses the small size of the community. Its location reinforces the Jewish presence in the land of Israel and contributes to the country's security. Being aware of this fact strengthens the sense of belonging and commitment that we feel toward the site and adds another dimension to the term "home."

For me personally, living in Gush Etzion in general, and in Netiv Ha'avot in particular, is an immense privilege. But the privilege comes with its challenges too. If I suddenly realize at ten at night that I forgot to buy milk, it'll have to wait for tomorrow. If my children feel like going swimming, they'll need to find a ride to the city nearby. Another challenge is the relationship with our Palestinian neighbors, with whom we share the roads, shop with at the regional supermarket, repair our cars at the local garage, and more. On rare occasions, the security situation challenges us and even comes at a high price, but it doesn't weaken us or undermine our belief in the lifestyle that we have chosen.

Despite all of the daily challenges, or perhaps because of them, our lives are filled with activity, as we build, maintain, and develop our community. We enjoy the rural air and try to draw inspiration from the founding forefathers of our country and our nation. We attempt to create a situation in which the physical home that we built is not very different than the home that our ancestors dreamed of throughout the Diaspora for thousands of years. This worldview is not unique to us, the residents of Netiv Ha'avot or Gush Etzion. It is a worldview shared by many Israelis, a worldview that is based on the knowledge that we are not strangers in our own land. This is our home, now and in the future.

You're invited to visit!

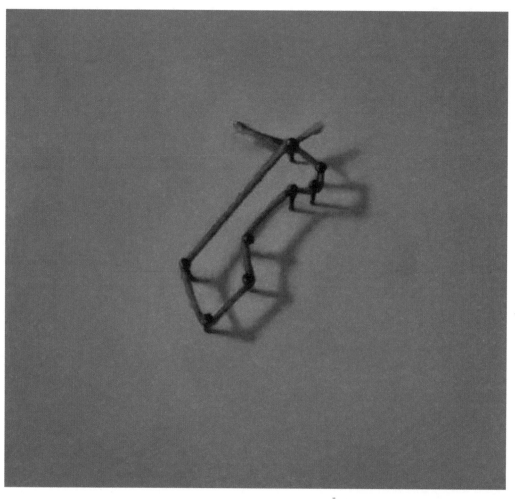

Eruv String Around Gaza, 2015
Oil on canvas
mounted on wood
20X20

14

Under the Hebron Skies

Michal Granot

Before my visit to Hebron in May 2020, I thought that people like me had no reason to go there.

Hebron is one of the largest cities in the West Bank (as the land conquered from Jordan by Israel in the Six-Day War in June 1967 is commonly referred to), home to about 220,000 Arab residents, living alongside approximately one thousand Jews. It is the location of the Tomb of the Patriarchs, the site where according to tradition most of the patriarchs and matriarchs are buried. This site makes Hebron the second holiest city in the land of Israel to both Jews and Muslims.

In my imagination, Hebron is a divided city; tension hangs in the air on its streets. I visited it once as a young girl. We traveled by bus from Jerusalem in torrential rain. Then, battling heavy winds (Hebron is at a high altitude of 3,050 feet), we stood next to a home that I was told used to belong to our family, until the 1929 riots, when sixty-seven members of the Jewish community of Hebron were massacred and the family home was abandoned.

The next time I thought about Hebron was on Purim of 1994, when Baruch Goldstein, an extremist Jew, entered the Tomb of the Patriarchs and murdered Muslim worshippers. Who would want to visit Hebron? A city of unrest. A city of fanatics. Settlers on one side, Palestinians on the other, and social activist groups in the middle, trying to guide complex tours.

I am the director of a tour guiding course, meant to train the next generation of guides, operated according to a training program authorized by the Israeli Ministry of Tourism. The Tomb of the Patriarchs in Hebron suddenly showed up on the list of tours. Strange, I thought, it wasn't part of the course I took a decade ago. What does that mean about today's course? That it has a more right-wing, religious agenda? And anyway, why do I immediately think of right-wingers and religious people when I see the words "Tomb of the Patriarchs"?

I was stressed about this tour. The day would begin with a drive along the ancient aqueducts that brought water to the Temple. We would drive next to the historic Path of the Patriarchs. The course that I organize is a special course. It's a tour guiding course given in English, in which two-thirds of the students are East Jerusalem Arabs, Muslims, and Christians, and a third are Jews who immigrated to Israel and usually have right-wing tendencies. The only Israeli citizen from birth is me, and I am one of three who have served in the IDF. Coming with such a diverse group to a volatile city like Hebron sounds to me like an exercise in mutual tolerance.

I discovered beforehand that in the Tomb of the Patriarchs, Jews and Muslims enter from different entrances and go into different halls. Jews visit the tomb of Abraham and Sarah, Jacob and Leah, while Muslims visit the tombs of Isaac and Rebecca. But what about our course? After all, we hadn't come to pray. We had come to learn about the site. What will the soldier guarding the entrance do with us?

Yes, we called to coordinate in advance.

Yes, we spoke with the commander.

But… he's not here, and the soldier simply doesn't know how to deal with the situation.

Since we came to learn, we won't give up and we won't let them separate our group. So we waited for an hour and a half in the sun.

I thought to myself that for once, the Jews in the group, myself included, on the sovereign side, can experience what it's like to see your destination but not reach it, because the soldier who met us was confused by the situation and didn't give us access.

In the meantime, we learned about the history of the building, which was apparently built toward the end of the Second Temple period by King Herod. We noticed its similarities to the structure of the Temple Mount in Jerusalem, with which we are so familiar. We learned about the Byzantine church that was built here, which became a mosque during the early Muslim period, and then reverted back into a church during the Crusader period, only to again be turned into a mosque in the Mamluk period. We mentioned that Jews, from the Mamluk period until 1967, a period of about seven hundred years, were not allowed to pray inside, and seven external stairs were built for them, on which they were allowed to stand and pray. We discussed the twenty special days throughout the year on which, for the past two decades, the entire complex is open either to Muslims or to Jews. How could that be? we wondered. Just then, we were permitted to enter.

We were only allowed to enter the Jewish part. Usually, Muslims are allowed to pray in this area on the date commemorating the birthday of the prophet Mohammad and on Islamic holidays. After 1967, under Israeli sovereignty, Jews and Muslims were allowed to pray in the entire complex. However, after the Baruch Goldstein massacre in 1994, in which twenty-nine Muslim worshippers were killed, and the ensuing unrest, the complex was split. Despite the division, the understanding was that there are certain days during the year when so many Muslims or Jews make the pilgrimage to this site that the complex cannot contain visitors from both religions. On these special days, the complex becomes either completely Muslim or completely Jewish for a few hours. Representatives from each religion are responsible for moving aside the chairs, books, pictures, and curtains so that the site looks appropriate for their own religious preferences during the event. There are lists that specify where to put the various books and chairs.

I was surprised. How could it be that in such a conflict-ridden city, at a site where sanctity is intertwined with nationalism, almost like the Temple Mount in Jerusalem, there is nevertheless a status quo arrangement that works? Later, I understood that what facilitates the situation here is in fact the detailed agreement.

In the early nineties, after many long years of bloody clashes between the Israelis and Palestinians, the atmosphere in the Middle East changed. In September 1993, the Oslo Accords were signed, a peace agreement between Israel and the Palestinians. The results of this agreement created the reality in the West Bank territories that can still be felt today. Four years later, when there was still an atmosphere of optimism regarding Israeli-Palestinian relations, the Hebron Accords were signed as an appendix to the Oslo Accords regarding Hebron in particular. According to this agreement, the city was divided into two parts, most of which remained in the hands of the Palestinians, with a small portion, including the holy site, the Tomb of the Patriarchs, placed under Israeli control. The agreement includes a section that permits converting the entire Tomb complex for either Muslims or Jews for a fixed number of days each year. The agreement is honored by both sides and operates under Israeli supervision.

So why don't people like me come to Hebron?

I am from a long-time, Zionist Israeli family. Like most Israelis, my entire family served in the army and even fought in Israel's wars. Like many Israelis, the Israeli-Palestinian conflict hit us as well in the form of beloved family members who were murdered in terrorist attacks and fell in battle. And like many Israeli families, the term Zionism is interpreted differently by different parts of the family.

We talk about the Israeli-Palestinian conflict at home. A conflict that began in the early twentieth century with the increase of Jewish immigration to the land of Israel, the purchase of land, and the Zionist settlement movement, all of which the local population, the Palestinians, was not too happy about. In November 1947, the United Nations approved the Partition Plan that proposed dividing the land into two states. That same night, the hostility erupted into a war that I, as an Israeli, refer to as the War of Independence, while the Palestinians call it the Nakba – the Catastrophe. The State of Israel, which had just declared its independence, obtained more land during this war than it had been allocated by the Partition Plan. The southern end of the Gaza Strip was conquered by Egypt, and most of the area designated for the Arab state, located on the West Bank of the Jordan River, the Hashemite Kingdom of Jordan conquered. This area was later conquered by Israel during the Six-Day War in June 1967. Different names have been given to this area by Israelis. There are those who call it the liberated territories, on the right side of the political spectrum, and those who call it Judea and Samaria, whom I refer to as indifferent. Among those who lean toward the left side of the spectrum, they are called the occupied territories. Sometimes, it seems like the Israeli-Palestinian conflict is centered exclusively on this area… the territories. But in fact, the conflict is everywhere here.

To what extent do I understand the conflict, and how much do I want to touch upon this subject? How do you explain the complexity of this conflict to a one-time visitor? How, on one hand, this conflict exists and is part of our entire existence here, impacting our daily lives constantly, while on the other hand, how easy it is for Israelis to shut their eyes and not see it. This might not be clear to someone who lives in a big city where there are immigrants from all over the world, and children from India, Iran, China, Israel, Guatemala, and America all learn in the same classroom. But here in Israel, even just a few feet from each other, Jews learn with Jews and Arabs learn with Arabs. Even in what we refer to as "mixed cities," we aren't really mixed. Each side is raised among their own people, on their own side, and it's easy not to meet each other. It's easy to only hear and be familiar with your own narrative. It's easy to live your entire life here without having one genuine, sincere conversation with someone from the other side, about the story of their family, about 1948 and what happened to them since then. We live alongside the conflict, and as long as there is no war or wave of terror, we put it aside. Everyone wants to earn a living respectfully and live their lives.

People like me don't visit Hebron, maybe because it's in the "territories" and it forces me to think and deal with the conflict. It also might be because I'm not a religious person and the tombs of the forefathers don't attract me. But for religious Jews, Christians, and Muslims, Hebron is literally the City of the Forefathers, a holy site that must be visited on their visit to Israel. It is the site about which the Bible says, "And Abraham weighed to Ephron the silver, which he had named in the hearing of the children of Heth, four hundred shekels of silver, current money with the merchant. So the field of Ephron, which was in Machpelah, which was before Mamre, the field, and the cave which was therein, and all the trees that were in the field, that were in all the border thereof round about" (Genesis 23).

And yet, here I am, visiting Hebron as part of a course with students who are Jews, Christians, and Muslims, and are interested in guiding tourists in this holy, captivating country. Some are Israeli citizens, while others, Arabs from East Jerusalem and Bethlehem, don't even hold citizenship, but they all want to be able to make an honest living. Life has brought us this opportunity to share a two-year course together, during which the distance between the Muslim Arab and the Christian

Arab lessens as they try to understand the Judaism classes together. Helping them with that is a rabbi, a new immigrant from the United States, who lives in a settlement. Here, the ultra-Orthodox Israeli, the secular left-wing Israeli, and the Palestinian social activist study about the sites holy to Christianity together. All of us stand together as "Hatikvah" plays at Independence Hall, out of respect for the country that enables this course to take place. That doesn't mean that we ignore, or even suppress, the Israeli-Palestinian conflict. It exists, it is fierce, and occasionally, to our great horror, it erupts and takes lives. It influences the economy, freedom of movement, our way of thinking, and essentially all areas of life for those who live in this land, where we live rich and complex lives in the shadow of the conflict. On this tour of Hebron, I discovered how many different facets a visit to this city can have, and how enriching a trip here is for anyone visiting the country. I can't wait until next time...

Brotherhood, 2013
Oil on canvas
mounted on wood
122X180

15

The IDF and Its Impact on the Israeli Soul

Yishay Shavit

I was born in the mid-seventies on a kibbutz in northern Israel. I grew up in the eighties in an environment where everyone served in the army. As a child, I don't remember even one person who didn't serve. I'm sure there were such people, but they were not part of the world in which I was raised. It was an accepted fact that after high school, there is another chapter in a person's life – military service. Among my friends, there were even those who physically and mentally prepared themselves in order to be accepted into the elite military units. My future army service was an integral part of my life, in the same way that every American child knows that one day, they'll have to go to work.

This attitude was not unique to the place or time that I grew up. It is a common mindset in Israel. Yes, there were and always will be Israelis who didn't and don't want to serve or who will try to evade military service, but among most of the population, army service is a fact of life. When you visit Israel, try talking to teenagers and ask them what they want to do during their military service. I can promise you that the conversation will be fascinating, and it will be based on the premise that they will definitely serve in the army one day. It's undisputed.

In Israel, military service is compulsory. Men serve in the Israel Defense Forces for about three years (the exact term of service varies) and women serve for about two years. After finishing their compulsory service, many Israelis will also do reserve duty, meaning that they will be recruited for military service for a set period of time every year, until they reach retirement age. This was how it was when the State of Israel was established, and this is how it still is today.

But not everyone serves. Arabs who are citizens of the State of Israel, and make up about 20 percent of the country's citizens, are not obligated to serve in the army. They can volunteer, and a small number of them even do so, but there is no requirement. Women can obtain an exemption from military service for religious reasons, as can ultra-Orthodox men studying in yeshivot – religious institutions of learning (about 10 percent of the population). Of course, those who are unable to serve due to various physical or mental reasons are exempt as well. Yet despite all of these exemptions, most Israelis still serve in the IDF for an extended period of time.

It is difficult, perhaps even impossible, to understand the way that most Israelis think without understanding the influence that military service has on our lives. It's not just the time spent in the army, or the understanding that Israel needs a strong military, so everyone should enlist. The impact that military service has on the lives of Israeli citizens is very deep, and accompanies us throughout our lives, from childhood to our senior years.

It begins long before recruitment. During high school years, many Israelis will be exposed to a state of mind that encourages them to pursue a meaningful military service. They will go on trips to famous battle sites, engage in conversations on the subject with teachers and friends, and some will even go on a week-long camp program that simulates military service. Schools in Israel are rated, among other things, based on the number of graduates who serve in the army. So it is no surprise that some Israelis feel that serving in a combat unit is a form of self-realization.

The years of military service themselves obviously leave their mark on the Israeli soul. There is no question that crises such as wars or other traumatic episodes leave scars on a person and influence the rest of their life. Unfortunately, there are too many Israelis who can tell such stories, and they are happy to share them with anyone willing to listen (and even those who aren't…). However, while most Israeli soldiers don't experience any incidents that are out of the ordinary during their military service, they will still undergo significant changes during this period of their lives. The years that we serve in the army are very formative years in the development of a young adult. Try to remember what you were doing during the period between your eighteenth-birthday celebration and your twenty-first-birthday celebration. Did you grow up? Fall in love? Study? Travel the world? Develop professionally and intellectually? Whatever you did, those were presumably formative years in your life.

A person's sense of belonging is also influenced by military service. It's been over twenty-five years, but to this day, I remember the State of Israel's forty-seventh Yom Ha'atzmaut (Independence Day), celebrated in May 1995. I was a young soldier in the Armored Corps and I was stationed at a small, forlorn army base in the Golan Heights not far from the Syrian border. Fate had it that I was assigned a three-hour guard duty shift that night. At first, I was really bummed out – guard duty on the night of Yom Ha'atzmaut! All of my friends were out celebrating, drinking, and having a good time, while I was stuck in the middle of nowhere guarding some deserted army base. Thirty minutes after I climbed up to the guard tower, I started to see flashes of light behind me. They were fireworks that were part of a Yom Ha'atzmaut celebration. Because of the high position of the base where I was guarding, I could see fireworks that were being fired from many different locations throughout the entire northeastern region of the country. Dozens, maybe even hundreds, of Yom Ha'atzmaut parties. A tremor spread through my body. I felt so proud. Thanks to the fact that I was standing here in this tower, my people could celebrate in peace and safety! Today I know that this was a bit of a naïve sentiment. Maybe it wasn't only because of me...

The feeling of national belonging that many soldiers experience during their military service is no trivial matter. Our service makes us better citizens, citizens who are more familiar with their country and its challenges, citizens who feel part of something bigger than themselves, and who are willing to sacrifice the best years of their lives, and sometimes even life itself, for their country. Citizens who care. I presume that this statement holds true for soldiers in many armies around the world, but don't forget – in Israel, most citizens were also soldiers at some point in their lives.

With all due respect to the moments when the soul soars to new heights during military service, most of the days and nights of a simple soldier are pretty dull and gray. Guard duty, kitchen duty, exercises, sleeping on hard beds, and so on. But this intensive routine creates new friendships that in certain cases become strong, inseverable bonds. These friendships stay with us, even after our compulsory service or reserve duty is long over, and they create an amazing social network. If my drain is clogged, I'll call my friend from the reserve unit who is a plumber. If I graduate Tel Aviv University with a degree in computer engineering, the first phone call I make will be to my friend from compulsory service whose father has a small high-tech company that is looking for employees. If I happen to hear about someone from the command headquarters who got divorced, I'll call him and ask if I can help him find a new partner. For many Israelis, this is part of the DNA of their daily lives.

Thus, military service has a lasting impression even after it is over. This goes beyond personal friendships. The employment market in Israel, the high-tech industry in particular, benefits from manpower with extensive experience in significant positions – manpower trained by the army. There are those who claim that this is part of the secret of Israel's successful economy. Think about it for a moment. The Israeli workforce is filled with people in their mid-twenties who hold an academic degree and have vast experience in planning or operating advanced systems in the field. Many of these young people are trying to find a way to apply what they learned in the army to their civilian lives. The result in many cases is the establishment of start-ups, some of which have even become large global companies. It is no wonder that an increasing number of teenage Israelis put great effort into preparing themselves so that they will be accepted into elite intelligence or technology units.

Israelis who served in a good military unit would be stupid not to mention their IDF record in a work interview. While the interviewer is not allowed to explicitly ask about their military service if it is not relevant to the position (so as not to discriminate), in many cases, there is an unspoken expectation that candidates will mention their military service. This isn't just an attempt to hear about the candidate's life experience in general, it is also a way of checking their credibility. The interviewer has probably also served in the army and knows exactly what the candidate is talking about. What's more, the interviewer has friends who they can call to ask about the candidate's conduct during their IDF days. This element makes it very hard for those who haven't served in the army. The absence of this social network can deal a mortal blow to the chances of an Arab or ultra-Orthodox candidate searching for employment in many cases, especially in the high-tech industry. The

State of Israel also suffers a loss when it misses out on the unique talents that have developed in these sectors of the population.

Another area in Israel that is influenced by military service is in academia. The average Israeli student is about three years older than their American counterpart. At this age, they are more experienced and have already seen a thing or two in life. This means that generally, more Israeli students know what they want to study, and the level of discussion in the classroom, at least in the humanities, is higher. The average Israeli student prefers not to live in student dormitories because they are already twenty-two years old, or in a significant relationship, or simply because they've had enough of sharing a room with other people in the army. In academia in Israel, campus life is not as lively as an American college campus. Israeli students will finish their required university classes and then go to work or head to an apartment they rent in the city. If you absolutely live for college sports – Israel might not be the place for you.

There are many other areas of life in Israel in which the impact of military service is evident, but I would like to focus on just one additional, emotional aspect that has to do with our families. When Israelis decide to bring a child into this world, we know that he or she will serve in the army in the future. This is a dramatic and difficult statement, but it's true. There are demographic scholars who claim that this knowledge even impacts the size of families in Israel. Think about it for a moment – when we have a baby, we know that in the future, he will risk his life in the army. When we accompany our daughter hand in hand to her first day of first grade, we know that she will serve in the army. When our son celebrates his eighteenth birthday, the level of apprehension and stress in the family moves up a level, and then come the years when every knock on the door makes your heart skip a beat.

Communities

Abundance, 2015
Oil on canvas
mounted on wood
60X25

16

A Mountain of Diversities

Minorities in Israel

Nimrod Shafran

When my wife and I lived in Jerusalem, we became close friends with our neighbors Adham and Sara Gaber. Adham and Sara, a Druze couple from Daliyat el-Carmel, a Druze town located on the top of the Carmel Mountain Range in northern Israel, were the first ones to hang an Israeli flag on their balcony in preparations for Yom Ha'atzmaut, Israel's Independence Day. Sara lost her older brother in a terrorist attack while he was serving in the IDF, and Adham served in the Israeli Navy as an officer. They both spoke fluent Hebrew, they loved the State of Israel, and defined themselves as Druze, Israeli, and Zionists.

In Israel, it's not a given that a couple that belongs to one of the country's minority groups would define themselves in this way. As an educator, I often think about the experience of the first-time visitor to Israel, having to navigate a complicated and sometimes confusing maze of minority ethnic groups and religious sites. As most tour guides in Israel often like to say: it's complicated. One of the regions where that complexity is most evident is in the Carmel Mountain Range.

Back to Daliyat el-Carmel, the Druze town where Adham and Sara are from. The Druze live primarily in Syria, Lebanon, and Israel. They are an Arabic-speaking ethnoreligious group, and even though the Druze faith originally developed out of Islam, the Druze do not identify themselves as Muslims. They are a fairly small minority in Israel – 1.6 percent of the total population of the country. So, what is the identity of Israel's Druze citizens? How do they define themselves? Firstly, it's important to note that Israelis have multiple identities, and the order in which the identities are described often reflect their respective importance. For example, there is a huge difference between a person saying he is a "Druze, Israeli, and Zionist," and a person saying he is "Druze, Arab, and Israeli."

One of the unique things about the Druze is that they have no national aspirations. They have always been loyal to the ruler of the land. This means that in Syria many will serve in the Syrian Army, and in Israel many of them will serve in the IDF. Their lack of national aspirations kept them neutral during most of Israel's War of Independence. This neutrality dramatically helped the Druze minority to integrate into Israeli society.

The Druze will always define themselves as Druze first. Some will define themselves as Israeli second while others will also define themselves as Arab before Israeli. The Druze are an Arabic-speaking minority and the Arab language plays a huge role in their culture. However, there is no real tension between their Arab and Israeli identities – they exist in harmony since their Arab identity is cultural and ethnic rather than national or political.

That is not the case for most of Israel's Arab citizens, who comprise more than 20 percent of the country's population. If you drive along the Carmel Mountain Range to the city of Haifa, Israel's third largest city, you'll be able to visit the colorful neighborhood of Wadi Nisnas, where most of Haifa's Arab residents live. Even in this beautiful and very touristy neighborhood – one of the symbols of successful coexistence and tolerance between Jews and Arabs – the majority of Arabs will identify themselves as Arab or Palestinian by nationality and Israeli by citizenship. Most of them will probably define themselves as Arab or Palestinian first, and Muslim or Christian second. Their Israeli identity will come last, if at all.

In the complicated reality of Israel, Arab citizens experience significant tension between their Arab and Palestinian identities and their Israeli identity. Their lack of identification as Israelis stems from the Arab/Palestinian-Israeli conflict, which dates back to the end of the nineteenth century. The rise of Zionism and the reactionary Arab nationalism led to over a century of wars and conflicts, mainly over land. In Haifa, for example, the Arabs comprised close to 50 percent of the city's population until Israel's War of Independence in 1948, after which time only a few thousand remained in the city. Today's Arab population in Haifa constitutes only 11 percent of the city's total population.

Not far from Wadi Nisnas lies the Bahai Gardens, the most distinct tourist attraction in all of Haifa, and one of the most visited tourist attractions in Israel. Due to the size and grandeur of the gardens, a first-time visitor to Israel would probably assume that there is a significant Bahai minority living in Israel, but that is far from being the case.

The Bahai faith is relatively a new one. Founded in Persia in the mid-nineteenth century, it has since attracted millions of followers from all over the world. Israel became central for this new religion since the founders of the faith were buried in Akko and in Haifa. Even though the Bahai holy sites are located in Israel, there is no real Bahai presence, and the holy sites mainly serve as pilgrimage sites. There are only a few hundred Bahai in Israel, mostly foreign residents who do not stay in

Israel, who come for short periods of up to a year to volunteer at the Bahai holy sites, only to be promptly replaced by other volunteers.

There are dozens of other holy sites spread around Israel – most of them Christian churches in northern Israel and in Jerusalem – that serve as pilgrimage sites for their followers, but do not have significant communities in Israel.

That is the case with the impressive Muhraka Carmelite monastery located on the southern slope of the Carmel Mountain Range. According to both Jewish and Christian traditions, it is here on this high ridge, overlooking the hills of the Lower Galilee, that the Biblical battle between the Prophet Elijah and the pagan prophets of Baal took place. The monastery is run by a couple of Carmelite monks and serves only as a tourist attraction and pilgrimage site, since there is no Carmelite minority in Israel.

Looks can be deceiving in Israel. You might meet Arabic-speaking citizens with very different identities. At the same time, you might see and visit some of the more iconic sites in Israel, that do not represent significant communities and minorities. The key to understanding the complexity of Israel is to dig deep and ask questions about the identity of different groups and sites.

17

I Did It My Way

A Story of an Arab Woman

Nadia Mahmood Giol

My name is Nadia Mahmood Giol. I am an Israeli Palestinian, mother to two children, and resident of the Galilee. All of these biographical details are significant parts of who I am. As a woman and an Arab in Israel, I have dealt with the ramifications of my complex identity throughout my entire life. To a great extent, they are what brought me to where I am today – involved in projects empowering women and a co-manager at a very special place – Sindyanna of Galilee.

Sindyanna of Galilee (the word "sindyanna" means "oak tree" in Arabic) is a nonprofit organization located in Kfar Kana, an Arab town in the heart of the Galilee with a population of twenty-seven thousand. The organization promotes social change by connecting Arab and Jewish women. This feminine dialogue has another purpose, aside from the bridges that it builds between the communities: female empowerment, with a special emphasis on the empowerment of Arab women. I believe that these two goals are intertwined. The profits from the Galilee olive oil that we produce are invested back into social initiatives to encourage women's employment, organic agriculture, a sustainable green economy, and bringing the communities closer together.

My connection to Sindyanna is no coincidence. Throughout my life, I searched for programs dedicated to building a shared lifestyle between all of the country's residents. At Sindyanna, I feel at home; I am proud of my opinions and my faith, and I can express myself in my mother tongue without anyone turning their head at the sound of Arabic. At Sindyanna, actions are more prevalent than words, especially because we believe that working together is a language that can build bridges and improve communication. Our space is a place where different people can meet each other personally and not rely on stories or prejudices. How is all of this related to my biography? To understand that, you need to get to know me a bit more deeply.

I was born in 1971 to an Arab Muslim family of refugees from the Palestinian village Saffuriya in the lower Galilee, not far from Nazareth. My family became refugees in their land as a result of the war in 1948. I grew up in the shadow of the Palestinian-Israeli conflict, on a small farm north of the Jewish town Zippori, which was established on the lands of my village. We called it "kherbet Roma." The farm was the only thing that my family had left after the war. Some of my family settled there, but others became refugees in the Ain al-Hilweh refugee camp in Lebanon.

When I was a girl, I remember sitting on the windowsill and looking southward at the tall fortress and the monastery, the only buildings in the village of Saffuriya that survived the Nakba, the catastrophe that befell my nation and my village in 1948. I would daydream about how my family's life could have been if not for the war. I thought about the new houses built behind the hill, the Jews living in them today who had replaced us, and of all the people of the village who had lived there for many generations before the war.

The window of my childhood bedroom, from which I looked at the world for the first time, was the window of the only room in our house, which was used as a living room and bedroom for my entire family. This room was built immediately after the war at the edge of my grandfather's goat and sheep pen. Under our feet, we could see the remains of a town from the Roman period that had stood here thousands of years ago. Every time I got angry at my family, I would tell my mother that I was going to run away and hide in the monastery, among the ruins of the village of Saffuriya, where no one would find me. My mother would laugh and say – first, let's see the authorities let you in there, and then we'll talk!

Every time we went to play in the fortress or gather wild herbs in the spring, the Jewish residents of the new Zippori would chase us away, claiming that we were trespassing on their private property. I always wondered how they could call us trespassers when it was our village, our land, and our home for so many years? It was the place that the country in which we live would not allow us access.

I was a very curious girl, and I always asked questions about the war and the conflict, and whether there could have been a different way other than war. Socially, I was considered rude and undisciplined. I wouldn't accept anything as a given. I grew up like a wildflower, strange and foreign in my surroundings. Even at the elementary school I attended in the nearby Bedouin village, I was treated as someone different. There, my family and I were the refugees who no one wanted to know.

As a teenager, the conflicts in my life increasingly worsened. Along with the Jews behind the hill who treated us like trespassers and the Bedouins who didn't want us, another conflict emerged – the need to follow the traditional social rules upon which I had been raised, rules that defined the world of women and that I didn't always agree to follow. Rules that shaped yesterday's world, the world before the war. Rules that didn't seem relevant to my life.

Luckily, I always had a role model to watch – my mother. My mother became a widow at the age of thirty-eight with eight children and stood strong in the face of all of the social and family challenges. My mother fought to raise us alone, despite all of the economic difficulty. She didn't know how to read or write herself, so she made sure that all of us, boys and girls alike, attended school. Due to the difficult living conditions in the partially dilapidated cabin where I was born, she sold the sheep and goats and gave up the land that we owned. With the money that she saved, she bought a plot of land in the nearby Arab village Rumat al-Heib, where we built our home. To support ourselves, we, the boys and girls of the family, worked in agriculture. Often, in contrast with the accepted conventions, we were hired by our Jewish neighbors who had settled on our land, and we sometimes even received assistance from them when we needed it. Some of the Jewish farmers would come to visit us with their children, but we never went to their homes. My mother always said: "الديـن لله والوطـن للجميـع" – religion is for God, and the homeland is for everyone. Every person should be respected as a fellow human being, regardless of his faith or origin. I grew up on these principles.

When I was fifteen, during my high school studies, it became clear to me that one day, I would head out into the big world. At the age of nineteen, I packed my belongings into a backpack and secretly left our family home and the village. The only one who knew of my plan was my mother, and to my surprise, she supported me and encouraged me to leave the village. She wanted a better life for me, and believed that the place where we lived would not facilitate it. Today, I know that she paid a heavy social price for supporting me. In those days, it was not acceptable for an unmarried Arab woman to go out to the big city alone. The traditional society in which we lived blamed her for my rebellion.

At this point, my new journey began. It was the journey of a young Arab woman who thought that she was an Israeli citizen with equal rights who could live wherever she wanted. I received my first slap in the face when I wanted to rent a house on a kibbutz, and my request was obviously denied because I am an Arab. Afterward, I moved to Jerusalem and naively thought that in the big, holy city, my chances would be better. But there, I discovered that as an Arab, I was not wanted on the Jewish side of the city, and as an Arab with Israeli citizenship, I was considered a traitor on the Arab side.

In the end, I decided to live in the monastery, in the international community in central Jerusalem. There, in addition to a place to live, I also found a job and studied for a degree in special education. But behind the walls of the monastery as well, I was considered a strange bird. I was the only Israeli, and they gave me the impression that they didn't know how to react to my complex identity. My friendships with young volunteers from all over the world and the cosmopolitan atmosphere that they gave the site helped me hold out there until I had completed my studies.

After I finished my degree in Jerusalem, it seemed obvious to everyone that I would want to return to my family's home. In those days, it was not customary in Arab society for young single women to live far away from their families. At first, I vehemently rejected this option, but when a difficult pressure campaign began, including serious threats, I decided to compromise. I returned to the Galilee but decided not to live with my family in the village, but instead in the nearby city of Nazareth Illit, a city with a large Jewish majority. At that time, my family didn't know that I was engaged to a Catalan Christian whom I met at the monastery. Our wedding plans were strange to the society in which I had grown up. It was not accepted, socially or religiously, for a girl from a Muslim family to marry someone from a Christian family, especially not from Spain... The only people who knew about my engagement were my oldest brother and my mother, of course. We decided to hide the news until the wedding. After a long and exhausting process, we got married in the Franciscan Catholic church Terra Santa, opposite the Prime Minister's Residence in Jerusalem. Our wedding day, July 2, 1994, was a historic day in the history of the Palestinian-Israeli conflict. It was the day that Yasser Arafat, the Palestinian national leader, entered the Gaza Strip after many years in exile. Large protests were expected in Jerusalem.

After our wedding ceremony, we thought that our problems were behind us and that we were beginning a new period in our lives. We tried to rent a home in Jerusalem, the holy city. To our surprise, we couldn't rent an apartment even as a married couple. Not on the Jewish side and not on the Arab side. It was again because the Jewish side weren't too happy about renting a property to an Arab woman, and on the Arab side, we were rejected because we were a mixed couple who communicated with each other in Hebrew. After three months, we gave up and decided to move to Spain to live with my husband's family. But even there, the subject of my identity chased after me. I couldn't get a job anywhere because no one wanted to hire a Palestinian with an Israeli passport. On November 4, 1995, Yitzchak Rabin, the prime minister of Israel, was killed by a Jewish assassin in Tel Aviv. Following the murder and the political events that ensued, I realized that I had to go home to fight for the country's character. I felt that I had to go back to deal with reality, instead of running away from it. In 1996, I returned to Israel and to the Galilee. I started from zero. Later, my husband joined me, and since then, we are here. Loyal to my belief in fighting for what I believe in, I became active in various initiatives that all deal with two issues: women's empowerment and racism. This belief led me to become a nonviolent communications instructor for multicultural groups, in addition to my work at Sindyanna of Galilee. I am currently pursuing an international certification in this subject.

These two issues are seemingly unrelated, but the truth is that in twenty-first-century Israel, it is difficult to separate them. In many traditional societies around the world that are undergoing an accelerated process of modernization, women are dealing with many challenges. The fight for freedom of movement, higher education, the possibility of employment, personal security, self-realization, and more – all characterize the efforts of feminist organizations around the world. The female Arab population in Israel is also fighting these battles, but at the same time, they are encountering additional obstacles related to their identities. Due to the national conflict, the options open to them among the Jewish population are very limited, and because of discrimination in government budgets, they must fight not only to acquire a proper education, but even to physically access their desired places of employment. After overcoming these obstacles, they still need to prove that they are clearly better than any Jewish candidate applying for the same position.

Over the years, parallel to my professional development, I was influenced by the philosophy of Mahatma Gandhi. I decided that in order to effect change, I must be an example of the change I want to see. After this decision, it didn't take long for me to reach Sindyanna of Galilee. Working with Arab women who had never joined the workforce and helping them, the joint Arab-Israeli activities, and working on a daily basis with olive oil produced in the Galilee – are all endeavors that are important to me. I feel a true sense of mission. I enjoy sharing my life story with visitors who come to Sindyanna of Galilee. I believe that it is possible to view my story as an example of the fact that regardless of a person's origin, religion, race, or gender, we are all human beings with emotions and needs, and the secret is in finding a way to help each other satisfy them, but not at the expense of one another.

Struggles for social change are never short struggles. Aside from time, they also require authentic contact with real people on the streets. Someone who has never experienced racism will have a hard time deeply understanding its paralyzing affects. Someone who has never experienced gender discrimination may think that it can be dealt with on a purely legal level, without comprehending the traditional social patterns. Someone who refuses to understand the connection cannot succeed in implementing real changes. If you would like to strengthen this effort, I invite you to talk to Arab women in Israel and visit Sindyanna of Galilee.

18

Living Stones

Christians in the Holy Land

Hana Bendcowsky

Growing up in a Modern Orthodox Jewish home in Israel, we never had the Church of the Holy Sepulcher on our list of places to visit in Jerusalem. It wasn't until I visited the city as an adult that I set foot in the place that is so important to the Christian world, the church erected on the site identified as the place of Jesus' crucifixion, burial, and resurrection. In the Israeli educational system, there was hardly any discussion of other religions aside from in history class, and Christianity was not part of the curriculum. My encounter with the Christian world and Christianity in the Holy Land actually took place at Hebrew University, when I studied European history. Studying Christianity was like learning a new language, enabling me to read the cultural, religious, and historical reality of Western society more adeptly. Curiosity, and a complex relationship with the library, spurred me forward, beyond the walls of academia, to study in what I believe is the "best classroom in the world" – the Old City of Jerusalem. My feet constantly drew me to the Christian Quarter, and to the Church of the Holy Sepulcher at its center.

First-time visitors to the Church of the Holy Sepulcher may be surprised. The current building is about 870 years old and was constructed atop the previous building from the fourth century. It does not look glorious. It is situated between many other buildings, cracked and dilapidated, even looking as if it has been neglected for years. I tell tourists that the condition of the church reflects, in a way, the situation of Christians in the Holy Land today. One would expect the holiest site in Christianity to be a magnificent, luminous cathedral, just as one might imagine that the Living Stones of the Holy Land, those descendants of the first Christian community in the world who lived in the holy city since the church's very first days, would be a large, well-known community with a significant presence in the city and in the Christian world. Yet this is not the case. The local Christian community, crumpled and compressed between the pages of history, is a small group that is fighting to survive and maintain a Christian presence at the holy sites, despite the changing powers and upheavals in the land.

There are usually clergy walking through the parvis (courtyard) of the Church of the Holy Sepulcher. Since the beginning of Christianity, religious people have moved to the Holy Land to live near the holy sites and to serve in the churches, so that pilgrims would be able to come to visit and pray. To this day, there are many who belong to Christian religious communities in the Holy Land who have chosen to dedicate their lives to God by serving the community. They spend their days conducting prayer services, singing at the holy sites, or serving the local lay community. They speak many different languages and are of varying nationalities. At times, people from ten different countries who all speak different languages can live in the same monastery.

To the left of the parvis of the Church of the Holy Sepulcher is Mar Yacoub Church, where the local Arab Orthodox community gathers to pray on Sundays. While the prayers follow the Greek Orthodox liturgical rite and the priest can speak Greek, the local community is Arab and uses an Arabic translation of the prayers. Similar to many in the Middle East, the local Christian communities adapted themselves to the spirit of the times back in the seventh century, switching to the use of Arabic not only as their everyday language, but also as their language of prayer. Here at Mar Yacoub, next to the church of the Holy Sepulcher – the cradle of Christianity, baptisms, marriages, and funerals are conducted for the local community, in Arabic.

However, most visitors tend to ignore the low entrance to Mar Yacoub as they rush forward into the Holy Sepulcher itself, disregarding the local Christians who have been preserving the Christian presence in the Holy Land throughout the years. They prioritize the possibility of an encounter with holiness in the place where Jesus was crucified, buried, and resurrected.

Those pilgrims and visitors will walk through the doors of the church, and once their eyes adjust to the dimness around them, they will discern an old wooden bench to their left, where Mr. Nusseiba sits. He is not a Christian, but he occupies this bench almost all day. His family and another family, the Jawda family, received the keys to the Church of the Holy Sepulcher and the right to lock and unlock it was given to the Nusseiba family about seven hundred years ago. Thus, the doors of the Church of the Holy Sepulcher are opened and closed every morning and evening by Muslims, the sovereign ruler of the land until a century ago. The holiest site in the Christian world has been subject to non-Christian control for hundreds of years. The relationship between Muslims and Christians in the Holy Land has waxed and waned throughout history. Years of living alongside each other produced a complex relationship of fraternity and cultural, linguistic, and national partnership, coupled with religious tension and disagreement.

The State of Israel is also part of this intercultural and interreligious encounter at the church, where the security and safety of visitors are the responsibility of the Israel Police. Police officers of the special unit of the Church of the Holy Sepulcher – whether Jewish, Christian, or Muslim – protect the safety of the visitors and worshippers. On holidays, when large crowds are anticipated at the site, the police put great effort into limiting the number of worshippers so that the traditional processions and ceremonies can commence, even when this means that freedom of movement is limited for pilgrims and tourists, who due to the narrow streets must remain outside the procession route. The presence of the Israeli Police must also be interpreted in the context of the complex Jewish-Christian relations over the course of history, taking into consideration the changes in these relations that have taken place during the twentieth century. A more respectful, open relationship is being built between the religions, and it is striking to remember that the State of Israel is responsible for the safety of worshippers at the holiest site in the Christian world.

Visitors continue into the church, passing the foyer and arriving at the heart of the church. This is the main hall where the most significant event in Christianity occurred – the site of the Holy Sepulcher. Pilgrims visiting the site have not come to see what is here, but rather what is not here. The tomb of Jesus is empty, according to the Christian faith here he was resurrected from the dead. For the visitors, spending time at the Church of the Holy Sepulcher connects them to an event that occurred in the past – the burial of Jesus and his resurrection, while providing encouragement regarding what will happen in the future, when Jesus returns. With his return, they will be resurrected by entering the Kingdom of God. The situation invites visitors to contemplate not only the past and future, but the present as well. They must stand in a long line, waiting an hour or two, to enter the empty tomb. The long wait in line provides an opportunity to scan the wide range of people standing there, Christians from all over the world, as well as members of other religions. It is a very diverse crowd, all waiting to visit the same sanctuary. Some wait patiently; others fidget. Some stand scattered, maintaining personal space between each other, while other groups stand close together, as if they are one cohesive entity. There are pilgrims who sing or listen to their guide, while others are engrossed in silent prayer. Thus, even if you attempt to focus on your own spiritual journey, you are exposed to the human richness, cultural diversity, and different experiences of the other visitors around you.

As I mentioned, the Church of the Holy Sepulcher is a dark place. Other than the light that seeps in through the round window in the large dome, there is hardly any natural light. When exiting the church to the courtyard, the bright sunlight reflecting off the Jerusalem stone can be surprisingly blinding. It is as surprising as the visit to the church itself. It is as surprising as the encounter between years of history and the vibrant reality of the local communities, churchmen, pilgrims, and tourists from all over the world. It is as surprising as the simplicity of the building whose sanctity is not expressed through architectural magnificence or golden decorations, but rather through the emotions of the visitors and the sounds of the prayers. It is as surprising as the Christian presence in the Holy Land today – small communities, most of which speak Arabic, a minority within a minority, holding on to the Holy Land to ensure that the silent stones will not remain barren as long as the "Living Stones" hold their prayers.

The Christian Arab communities in the Middle East, specifically the Palestinian ones in Israel and the West Bank, emphasize the importance of their presence in the Holy Land, quoting the letter from Peter: "You also, like living stones, are being built into a spiritual house to be a holy priesthood, offering spiritual sacrifices acceptable to God through Jesus Christ" (1 Peter 2:5). This letter speaks of a spiritual house that replaces the stone structure of the temple. The members of these communities ask visitors to the Holy Land to pay attention to them, not just to the structures of the churches and the tourist sites – but to see the communities, listen to their stories, and discover their heritage and deep connection to the land. They call to notice their challenges as a minority in a society with a Jewish majority, and being Christian among the Muslim Arab population. They ask to consider the place of the church in maintaining their unique identity, alongside the process of distancing from the churches as part of the shift toward modernization and secularization that the communities are experiencing. The communities, like the Church of the Holy Sepulcher, ask you to look beyond the external façade.

19

The Long Shadow of Ethnicity

Rivka Brama

When I was six years old, we moved from a small neighborhood next to Hebrew University to our new home in a suburb of Jerusalem. On my first day in the neighborhood, I courageously set out to explore our new street and neighbors. During my first encounter with the neighborhood kids, I was asked, "What are you?"

"What do you mean, what are you?" I replied, confused. "I'm Rivka. I'm starting first grade."

"No, no," the new neighbors explained. "What are you – Ashkenazi? Moroccan?"

I vaguely remembered hearing those terms in the past, but I didn't really know what they meant. I quickly ran up the four flights of stairs and asked my mother, "What am I – Ashkenazi or Moroccan?"

My mother smiled and said that I was both.

My father was born in Paris and came from a family with deep roots in Alsace that traced back to the period of the emancipation. They successfully integrated into French society and reached impressive professional heights. My mother was born in Casablanca to parents from Morocco and Tunisia. When her family moved to Kibbutz

147

Tze'eilim, which was established by one of the first and only *garin* groups from the Zionist youth movement in Morocco, she was the only child to live on the kibbutz. My Moroccan family never spoke Arabic, and most of my culinary experiences involved eating an unidentifiable kugel in the kibbutz dining room while listening to wistful stories of my great-grandmother's couscous. My Ashkenazi family never spoke Yiddish. The Holocaust was referred to as "the war" and the only meal that didn't include wine was breakfast.

Was Ben-Gurion's vision of an ingathering of the exiles and the creation of the new Israeli realized in little me? Did we indeed create a society here where ethnicity has no impact on a person's worldview, political opinions, and socioeconomic situation?

The same historic reality that saw the absorption of the pioneers of the first waves of aliyah also witnessed the arrival of masses of new immigrants from North Africa and the Middle East in a short period of time. The consequence is the reality we are faced with today – considerable injustices and challenges whose imprint is still visible. Most of the key positions in public administration, the media, and centers of power were in the hands of the dominant political party at the time, Mapai (Labor Party), resulting in ongoing discrimination and neglect. Whether the discrimination was the product of circumstances or caused by inherent racism and a sense of supremacy continues to be a burning question in the Israeli consciousness.

During the first three years of independence, Immigrants from North Africa and the Middle East, together with Holocaust survivors, arrived all at once in droves, about two hundred thousand Jews per year – making it very difficult to provide them all with education, health services, and housing. Thus, enclaves of neglect developed in the immigrant transit camps (*ma'abarot*), development towns, and neighborhoods "abandoned" by their Arab residents in 1948 and resettled by the immigrants. The ramifications of the reality that developed under these circumstances are, to this day, felt in Israel.

Many claim today that this sense of discrimination is a thing of the past, the result of insensitivity and necessity dictated by circumstances rather than a sense of supremacy among European Jews toward other ethnicities in Israel. However, by browsing confidential minutes from government meetings and the writings of various Zionist leaders, a problematic and disturbing picture emerges of a genuine sense of Ashkenazi supremacy over non-Ashkenazi Jews and their traditions.

The vast gap between the senior, governing Ashkenazi elite and the new Mizrahi immigrants reached its boiling point in 1959 in riots that broke out in Wadi Salib in Haifa. It ended with several wounded, and a commission of inquiry, the conclusions of which were unclear and not actually implemented. Several years later, in the early seventies, a civil disobedience movement was formed that called itself the Black Panthers, inspired by the parallel movement in the United States. The movement organized angry protests and strikes in various locations in Israel, following which the movement's leaders would meet with government representatives in order to obtain funding to narrow the gaps, rehabilitate neighborhoods, and raise awareness of the plight of Mizrahi Jews in Israel.

After one of these meetings, Prime Minister Golda Meir was asked her opinion of the protest representatives and remarked: "They're not nice," a comment that is still quoted today and characterizes the surprise of the classic Zionist establishment at the fact that the stereotype of the simple, happy-go-lucky Mizrahi immigrant did not match reality. To this day, there is a small alley in Jerusalem's Musrara neighborhood that is called "They're Not Nice." The alley received this name forty years after the riots to commemorate the struggle, though the name was never officially recognized by the authorities.

The homes in Musrara were built by Arabs who had left the Old City at the end of the nineteenth century, and was a high-class neighborhood until the establishment of the State of Israel. In 1948, Arab residents abandoned the neighborhood and it remained adjacent to the municipal borderline, which was exposed to Jordanian sniper fire. Immigrants from North Africa were placed in this dangerous neighborhood, which suffered from neglect that continued even after both parts of the city were reunited in 1967, following the Six-Day War. Over the years, the neighborhood was characterized by crime and high unemployment rates, and it is no wonder that it was home to many of the leaders of the protests.

The ninth Knesset elections in 1977 are still referred to as the *mahapach* – (electoral upheaval). The left-wing Alignment Party (its predecessor was the historic Mapai Party) led by Shimon Peres lost the election to Menachem Begin and the Likud party, surprising the media and the Israeli public.

There were several factors that contributed to Likud's rise to power. One of them is related to the fact that historically, most citizens of eastern descent supported Menachem Begin and his party. Although most of its leaders were of Ashkenazi descent, the party was considered attentive to Mizrahi voices. It's a popular joke that many are still convinced to this day that Menachem Begin, who was of Polish descent, was actually a Moroccan Jew.

Another important milestone in the division of Mizrahi votes and the ascent of the Mizrahi voice to the forefront was the founding of Shas, an ultra-Orthodox party whose spiritual leader was the former Sephardic Chief Rabbi, Rabbi Ovadia Yosef. The party was established as an antithesis to the Ashkenazi ultra-Orthodox political parties that were in office but did not take the needs of ultra-Orthodox Sephardim into account. Over the years, Shas became the party for which many Mizrahi Jews, even those who are not religious, cast their vote.

The very fact that a party declares itself as Sephardic, and that many politicians use tribal, ethnic terms in their rhetoric, is proof that discrimination still exists, and the chasm between Mizrahi and Ashkenazi Jews is still substantial. The popular jargon of identity politics in the Western academic world has trickled down to political discourse as well. Sometimes it is above the surface, and sometimes below. Every political move is framed as an act that is characteristic of a certain tribe, regardless of the ideological basis upon which its stands.

Ben-Gurion's vision is still far from being realized, and questions of distributive justice, racism, and dominant, non-permissive culture have remained open and have become even more pointed with the rise of a new generation of Mizrahi Jews who are less involved in survival and have more time to redefine their identity. We are witnesses to the flourishing success of Mizrahi culture. Classic Mizrahi music has made a comeback and traditional liturgical songs (piyyut) have gained momentum. Mizrahi pop is the most popular music in the country. Poets and authors of Mizrahi descent are read and printed, and more Mizrahi families are being featured in television shows on prime time. The common Jewish-American question, "Are you more Jewish or more American," or its Israeli parallel, "Are you more Jewish or more Israeli," has another dimension – are you Ashkenazi or Mizrahi. The answer will depend significantly on the identity of the person asked. I believe that "Jewish" and "Israeli" (not necessarily in that order) will rank higher than the question of ethnicity, but ethnicity will still be there, somewhere at the top of the list.

Often, when I meet US tourists who are interested in hearing about the burning issues in Israel, the questions often revolve around our relations with the neighboring countries, security challenges, the complexity of politics and diplomacy, and the relations between Jews and Arabs. But the truth is that in our daily lives, questions of descent and ethnicity may have a stronger impact on Israeli society. It is possible and important to understand the political divisions through the prism of Mizrahi Israel and the periphery, versus homogenous Ashkenazi Israel, and the way they impact processes today. For many Israelis, the question of their parents' ethnicity is still a relevant and influential (though not absolute) factor in the way they vote, their taste in music, their level of education, and their economic situation.

The struggle between what is considered "Mizrahi and common" versus what is considered "Ashkenazi and elitist" (a stereotypical division that is ridiculous, of course) is alive and kicking, and used sarcastically by political leaders and the media. If we treat reality television as a mirror of society, there will always be that point when one of the contestants accuses the other of being racist and elitist, evoking the counteraccusation that he is picking a fight and is uncultured. These will be minutes that produce high ratings and extensive social media buzz. Was the argument staged to boost ratings? Regardless, it's proof that this is a sensitive subject.

Looking at my own children, with a half-Ashkenazi, half-Moroccan mother and a father of Polish Ashkenazi descent, I notice that they have a heightened awareness of the question of ethnicity than I had at their age. I have no doubt that the divisions are artificial, stupid, and most of all divisive, but if the price of giving them up is a blurring of identity and singularity, maybe it's better this way.

When you visit the country and meet the people, the cultural, musical, literary, and culinary richness that Israel has to offer is definitely impressive, but also remember that behind it all, there are also social complexities and feelings of injustice and discrimination. Israel may pride itself for its multicultural society, but there is also a struggle underway between the different populations regarding the dominant character of Israeli society. Will the ultimate Sabra (native-born Israeli) always be the child of European descent who grew up in a community in the Galilee, or could the ultimate Sabra also be the child of Iraqi descent who grew up in a development town?

I feel that the struggle is essentially about recognition of the pain. When we speak about pioneers and the builders of the country, we should not only mention the founders of the kibbutzim, but also those who settled in distant periphery towns and built cities from the ground up. Remember the thousands of students who were directed toward a worker lifestyle, rather than higher education, yet still managed to develop great careers and flourishing businesses. Remember those whose culture was pushed into a corner and who had to maintain it without budgets and without government recognition yet managed to preserve their rich cultural heritage.

The dream of a new "mixed" Israeli has indeed come to fruition in my children, but they too are aware of the depth and richness of the different cultures at the basis of this mixture, and they understand that our multiculturalism is also testimony to the pain that has not yet healed.

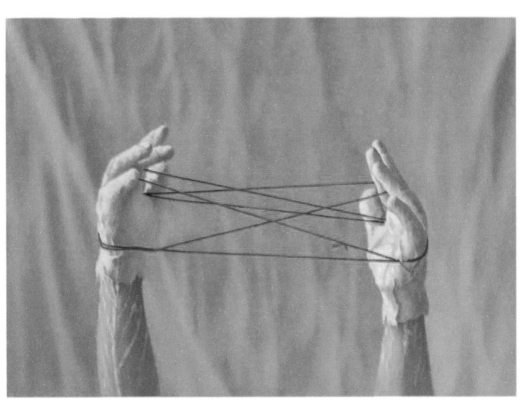

Cat's Cradle 1, 2016
Oil on canvas
mounted on wood
45X65

20

Does Jerusalem Belong to Me or Do I Belong to Jerusalem?

Ya'acov Fried

I t's 1857. Herman Melville, one of the most important American writers, and author of the famous novel *Moby Dick*, sets out on a seven-month journey in the eastern basin of the Mediterranean Sea. The purpose of his trip was to improve his poor health and raise his low spirits, caused by years of intensive and frustrating literary work that had not yet resulted in the acclaim he desired. On his trip, Melville visited Egypt, Turkey, Lebanon, and Greece, but the highlight of the journey for many reasons was his visit to the land of Israel.

It seemed that Melville had focused all of his hopes and dreams for spiritual gratification on this visit. He saw Jaffa, Ramle, and the Dead Sea, but he spent most of his time wandering the alleyways of Jerusalem, searching for remnants of its former glory and spirituality. The impressions from his visit to Jerusalem left a deep imprint on the author's soul, later appearing in his trip journal, poems, and books. In his book, *Clarel: A Poem and Pilgrimage in the Holy Land*, Melville proved to be an astute observer, like the Hebrew idiom – "an occasional visitor who sees all faults." He wrote: "Jerusalem is surrounded by cemeteries and the dead are the strongest guild in it. The dead 'run' the city and serve in every possible position."

For many years, this statement by Melville echoed in my ears incessantly. I wonder if behind the shoulder of every political, religious, or social leader stands an "honorable dead person," someone from the past who determines how the city is run and where it is headed. Perhaps behind each one of us who live in the city or feel a soul connection to it, there is an "honorable dead person" who stands and essentially dictates that we act in a certain way, not allowing us to make logical, sensitive decisions regarding those who are different than us. Maybe this is what prevents us from living a life of freedom in the city.

I think back to my childhood in Jerusalem, torn between my deep love for the city and the sense of loss that I feel regarding the direction in which Jerusalem has headed and is heading. It's only in the last two decades that I have felt that perhaps the city has betrayed me.

I was born in Jerusalem in a neighborhood called Kiryat Moshe, next to the entrance to the city. My childhood memories in Jerusalem do not include far-reaching overlooks – not from Mount Scopus, the Mount of Olives, nor the promenade in eastern Talpiyot. Those are overlooks that I only discovered after the Six-Day War in 1967. My childhood in Jerusalem was one of open fields, mountains, rocky soil, puddles, a narrow entrance to our capital city, and a border with Jordan just a few kilometers from my house. I was born and raised in a Jerusalem home in a housing complex called the "discharged soldiers complex," built for people like my father who fought in the War of Independence in 1948. The country felt obligated to care for their housing needs. But there was nothing majestic about my housing complex. It was not built of Jerusalem stone. It was built of bricks covered in gray mortar. It didn't have magical alleyways like the old neighborhoods or potted geranium plants peeking out from its windows, like the ones so characteristic of

Jerusalem. My Jerusalem was a Jerusalem with a community and mutual assistance: conservative but with a tolerant attitude of "live and let live." In the housing complex, every family had a small garden where they could grow fruits and vegetables. (The smell of the soil after the rain is something that never left me.) Next to us, in the neighborhood of Givat Shaul, there were dairymen who raised cows and cultivated the land.

My parents were very different from each other in their personalities and cultures. What they did have in common was a shared sense of awe and holiness toward Jerusalem. My mother, a "sabra" born in Jerusalem, worshipped the character of the city in the late fifties and sixties – the modesty, the conservatism, and especially its stark contrast with Tel Aviv. One of the sentences that I remember her saying was, "Here in Jerusalem, we don't sit in cafes. Here in Jerusalem, we work, look out for each other, establish Israeli families. Jerusalem is like a womb that protects us." My father, who immigrated from Romania to Israel after the Holocaust, came from an ultra-Orthodox home and continued to lead a very traditional lifestyle. He worshipped the religious, cultural, and historical sanctity of the city. He took me on trips from one end of Jerusalem to another, with tremendous excitement, reveling in the feeling that we were living a miraculous, holy life. He did this while building and managing construction projects in the city; the values of work and equality were of utmost importance to him.

There were three public institutions in my neighborhood: the Diskin Orphanage, the Jewish Institute for the Blind, and Kfar Shaul Mental Hospital. From each institute could be heard shouting; each institute had its own locks and bolts; each institute taught me a different lesson for life.

I remember the children from the Institute for the Blind with great warmth and love. As children, we were invited into their magical garden. Their vision of the garden was the fruit of their imagination, a vision that we couldn't see. I remember playing regular children's games during which we acted as their eyes but discovering their sharp intuition and their senses was one of the biggest and most important lessons of my childhood. I also remember how much these blind children wanted to play with us, but their teachers prevented us from getting together out of a fear that it would be too difficult for them to spend time with us seeing children.

The Diskin orphanage, a few hundred meters from my home, brings back some sad feelings. It was the Diskin orphanage that made me aware for the first time in my life that there are children who don't live in a loving, warm home. I remember the children's eyes, so desperate for human contact with us children outside of the institution walls. When we had an opportunity to play with the children from the orphanage, the expression in their eyes instantly warmed up and brightened.

The Kfar Shaul Mental Hospital, on the other hand, was an institution that was ahead of its time. It allowed people with mental illnesses to receive treatment and shelter while still having contact with the community. I remember taking a walk with my father one Shabbat. He held my hand and said, "Yankele, don't be scared of that strange man talking to himself. He won't hurt you. He won't do anything to you." He uttered that reassurance while waving to the man and then gave him some of the peanuts that we were snacking on during our walk. The sense of communal responsibility and commitment, and the lack of isolationism, that characterized Jerusalem during my childhood never left me.

For elementary school, I attended Beit Ruth, which was part of the Beit Hakerem school, in the neighborhood next to ours. I remember receiving my first Bible, which was presented to me by the legendary school principal David Benvenisti, a geographer and educator who even won an Israel Prize for his achievements in education and geography of Israel. I remember how excited I was to be handed my first

Bible in preparation for studying the Torah. Before the ceremony, my parents told me that David Benvenisti was from a distinguished family of rabbis in Thessaloniki and one of the greatest educators in Israel. He established the Palestine Hikers Association in 1927, which was one of the first groups to organize guided tours by foot and by car throughout the land of Israel. Essentially, he established the first tourism organization. I remember David telling us at the ceremony that the Bible can and must be our tour guide when we hike with our families or with our class in Jerusalem. David Benvenisti wrote geography books about Jerusalem and the land of Israel, and for my bar mitzvah, I received his book, *Biblical Atlas and Cities of the Bible.* I have often wondered whether this is where my love for Jerusalem took root and became such an importance presence in my life.

Prior to the Six-Day War, I would often ascend to the rooftop of my grandparents' home in Meah Shearim, where we could see the eastern side of the city. The city that we couldn't visit, there on the other side. I heard stories from my parents and grandparents about visits to the Old City before 1948, about my uncle who was taken captive by the Jordanian army during the battle in the Old City, about friendships with Arab residents of the Old City, and about the hope to return one day. A few months before the Six-Day War, I was listening to a musical performance on the radio when I heard the song "Jerusalem of Gold" for the first time. It left a very powerful impression on me. Since then, every time I hear it, I remember that Wednesday during the Six-Day War and the moving announcement of the liberation of the Old City and the Western Wall. Even today, thinking of that first visit, walking through the alleys of the Old City and reaching the Western Wall, makes me feel like I'm floating. Every year our family feels uplifted and giddy during the Yom Ha'atzmaut parade in Jerusalem, coupled with the belief that the era of wars is over.

I spent the best years of my life at Hebrew University in Jerusalem. The first years were at the Givat Ram campus, while in our final year, we ascended. We returned to Mount Scopus and to the views it offers of the city, even down to the Dead Sea and the Moab Mountains.

There is no place that compares to Jerusalem in terms of the beauty of its landscapes, the crisp air that never loses its cool touch even on a hot day, the sweet peacefulness that descends upon the city as Shabbat begins. There is nothing like Jerusalem's heavy, weighty historical baggage that layers the ground that we walk on with meaning. Layers of realization, of yearning, of dreaming, praying, longing generations. Therefore, it was hard for me to understand my friends who left the city in the eighties and nineties. I watched them with sorrow and pity.

Jerusalem demonstrates the complexity of Israeli existence. It is a city of sharp contrasts: the most Jewish of all, but at the same time, the most universal city, belonging to the entire world. Jerusalem joins together the Holocaust, wars, and independence; Yad Vashem, Mount Herzl, and the sovereign institutions of the State of Israel that embody the revival of our nation in its homeland. Jerusalem represents destruction and redemption. It expresses the dream of one united city, and simultaneously the broken pieces of that dream. This is a city whose two parts weren't really united, and even if you can cross over from one side to the other, a wall still remains at its heart. More than anything else, it embodies the hope of peace and the danger of war and loss. It is the junction that we face: do we actually have free choice or are our decisions predetermined by "one of the dead"?

The historical fate of the city, and especially its destructions, serves as writing on the wall. A warning against the sin of pride, extreme behavior, and loss of a sense of reality. Jerusalem represents the beauty and sublime of Jewish culture; the commitment to law and charity, to justice and kindness, and the understanding that neither ritual nor the sanctity of the site are what's most important. The three charitable institutions that surrounded my childhood home in Jerusalem do not permit me for even one moment to forget our commitment as Jews to social justice.

Jerusalem represents peace, not just as a vision for the end of days, but as a dream that we should strive to obtain at all times, tirelessly and relentlessly. For peace to be obtainable, I believe that it's not enough to recognize and see our own version and perspective of justice. We cannot be blind or closed off to those who are different than us. It is important to open our hearts to the injustices that others are experiencing too. Without peace with the Palestinian side, without a fair and humane solution with our neighbors, where there is room for their dreams and needs, Jerusalem cannot be complete. It will remain an unfulfilled promise.

There is a dish that I really love that originated in Jerusalem, and it's called Jerusalem mixed grill. I have always felt that this dish can only be really appreciated by people who live or have lived in Jerusalem, and visitors are missing some of the secret of its magic and flavor. The name "Jerusalem mixed grill" also holds part of the secret to understanding the unique complexity of Jerusalem's existence.

Today, there are almost a million people living in Jerusalem. In Tel Aviv, the second largest city in Israel, there are about 460,000 people. Jerusalem is the only city where groups from all of the main populations in Israel live together side by side in significant numbers: secular, religious Zionist, traditional, ultra-Orthodox Jews, and Arabs. The demographic changes in Israel mean that the reality in Jerusalem is a sign of what is to come in Israel in a generation from now. I feel that what is happening and will happen in Jerusalem over the next few years will be characteristic of what happens in the entire State of Israel in the future.

The encounter between these entities, or if you will, these "tribes," can be of an oppositional nature. They can also be mutually productive. As of today, the oppositional encounters attract the most attention. The tension between ultra-Orthodox and non-ultra-Orthodox Jews is even worse than that between Arabs and Jews. The reality of a growing ultra-Orthodox demographic force that feels a very limited sense of responsibility toward the general population creates a feeling of intense ongoing stress regarding the future of the city and ultimately drives Jerusalemites away from the city. While there are positive attempts at dialogue and contact, I feel that most of the city's residents are not yet prepared to really live together. The process of each population isolating itself in its own world only exacerbates the sense of alienation and the waves of migration.

On January 6, 1857, Herman Melville began his visit to the Holy Land at Jaffa Port. "A large wave hit our ship, and then we saw the breakwaters in front of the city. We descended the ship and the sailors who received us tried to take advantage of our tourist apprehensions." He summarized his visit after the trip to Jerusalem, saying: "Before boarding the French ship, headed toward Alexandria, I stayed in a room on a rooftop in Jaffa. Parting was very difficult. Jaffa is located on a steep hill that ascends from the sea and slopes down into the coastal plain. It is surrounded by a wall and guards. Its homes are old, dark, decorated, and arched. The house where I am staying is at the edge of the hill. It is the tallest of all of the homes. From the rooftop, I can see the Mediterranean Sea, the plain, and the mountains of Ephraim. A wonderful view. To the north, I imagine that the closest point is Beirut. To the south is Gaza, city of the Philistines, whose gates were broken open by Samson. I am the only tourist here in Jaffa. I enjoyed being alone and am beginning to feel like the prophet Jonah. The wind is getting stronger, the waves are rising and crashing on the breakwaters. The foam is like a huge blanket spread across the coast to the north and south as far as the eye can see. Jaffa was a port from before the Flood. Compared to Jerusalem, it has no antiquities worth mentioning. Jaffa is ancient and abandoned. I am able to maintain my cool only thanks to firm, cold self-control. I took a boat and rowed out toward the boulders outside of the port. I remember Jerusalem, with ghost names like Jehoshaphat, the Valley of Hinnom, and more. I think of the Via Dolorosa, women panting under their heavy loads, the melancholy looks on the faces of the men. I remember wandering in Jerusalem around the tombs until I start worrying that perhaps I too have been possessed by a spirit. A range of different tombs with steps, stones next to the Tomb of Absalom, headstones next to the tomb of Zacharia, the Church of the Holy Sepulcher, a broken dome, stone lamps, pilgrims, and resting in the Armenian monastery. The view from Mount Zion, stones and pebbles strewn everywhere. The heart is crushed at the indifference of nature and man and everything that makes this place holy."

About twelve years ago, after much deliberation, I decided to move from Jerusalem to Jaffa. I felt that I no longer wanted the dead to run my life.

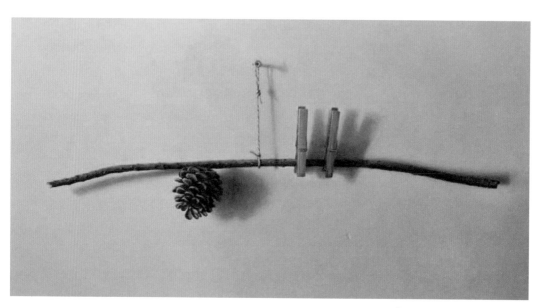

Equilibrium, 2014
Oil on canvas
mounted on wood
45X70

21

Between Two Squares

The Haredi Community

Netanel Zelicovich

Summer in Jerusalem, Saturday night. I am performing the Havdalah ceremony – a festive farewell to the holy Sabbath. I recite the blessing over a cup of fine wine, breathe in the scent of the cloves and myrtle leaves. This is a custom that is meant to ease the abrupt descent from the spiritual elevation of Shabbat to the mundanity of the week. I recite the blessing commemorating the discovery of fire by Adam at the end of the Sabbath day; this was the beginning of civilization and human creativity, according to tradition. I prepare for the upcoming week. I still have a few Saturday night chores to do. I must put the candlesticks and the Kiddush cup back into the glass-fronted display cabinet and wash the dishes. Once done, I can put on my running shoes and a shirt suitable for exercising. We have parted from the Sabbath, and now I must try to part with the many calories from the rich meals that I shared with my family throughout the holy day.

I leave my house and turn to the main square at the edge of the neighborhood where I live. The tranquility of night is interrupted by a buzz. Commotion. Familiar noises. I get closer, and the sharp smell of burned plastic hits my nostrils. At the center of the square, dumpsters are ablaze, like torches, emitting light, flames, thick black smoke, calling to the masses to come out and join the protest. On the surrounding walls, I see the blue and red lights of the police cars and firefighters. Of course, it is hard to miss the throngs of journalists and photographers covering the story. I approach one of the young people who are quickly gathering in the square, their fists clenched and throats sore, those same young people who ignited the dumpsters and the protest, and I ask them – what's the story? What are you protesting? What is the reason you are willing to risk being arrested?

We are fighting for our values, they explain to me. We feel that the state and the establishment are crushing us – the values that are most important to us. Time after time, we try to make our voices heard in the regular ways, but it doesn't work. We simply have no choice but to come to the square and burn dumpsters.

If you are familiar with Israel, or follow the Israeli news, there is a good chance you will be able to guess which square an ultra-Orthodox Israeli would be referring to – or what the young men there are protesting about. That's right – Shabbat Square (Kikar HaShabbat), which is at the entrance to the ultra-Orthodox, isolationist Meah Shearim neighborhood, and the location of passionate protests for the past several decades. The protestors are probably young ultra-Orthodox men from the extreme factions of the Eida Hareidit, the ultra-Orthodox council of Jerusalem, and are probably protesting about the desecration of the Sabbath, the Pride Parade, the enlistment of yeshiva students into the army, or one of the other many topics that are a bone of contention in the conflict between religion and state in Israel.

Well, you would be wrong. I am not referring to Shabbat Square, but to Paris Square (Kikar Paris), located opposite the Prime Minister's Residence. The protesters are not ultra-Orthodox yeshiva students, but rather young Israeli men and women, mostly secular, protesting and calling to replace the government. The topic is not desecration of the Sabbath or a demand for gender separation, but rather a call for Benjamin Netanyahu to step down as prime minister.

The geographic distance between Shabbat Square and Paris Square is very small, less than a mile. However, there is an enormous ideological distance separating the two in the State of Israel. Conservativism, isolationism, and withdrawal, versus democracy, humanism, and liberalism. But somehow, to my great dismay, the pain and feeling of helplessness that can lead to such extreme demonstrations of protest are identical in both places. In both places, young people who believe that their values are being threatened go out to the square to protest; in both places, police forces apply violence to disperse them – the citizens whose future is tied up in the State of Israel.

For many years, dumpsters burned in Shabbat Square. In the summer of 2020, dumpsters burned in Paris Square too.

My name is Netanel Zelicovich. I am an ardent ultra-Orthodox man. For those unfamiliar with the terminology, I will explain that I am an observant Jew who makes every effort to live a rich Jewish lifestyle according to the customs of my ancestors. The ultra-Orthodox sector in Israel is very diverse and includes many people who have differing opinions; therefore, it is hard to precisely determine how many ultra-Orthodox people live in Israel today. Roughly, the estimate is slightly more than 10 percent of Israel's citizens.

In contrast with many ultra-Orthodox people who prefer to live in neighborhoods with a religious character that suits their worldview, I chose to live in Rehavia, a neighborhood with a secular character that is one street away from the center of the protests at Paris Square.

I was born into an ultra-Orthodox family with deep roots but was raised in a town in northern Israel where there were no other ultra-Orthodox people. My parents moved there as part of a significant educational position that they held. Throughout my life, I was surrounded by two conflicting worldviews. On one side was the ultra-Orthodox attempt to preserve the world of content, values, and tradition that are so important to us in an ever-changing world. On the other side was the secular lifestyle. From a young age, I was exposed to a sense of bitterness that developed and was expressed toward the ultra-Orthodox population, mainly arising as a result of misunderstandings regarding our lifestyle and the fear of religious coercion and political manipulations on the part of ultra-Orthodox parties.

The ultra-Orthodox population, of which I view myself as a member, deeply believes in the values of Judaism and in tradition. The desire to follow Jewish law with all of its commandments, together with an adherence to a traditional lifestyle and customs, defines our lives in many ways. Teaching our children in the spirit of the Torah is very meaningful to our existence. We strive for them to continue our lifestyle, which is sometimes demanding and rigorous, but is precise and correct, according to our understanding, of course. We put emphasis on learning the Jewish holy writings and on the Jewish behavior that stems from the learning. An agenda and curriculum that enables this type of education is materially different from the secular agenda and curriculum. Secular education is perceived as being outwardly critical of ultra-Orthodox beliefs. The lack of gender separation and the permissiveness, coupled with the liberal values characteristic of academia in Israel, could lead to processes of secularism and leaving the faith, according to our viewpoint. This concern causes many members of the ultra-Orthodox population to attempt to limit their exposure to this world. As a result, many stay away from academic studies and from employment in secular work environments. Many attempt to avoid using technology, which provides access to a culture that many perceive contradicts ultra-Orthodox beliefs.

The ultra-Orthodox population does not operate in a vacuum. We are citizens of the State of Israel and we are influenced by events that take place here. Therefore, together with our loyalty to our heritage, we have experienced changes over the past generation that have challenged our worldview. These challenges are not unique to the ultra-Orthodox population, but here, they take on a different shape. One example of this is the struggle for economic survival. The Israeli economy changed over the past generation. The road to earning a respectable living today is more complicated than in the past, and it requires academic degrees and technological orientation as well as longer work hours and knowledge of different languages. These demands conflict with the lifestyles of many ultra-Orthodox people, making it harder for the family to manage on a daily basis. The Israeli economic success, the sense of abundance, and the consumer culture that developed here influences the agendas of the younger ultra-Orthodox generation, who accept the dictates and standards that the rest of society has set. Of course, these trends are changing the traditional ultra-Orthodox agenda, which espouses values such as Torah study, acts of charity, sufficing with less, putting the community above the individual, and so forth.

The economic and social changes come with another challenge – the leadership challenge. In the generation after the Holocaust, the ultra-Orthodox population had strong leaders. It was a generation of giants whose leadership capabilities helped rehabilitate and build after the decimation and tragedy that had occurred. Many in this generation of leaders lived to a ripe old age. In our generation, as the ultra-Orthodox population grows and increases, the leadership is dealing with challenges of different dimensions. This strain, coupled with the social and economic changes that many ultra-Orthodox communities are undergoing and the development of ultra-Orthodox media channels and the world of social media, challenge the old, familiar model of leadership inherited from the past generation.

The changes that the ultra-Orthodox world is experiencing are not uniform across the board. True, there are communities who accept the changes and adapt to them in various ways, such as by developing applications that screen content on the internet, or by encouraging studies in academic institutions that meet the community's standards. But most of the communities are opposed to these solutions and do everything in their power not to adopt these changes, or at least to delay them. Others feel confused and torn between the desire to keep tradition and the winds of change and demanding everyday necessities. All of this takes place far from the eyes of the average Israeli. As someone exposed to both worlds, it is clear to me that the secular community does not even have the tools to understand what is happening in the ultra-Orthodox world. Someone who has never occupied the benches of a traditional study hall or yeshiva cannot understand the ultra-Orthodox way of thinking. Someone who only consumes secular media channels does not know what the residents of Meah Shearim really care about. Someone who has not walked the packed streets of the ultra-Orthodox neighborhood of Geula has no idea what daily ultra-Orthodox life looks like. For many secular Israelis, this lack of familiarity with the challenges faced by the ultra-Orthodox population leads to fear or even, most unfortunately, to hatred. This fear is expressed in various ways in politics, in society, and even in the terminology that people use to describe the ultra-Orthodox world.

In 1952, David Ben-Gurion, the prime minister of the State of Israel, visited the ultra-Orthodox city of Bnei Brak. He met with the Chazon Ish, the prominent leader of the ultra-Orthodox population at that time. During their discussion, Ben-Gurion mentioned that, "this rift between the ultra-Orthodox and the state of Israel scares me more than anything else, more than the security threat that we face. I am afraid that it will blow up in our faces." Many years went by, the ultra-Orthodox population grew and developed, governments rose and fell due to this tension that Ben-Gurion spoke about, and the solution is still far away.

I personally believe that dealing with this rift is essential to our lives here in Israel. As a guide, I take people from Israel and from all over the world on a journey into the ultra-Orthodox world. On this journey, people actually step into the yeshivas – the ultra-Orthodox study institutions. They are exposed to the amazing abundance of social activism and philanthropy within the communities. They taste the best kugel in the entire world. They hold an ultra-Orthodox children's book in their hands for the first time. They learn about the different types of hats and the ultra-Orthodox lifestyle. For many on my tours, the highlight of the visit is a conversation with real people, those who are busy with their everyday work, seeking to live respectably, according to the traditions of their ancestors, in a changing society.

The exposure to the real ultra-Orthodox world, a world infused with faith that deals with the challenge of life in modern-day Israel, gives the visitor a glimpse of a society that is unapologetic. A society proud of its heritage; a dynamic, developing society. A society that is no longer prepared to tolerate the fact that its defining values are being ignored. A society where, just like the secular society in the summer of 2020, so many people feel that their emotions and beliefs are being overlooked. If Israeli society wants to create a better country, it must attempt to understand the sentiments of the ultra-Orthodox public. If you are interested in becoming deeply familiar with Israel, you must see the world where I live. The ultra-Orthodox world.

Again, the Sabbath is about to begin. Another week is about to end. Soon, we will light the candles, I will go to pray at the synagogue near my house, and then I will sit down for the Sabbath meal with my family. The silence of the Sabbath and the disconnection from the everyday world allows me to focus on my actions and the actions of my fellow social activists in the ultra-Orthodox world. We will continue to try to change the situation, opening our hearts and our doors to people who are not familiar with our world. We are not only doing this for altruistic reasons. For many long years, many secular Israelis ignored the emotions of the ultra-Orthodox population. I feel that the protests of the liberalists come from a similar point of origin. When people feel that their most basic values are being threatened and that no one cares about what they view as an essential part of their lives – they go out to the streets. To my great dismay, some of them will also behave violently, something that the leaders of the ultra-Orthodox population have firmly denounced, as have the leaders of the secular protestors. Maybe the distance between Paris Square and Shabbat Square isn't that great after all.

Jews and Judaism

Next to Each Other, 2015
Oil on canvas
mounted on wood
70X40

22

For These Things Do I Weep

The Struggle for Pluralism in Judaism

Lana Zilberman Soloway

For these things do I weep, my eyes flow with tears;
far from me is any comforter who might revive my spirit;
my children are forlorn, for the foe has prevailed.

– Lamentations 1:16

The Jewish nation is an ancient one. A nation of individuals. A nation of families. A nation of many opinions. The rifts within the Jewish nation between those who favor unity and those who favor uniformity have existed for over two thousand years, since the Second Temple period. This rift is the enemy among us. The ancient claim of some individuals that their way is the only true way and everyone else is wrong has been preserved within the Jewish nation to this day. In this essay, I would like to suggest that there is no single form of Judaism, no one way to live a Jewish life. There are many diverse paths. Walking down these paths, it is possible to remain unified even if we are not uniform.

The Rift

On the day after the Ninth of Av in 2018, at five in the morning, a rare occurrence took place at the Western Wall. One of the stones in the wall loosened and fell from very high up onto the egalitarian prayer plaza. At the time, there was only one woman there and luckily, she was unhurt.

The Western Wall is a holy site for Jews, and as such, it is run like an Orthodox synagogue, with men and women praying separately. The egalitarian plaza, Ezrat Israel, was established in August 2013, in response to the claims of Women of the Wall. The women of this organization, who are Reform, Conservative, and Modern Orthodox, sought to pray in the traditional women's section while wearing kippot (head covering for Jews) and prayer shawls, donning tefillin (small black leather boxes containing scrolls of parchment inscribed with verses from the Torah) and reading from the Torah – all rituals that are not customarily performed by women according to Orthodox Judaism. According to Orthodoxy, nothing in the Torah should be changed. The wholeness of the Torah should be preserved, especially when some Jews attempt to interpret it differently. As the Chatam Sofer, a leading nineteenth-century rabbi, famously said: "New is forbidden by the Torah."

After thirty years of a determined struggle that sometimes turned violent, the women petitioned the Supreme Court and asked for official permission to pray as they saw fit. This request was met with vehement opposition from the Orthodox side. In August 2013, the Israeli government initiated the establishment of Ezrat Israel, next to the existing plaza used separately by men and women, as a temporary solution, until the court ruled in favor of the women in 2016 and decided on the establishment of an equal prayer plaza. This plan is known as the Kotel Compromise. Due to opposition from ultra-Orthodox parties, however, the prime minister rescinded his approval in June 2017, and since then, the subject has been frozen. This issue shows how much power the ultra-Orthodox population has over daily life and the decision-making process in the State of Israel.

According to the Central Bureau of Statistics, beginning in 2020, the ultra-Orthodox population in Israel makes up about 11 percent of the total Jewish population. In the Knesset, about fifteen (out of 120) members are ultra-Orthodox; they are coalition members with significant influence. How did a minority population become so strong and influential?

One explanation is the status quo letter, which Israel's first prime minister, David Ben-Gurion, sent to Agudat Yisrael in 1947, when he was still serving as chairman of the Jewish Agency. At the time, Agudat Yisrael included four hundred ultra-Orthodox young men who were studying in yeshiva (Jewish educational institution that focuses on the study of traditional religious texts). In this letter, Ben-Gurion promised that the future state would be Jewish, specifying four elements. One, the weekly day of rest would be Saturday. Two, all public kitchens would adhere to the laws of kashrut. Three, personal status and family laws would follow Jewish religion. Four, the ultra-Orthodox would have autonomy over their own educational institutions, without government intervention in their curriculum. All four of these promises were kept in full and are part of the Israeli reality in the twenty-first century.

Another reason the ultra-Orthodox are so powerful is Israel's political structure: a parliamentary democracy with a large number of parties. In order to obtain a majority and form a government, cooperation is vital. Over the past decades, ultra-Orthodox parties have been partners in almost every coalition, so they have the ability to pull strings, apply pressure, and further their interests. Binyamin Netanyahu, for example, who has been the longest serving prime minister in the history of

Israel, almost always has to concede to the demands of the ultra-Orthodox population in order to preserve his coalition.

When that stone fell out of the Western Wall on the day after the Ninth of Av, the date on which Jerusalem and the Temple were destroyed, some ultra-Orthodox groups took this as a divine sign that Ezrat Israel was a mistake. This probably explains why the part closest to the Western Wall in the plaza – where the stone fell and was subsequently put back in place – was not reopened to the public and remains closed to this day. Two years have passed since that unfortunate incident. The Ninth of Av arrived once again, and this year, like last year, Jewish men and women could not come to the only place where they can stand together, men and women, and pray with their hands on the Wall, as their lips murmur the verses of Lamentations, "For these things do I weep…"

What is the rabbi of the Kotel afraid of? Rabbi Shmuel Rabinowitz, an ultra-Orthodox rabbi, has been serving in this position for twenty years. His precise job title is Rabbi of the Western Wall and Holy Sites. Rabbi Rabinowitz, like the vast majority of ultra-Orthodox Jews in Israel, is interested in ensuring that the sovereignty, the "status quo," and all decisions made about Jewish religion and its holy sites, remain in the hands of the Chief Rabbinate, which is Orthodox. In this way, both Orthodox and ultra-Orthodox Jews (who compose about 35 percent of the total Jewish population in Israel) can continue to live according to Jewish law, and the Chief Rabbinate can maintain the status quo and determine their conduct. In contrast, women and men from the remaining 65 percent of the Jewish Israeli population, including secular, traditional, Conservative, Reform, and other Jews, either use the Chief Rabbinate's services for life cycle ceremonies (births, bar mitzvahs, weddings, funerals) or will do everything they can to avoid any contact with this institution, which some feel does not respect them.

Why wasn't it possible to repair the area where the stone fell in the egalitarian plaza? Why did Rabbi Rabinowitz say that there was a need to clarify the standpoint of Jewish law regarding restoration of the stone, which some viewed as a hint to a divine sign of opposition to the mixed plaza, despite the issue's importance to the liberal sects? If a similar incident had occurred in the main Western Wall plaza, this rabbi would have brought in engineers and fixed the spot that same day, without clarifying the Jewish law and giving other excuses. The simple reason is that it has nothing to do with the wall; rather, it is meant to preserve the Orthodox hegemony in the State of Israel using political tools.

The responses to this situation among the Israeli public are diverse. On the one hand, there is increasing opposition to, and even resentment toward, the Orthodox hegemony and the Chief Rabbinate. Over the years, the word *religion* has even started to conjure negative associations, based on the perception that religion is only for the Orthodox. Many Israelis are not even aware of the fact that there are alternatives, so the synagogue that they don't attend, or the synagogue that they attend once a year on Yom Kippur, is an Orthodox one. On the other hand, there are quite a few Israelis who have already given up on their Judaism. They define themselves as "secular" and they identify as solely Israeli, but not Jewish.

This polarity is not necessary. In Midrash Rabbah, it is written that there are "seventy faces to the Torah." In Jewish tradition, this means that there are different answers to each Jewish halachic question. In the State of Israel, there is more than one path that can be taken in order to answer those questions by those interested in them. Every man and woman should be free to choose how to get married, how to celebrate a bar or bat mitzvah, how and where to pray, how to spend the Sabbath day, how to convert, how to be buried, and so on. I will give a few examples.

Seventy Faces to the Torah

Weddings

In the State of Israel, there is no separation of religion and state. As a result, anyone interested in getting married can do so only via the religious institution to which they belong. Since there are no civil marriages in Israel, most people choose to get married via the Rabbinate. It is important to remember that for many years, there were no alternatives to the Chief Rabbinate in terms of marriage licenses. But today, there are. There are people who choose to get married in a different way. I personally chose such a way. I made aliyah from the Former Soviet Union and grew up in a family where everyone only married Jews. My parents, grandparents, and great-grandparents all had traditional Jewish wedding ceremonies. My husband made aliyah from the United States, and also grew up in a Jewish family that married in the traditional Jewish way for many generations.

The Chief Rabbinate makes couples who want to get married "prove" their Judaism in various, often unpleasant, ways, especially those who weren't born in Israel. Daniel and I could have "proven" our Judaism, but we didn't want to. We didn't want to start our lives together with an institution that we don't believe in. So we got married through the Conservative movement by a female rabbi in a proper, egalitarian, unique, and moving ceremony. We signed an egalitarian *ketubah* (Jewish marriage contract), written in Hebrew. We blessed each other and exchanged rings. It was a ceremony in which we were both active participants.

This description might sound totally normal and appropriate, but the reality is that most Orthodox weddings look different. Not only is the ceremony not egalitarian (for example, only the husband "takes" the wife and only he gives her a ring), but it is not understood by the couple or by the guests at the event. Such a wedding ceremony requires prior learning, preparation, and explanations, for the couple itself, the participants, and the general public. An example of this lack of understanding is the *ketubah*, which is written in Aramaic. Most couples who get married in the modern State of Israel are not familiar with this ancient language, but that doesn't prevent them from signing the document without understanding what it says. Each of us has the right to know what is happening at the ceremony that symbolizes our shift from being single to being married. To me, this example demonstrates that there needs to be an alternative to the Orthodox Chief Rabbinate.

In addition, marriage through the Chief Rabbinate is only open to couples who are both Jewish according to Jewish law, meaning that their mother is Jewish. For Jews whose mothers are not Jewish, and for same-sex couples, there is no legal way to get married in Israel. This creates a situation in which there are many citizens who cannot get married in their own country. At the moment, there are about 250 male and female rabbis, belonging to the Conservative movement, the Reform movement, and the Israeli rabbinate movement, who conduct significant life cycle ceremonies, including weddings. There are also organizations such as Havaya and New Family that are happy to conduct Jewish, meaningful, and inclusive wedding ceremonies to any interested couple, customized to the lives of the couple. Some of these rabbis and organizations will agree to officiate at ceremonies for Jews who are not Jewish according to Jewish law, as well as same-sex couples, thereby providing every person and citizen with respect and basic rights.

It is important to note that couples who decide to get married outside of the Chief Rabbinate are not entitled to register with the Interior Ministry as married unless they also get married in a civil ceremony outside of Israel. My husband and I had a Jewish wedding in Israel, and a civil wedding in the United States. When we went to register as married at the Interior Ministry in Jerusalem, we presented our egalitarian *ketubah* alongside our American marriage license. The only document that was accepted in the Jewish State of Israel was the American document. In our case, the person who signed the American marriage license happened to be a rabbi. But in most cases, when Israeli couples get married abroad, the signatory on the marriage license is not Jewish, so this reality is absurd. A *ketubah* signed by an Israeli male or female rabbi (who is not Orthodox) is not accepted at the Israeli Interior Ministry, but a document usually signed by a non-Jewish judge abroad is.

Conversion

Anyone interested in joining the Jewish nation needs to undergo a conversion process. This is a long process of serious, deep study, declaration of intentions, close guidance, and finally an oral examination before three rabbis on a Jewish court, immersion in a mikveh (ritual bath), and circumcision for men. The only conversion process recognized in Israel today is Orthodox conversion. I have often met people who went through this long process, while observing all of the commandments, but the moment they converted and registered as Jews at the Interior Ministry, they instantly changed their dress and their lifestyle from completely religious to completely secular. I would say that this is a bit hypocritical. Someone who chooses to join the Jewish nation and live an Orthodox lifestyle should in fact convert via the Chief Rabbinate. But what about someone who is interested in joining the Jewish people but isn't interested in observing Jewish law? In my opinion, this needs to be considered equally legitimate by the authorities.

Both the Conservative and Reform movements perform conversions today according to all of the laws and rules, but in a more liberal, egalitarian, and accessible way. At the end of this process, the candidates still stand before a court, immerse in a mikveh and perform circumcision, but the process is much more similar to the lifestyle that they will lead afterward. In 2005, a historic decision was taken by the Supreme Court recognizing Reform and Conservative conversions performed abroad, for the purpose of granting citizenship approvals by virtue of the Law of Return. (According to the Law of Return, any Jew, up to three generations, is entitled to move to Israel and receive immediate citizenship by virtue of their Judaism.) People who underwent a Reform or Conservative conversion abroad are entitled to make aliyah, receive Israeli citizenship, and register at the Interior Ministry as Jews, but they will not be entitled to religious services as long as the Orthodox hegemony continues. The question is obvious: why are Reform and Conservative conversions accepted when they are performed abroad but are considered invalid when performed in Israel? This is completely illogical. Again, freedom of choice must be respected. All the rabbis I mentioned earlier who conduct weddings would be happy to perform conversions as well. The truth is that they already do so, although the state doesn't officially recognize the conversions yet.

Bat Mitzvah

In 1994, when I turned twelve, I was in sixth grade. The annual theme that year was "bnei mitzvah year." All of the students in the class wrote genealogy essays, and we took a trip to Jerusalem and visited the Western Wall. All of us, boys and girls together. But, when the subject of bar/bat mitzvah celebrations came up, it was clear that the boys would be reading from the Torah and the girls would be having a party. To complete the process, that same year, we all received a bar/bat mitzvah certificate, signed by the chief (Orthodox) rabbi of Netanya, the city I grew up in.

Why didn't I or any of the girls in my class read from the Torah? Why weren't we even offered the option of learning the Torah reading?

I wish that every boy and girl in Israel would learn about all of the options and then be able to make a choice regarding which best suit their lifestyle: whether to read from the Torah, and if so, how; whether they want to learn with a male or female rabbi; which ceremony they want; or if they just want a party. I was twenty-eight when I got to read from the Torah for the first time. I wish every twelve-year-old Israeli girl had such an opportunity, if she chooses to do so.

Conclusion

We have become accustomed to living under the Orthodox hegemony for many years, as it controls many areas of life in the modern State of Israel. Now, it is time to implement the vision of the prophets of Israel and allow for the establishment of a Jewish, democratic state based on the tenets of liberty, justice, equal social rights, and freedom of choice. This type of change is a process that will take time and will require a lot of patience. My hope is that one day, every Jew in the State of Israel will be able to choose how to get married and how to celebrate life cycle events, according to their beliefs, and that every such decision will be accepted with respect by all of the relevant bodies and authorities. May we succeed in proving that it is truly possible to live in unity, even if not in uniformity, because after all, we are brothers and sisters.

23

Shades of Tradition

Hillel Meyer

I have a friend who defines herself as an atheist. As soon as she hears someone mention the seven days of creation, she jumps into a deep conversation about the Big Bang. She usually spends Yom Kippur abroad, or hosts a shrimp and movie party at her house. When someone wishes her lots of success – with God's help, she snickers and says that she'll be successful despite His help. As far as she is concerned, Judaism is a culture that you are born into, and a person can decide to change cultures at any given time.

Yet when her son was born, after three daughters, I received an urgent telephone call from her asking me to recommend a *mohel* (circumciser) who is also a physician. Usually, *mohels* are rabbis who don't have medical training, a fact that frightens some parents. "You know what circumcision symbolizes?" I asked her. "It's the covenant between the Jewish nation and God. It's what makes the Jewish nation unique, something that transcends culture."

"Yes," she said firmly. "I know, but there are things that even an atheist like me is not prepared to give up." She isn't alone. According to the most recent survey conducted by the JPPI, the Jewish People

Policy Institute, about a quarter of the Jewish residents of the State of Israel define themselves as completely secular, non-traditional Jews. When asked if they believe in the existence of God as creator of the world, only 20 percent of that quarter responded in the negative. If you do the math, this means that just 5 percent of Jews living in the State of Israel view themselves as complete atheists. All of the rest have some affinity toward tradition.

This is a significantly lower figure than in other democratic countries. How can it be explained?

In order to understand Israeli reality today, we need to go back in time to the years following the establishment of the state.

When the State of Israel was founded, one of the many ministries that was founded was the Ministry of Religious Affairs, which is the executive branch for religious services in Israel. It was controlled by representatives from the Orthodox parties. The secular character of the governing bodies of the future state aroused the concern of groups from this population, to the extent that there were even those who called to oppose the establishment of a secular State of Israel. David Ben-Gurion, the prime minister at the time, sent a letter to the religious parties in response, clarifying that the new state would make sure to maintain the kashrut laws in government kitchens; the weekly day of rest would be Saturday; a special court (*beit din*) would be established to hear marriage and divorce cases, and full autonomy would be granted to all sects in the field of education, including ultra-Orthodox education.

This letter calmed the Orthodox organizations, most of which supported the establishment of the state, and it constituted the basis for the balance of religion and state in Israel as we know it, referred to as the "status quo" between secular and religious Jews. In order to provide government religious services, the young state adopted an organization called the Chief Rabbinate established by the British, and appointed two rabbis to lead it – one an Orthodox Sephardic rabbi and the other an Orthodox Ashkenazi rabbi.

Over the years, the status quo was more or less preserved without issues. The young state was dealing with other challenges, and its Jewish residents accepted the involvement of the Chief Rabbinate in their daily lives as a given. This was not the case in communities with a pronounced secular orientation, such as on the kibbutzim, which created their own traditions based on their interpretation of Jewish culture and tradition.

At the end of the forties and during the fifties, a large wave of immigration arrived from Arab countries, referred to as Mizrahi (eastern/oriental) Jews. Most of the immigrants were observant Jews who kept the same rules preserved by the status quo. Despite the cultural differences between them and the population in Israel, most of whom had come from European countries, they found Israel to be a comfortable place to practice their religious traditions. The rabbis who had been their leaders in their countries of origin became community leaders here as well, conducting their life cycle ceremonies. Some Mizrahi Jews brought with them a new concept that had not existed among Jews who immigrated from Europe – the "traditional Jew." What is a traditional Jew? Until this point, the division in Israel was between those who observed the commandments and those who did not. A traditional Jew, on the other hand, observed those commandments that were important to him family-wise and community-wise, like kashrut and praying in synagogue on Shabbat, but after prayers on Shabbat, he might drive to the beach or listen to the radio. It is said that Rabbi Mashash, who was the Chief Rabbi of Morocco, ruled to turn a blind eye toward those community members who opened their businesses on Shabbat, as long as they were still keeping kosher and attending synagogue. He ruled in this way in order to save the community's Jewish youth from completely leaving the faith.

The second generation of Mizrahi immigrants preserved this atmosphere. In contrast with the youth from the kibbutzim, who rejected any religious symbol from their parents' countries of origin, the children of Mizrahi immigrants still observed some of the commandments and customs. They are mostly conservative in their views, and have a difficult time accepting the pluralistic communities that are developing in Israel. While they will take pride in their fashionably dressed wives who are not maintaining traditional modesty rules, they won't accept the fact that a woman can serve as a female rabbi. They will travel abroad and frequent non-kosher restaurants and clubs, but intermarriage is strictly out of the question.

Personally, I was born in Canada and define myself as Orthodox. I am raising my children with their secular mother, whose family immigrated from Iraq in the early fifties. The fact that she is of Mizrahi traditional descent makes it much easier to build a bridge between my religious lifestyle and her chosen secular lifestyle. Flexibility is the name of the game. My children attend a public secular school, but they go to synagogue too. We keep a kosher kitchen, but outside of the home, my children and their mother will eat at restaurants that do not have kosher certification – though they won't touch pork. At the Shabbat table, everyone wears a kippah (skullcap worn by Jews) and sings Kiddush and Grace after Meals, and then they go to a different room to watch television, without me.

The Religious Zionist movement in Israel demonstrates openness to the population that does not observe the commandments but still wants to experience Jewish tradition. For years, the movement has prided itself on its successful combination of strict observance and active participation in public and cultural life. Religious Zionism carries the banner of "Torah and Avodah" – Torah representing the spiritual aspects, study and observance of the values of the Bible, and the commandments, and Avodah representing the physical aspects of life, serving in the army, learning a profession, and finding a job. There are many communities whose ideology is based on these principles. One such community is Alon Shvut, located in Gush Etzion. Aside from the wonderful landscape, the crisp clean air, and the breeze that always blows through this mountainous settlement, Alon Shvut is considered one of the flagship Religious Zionist communities. It is home to the prestigious *hesder* yeshiva (a yeshiva that integrates Torah study with military service), Har Etzion. Local residents are highly involved in the military, the media, various industries, and Torah study in Israel. During the week, they will leave the yishuv (community) to work in nearby cities, while their children participate in local soccer leagues. They will eat at kosher restaurants of course, watch movies and shows, and take vacations abroad. The gates of the yishuv are open to visitors and guests throughout the week, but when Shabbat begins, the gates are locked and no vehicle is permitted to enter the yishuv, which is entirely Shabbat observant. The residents will put on their festive clothes and walk to the various synagogues throughout the yishuv to pray.

Not all of the children, however, choose to follow in their parents' footsteps. When they reach the army, some choose to leave the path of Torah observance and become secular. Secular but not atheist. They still want to be part of the family and celebrate Shabbat meals and Jewish holidays with them, though they will not take part in the religious practices of prayer and observance of the commandments. This population has been named Datlash – an acronym that means "formerly observant." At first, families had a very difficult time accepting their children's decision to stop leading an observant lifestyle. After consulting with Religious Zionist rabbis, who viewed the phenomenon as a worrying one that threatened to shake the children's religious foundation, they set a condition. In order to visit the family on Shabbat by vehicle, they would need to arrive before Shabbat while the gates were still open, enter the yishuv, change into festive clothes, put on a kippah and go to synagogue.

This created a rift in many families. Over time, everyone understood that in order to keep the family united, it was necessary to find a middle ground. Today, if you visit one of these communities, you will surely notice the row of vehicles that arrive before and after Shabbat begins and park outside of the gate. The Datlash child, their spouse, and children will get out of the car and walk straight to the family's home, where they will eat the Shabbat or holiday meal together. At the end of the meal, they will again walk to the entrance of the yishuv and drive home.

The Datlashim, along with the traditional Mizrahis, created an unofficial group in Israel, or more precisely a new variety, that respects tradition but does not observe the commandments. They live among the population that is secular from birth, and they are often the connecting link between the religious and secular groups in Israel, because they are familiar with the customs of both groups. Some Datlashim look for community and tradition among the pluralist groups, while others prefer to maintain a connection with tradition by keeping in touch with the community where they grew up.

Parallel to the observant community, there are many families for whom Saturday is not a holy day. According to dry statistics, these families can be characterized as secular families. But even in these families, their child will bake a challah in honor of Shabbat in kindergarten, the entire family will light Shabbat candles together, and the Friday night meal will be more festive than a regular weeknight dinner. Many secular families will dine on Friday night with relatives or friends whom they haven't seen all week. I would like to emphasize that these are not families who consider themselves traditional. These are families like my friend – who consider themselves strictly secular.

In Israel today, there are many ways to be Jewish. Orthodox, traditional, pluralistic, Datlash, or secular are all just labels. Essentially, most Jews in Israel deal with their identity every day by virtue of their residence in a country that has a Jewish majority. Questions such as Shabbat observance, eating kosher food, marriage according to Jewish law, or circumcision, are questions that cannot be avoided and must be decided on a personal and almost daily basis. The result is a huge range of Jewish lifestyles. Seventy shades of Judaism.

Not everyone likes this infinite diversity in Jewish life. Ultra-Orthodox leaders claim that Israel is heading toward Jewish atrophy, and in a generation or two, we will no longer be the Jewish state. In contrast, many secular Jews claim that the state is becoming increasingly religious, and in a generation or two, we will look like countries such as Iran. And at the center? The center is liquid, sliding from side to side, and is composed primarily of traditional Jews, but also a growing number of pluralistic and Datlash Jews. If up to a decade ago, the educational system in Israel was divided into ultra-Orthodox, Religious Zionist, and secular schools, today, in almost every large city in Israel, there is at least one joint school whose population includes both religious and secular families, out of an understanding that it is necessary to create a bridge between these worlds. Will this lead to an expansion of the traditional center and an understanding that there are different shades of Judaism? Time will tell. Until then, all of us – the Orthodox, secular, and everything in between – will continue to uphold tradition: we will continue to affix a mezuzah to our doorpost, we will light the menorah on Hanukkah, we will wish each other Shabbat Shalom, and when someone asks us how we're doing, we'll answer "Thank God," even those of us who don't really believe that He exists.

Death Mask, 2015
Oil on canvas
mounted on wood
30X30

24

Choosing to Be
with the Chosen People

The LGBTQ Community

Hillel Meyer

Seventeen-year-old Arik stood at the entrance. A small metal plaque bearing the words "Rabbi Epstein, Specializing in the Jewish Soul" was affixed to the brown, wooden door. He already knew what was waiting for him behind the door. After all, he had come here every week for the past six months.

After a light knock, he heard the pleasant, familiar voice: "Come in," turned the handle, and went inside. When he entered, an older man with a dignified beard nodded at him and extended his hand. This was Rabbi Epstein, with his familiar, warm smile and his kind, wise eyes that peered from behind his glasses.

It was the mid-eighties. There was a storm thrashing outside. Not a storm with wind and lightning, but rather with photos and articles coming from the United States of a terrible plague that kills homosexuals. The only homosexuals in Israel who had come out of the closet during those years were more extroverted. Bohemians, drag queens, and prostitutes. AIDS was the punishment for all of those deviants. Homosexual orientation was an ancient criminal offense from the days of the Ottomans, and until 1988, homosexual intercourse was prohibited according to Israeli law, punishable by ten years of imprisonment. Meeting points were in dark parks and public bathrooms. Arik, who had visited Independence Park in Jerusalem a few times, met married men who were betraying their wives, and teenagers his age who had been thrown out of their homes and turned to prostitution. Arik knew it all, and was afraid of it all. When he told his counselor at yeshiva about his attraction to men, the counselor's reaction was that it was a death sentence, that homosexuality is a disease, and if you don't recuperate from it, the result is life without a family, community, friends, children, or love. He said that God was taking revenge on the gays by sending them AIDS. Arik should take care of it as soon as possible before he gets infected too. The next stop was a talk with the head of the yeshiva who sent Arik straight to Rabbi Epstein, who had a conversion therapy center in the Jerusalem mountains.

Conversion therapy was the remedy that the religious and conventional world proposed for the "illness" of homosexuality. While this wasn't an officially recognized therapy in Israel, the state turned a blind eye to these treatments. According to Jewish law, male intercourse is an abomination, and in the distant past, the punishment for it was stoning. In the Torah reading during the Mincha prayers on Yom Kippur, the prohibition is read aloud. "You shall not lie down with a male as with a woman: this is an abomination" (Leviticus 18:22). Arik, who was taught to understand that treatment was the only realistic option, was anxious to begin. He had already notified the head of the yeshiva that he would be absent for a few weeks, and he told his parents that he was going to visit a different yeshiva, at the encouragement of his own yeshiva (at the time, this was a regular practice).

Arik was lucky. His father suspected that something was off, and after checking a few things, he discovered that his child was about to undergo a dangerous and unfamiliar psychiatric treatment. He prohibited his son from going. Instead, he sent him to a conventional psychologist, hoping that this stage in Arik's life would pass, and that he would continue on the familiar path: studying at a yeshiva, army, marriage, children. They hoped that he would belong to a community of people like him – straight, religious Zionist people.

The beginning of the nineties in Israel were golden years for the LGBTQ community that began to develop in Israel. The centrist-left government led by Yitzchak Rabin heralded a new era in the region. Gay cafes and pubs were opened, and the first pride parade marched in Tel Aviv. A group of gays and lesbians visited the Knesset and told their story, and important popular figures started to come out of the closet, including Dr. Uzi Even, a nuclear energy specialist. At the end of the eighties, when male intercourse was no longer illegal, laws were written to fight discrimination against the LGBTQ community.

Arik tried to suppress his attraction toward men with all of his might. He continued with the psychological treatments until the end of high school, telling his parents that the tendency had gone away so that they would leave him alone. He enlisted in the army, and in addition to his girlfriend, whom he planned to marry, he continued to visit the public parks. Before entering the park, he would take off his kippah (skullcap worn by Jews), meet whoever he met, and leave with a strong sense of self-loathing. One night, he met Avner, a medical school student. The two became engrossed in a deep conversation until the early morning hours, and realized that there was more here than just a sexual attraction. It was the first time that Arik fell in love.

Twenty-year-old Arik realized that he wasn't going to be cured from this "illness," and that he would need to choose. The religious institution would not accept a couple composed of two males, and among

Avner's circle of friends, Arik, as an Orthodox Jew, represented those who refused to accept them. Arik decided to stand up and do something. He broke up with his girlfriend, asked to meet with his parents, and there in their living room, he told them that he was homosexual, and that he had met someone who planned on becoming a doctor. He explained that he was in love and wanted to share his life with him. His parents' reaction was shock, tears, and screaming, ending with a threat that if he decided to pursue his intentions, he was not welcome in their home anymore. He shouldn't show his face in the neighborhood and shouldn't make contact with his siblings.

Arik angrily left the house and drove straight to the Western Wall. There, opposite the last remnant from the Temple period, he prayed to God and asked for the answer to the question that was agonizing him. He turned to God in anger: Why did You create me like this? How am I supposed to know how to live? He didn't receive an answer. Arik stood there for a few hours, and as time went by and he didn't find a solution, he understood what he needed to do. He called Avner, who was on shift at the hospital, and they decided to meet at the cafeteria at the entrance. When Avner arrived, he noticed that something was different. Arik wasn't wearing his kippah anymore. From that moment, Arik decided to leave the religious community in which he had grown up, as well as his family and his friends, and to follow his love. He felt angry at the religious community, which had been unwilling to accept him.

The murder of Yitzchak Rabin in 1995 was a turning point for Arik and Avner. They watched as everything collapsed around them, all of their dreams and hopes for a new, more inclusive world. The nation chose a right-wing government. Arik finished his degree in computers with honors, and his relationship with his family was polite. They accepted Arik as their son, but not his partner. When Arik was offered a chance to move to the United States, to the Silicon Valley area, Avner, who was already a physician, also received a research position at one of the medical centers in San Francisco. They both seized the opportunity, moving straight to liberal California and to San Francisco, with its reputation as a city with a developed LGBTQ community which possessed rights.

The Israeli couple was welcomed with open arms in this city, and they became involved in social life and in academia, signed up for the local gym, rented a gorgeous apartment, and felt happy about the move and the chance at a new beginning together. The only Jewish symbol was the mezuzah that they affixed at the entrance of their home. Despite the comfortable lifestyle and the Hebrew that they spoke at home, Arik felt that something was missing. The sudden disconnection from the religious environment of Jerusalem, working late on Fridays, the lack of the special atmosphere on Jewish holidays, and the absence of a Hebrew-speaking community all hit Arik, the yeshiva graduate.

Avner didn't feel like anything was missing at all.

As Passover approached, Arik's mother asked him during their weekly telephone call where he would be celebrating the Seder (she was still ignoring Avner's existence). Arik, who didn't want to lie to his parents, promised that he would celebrate the Seder in his home. Avner's reaction was a shrug of the shoulders and a comment that it would be pretty pitiful for the two of them to celebrate alone. Arik decided to do something else. It turned out that at his workplace, there were quite a few Jews, and he decided to invite them to the Seder, an evening that would end up changing his life.

While cooking and cleaning in preparation for the meal, he felt the excitement that comes with everything familiar and beloved, and reveled in the emotions. He went to buy kosher-for-Passover products at the kosher store in Berkeley and called his mother to ask for recipes. In the evening, Arik led the Seder, while Avner made sarcastic comments about his partner's sudden religious fervor. Arik taught songs, discussed the story of the exodus from Egypt with his guests, and drank all four cups of wine, and a bit more. One of the guests was a member of the Reform synagogue Sha'ar Zahav, affiliated with the LGBTQ community in the city, and he invited them to attend the Friday night prayer service.

Arik and Avner arrived for the Kabbalat Shabbat prayers. Everything was strange and different: a female rabbi, a sermon in English, a prayer on behalf of the president of the United States, unfamiliar tunes. Avner snickered quietly and said that it was more like a church than a synagogue, telling Arik that he wasn't planning to go back there again. Arik continued to attend; for him, this was his connection to his family home and his childhood. The community was completely composed of LGBTQs and their families, and this was the first time Arik saw that it was possible to combine a strong Jewish identity with homosexual orientation.

This was Arik's first step back toward religion and the customs that he loved so much. As a first step, he decided not to drive on Shabbat anymore and would walk about an hour each way to attend synagogue. The next stage was that he asked Avner about making their kitchen kosher, buying new dishes, and running a kosher home. As Arik came closer and closer to his religion, Avner became more and more distant, and they separated in 2001. Arik found himself a new job in a different city, on the East Coast.

In his new location, Arik joined the liberal Orthodox community in the city and was an active participant in community life, but hid the fact that he was gay. After a few months, when the young rabbi of the community asked Arik about the fact that he was single (a question that is always asked to determine whether the person is interested in matchmaking), Arik answered hesitantly, "I'm gay, and I'm religious. I try to observe all of the commandments, but I'm gay." To his surprise, the rabbi wasn't appalled, and instead invited him for a Shabbat meal to meet his wife and children.

During the meal, the rabbi's wife, who was also the principal of the Orthodox Jewish day school in the city, asked Arik if he would be willing to help the school with Hebrew and Jewish studies subjects. Arik replied that he had to think about it, and shot a glance at the rabbi to see his reaction. "If you're worried about the reactions of the parents regarding your sexual orientation, you can rest assured that you will receive the support and backing of most of the community," the rabbi told him. Indeed, the rabbi had to fight a few influential families in the city who threatened to pull their children out of the school, but he won. Arik became part of the community leadership and was loved and embraced by everyone. He felt wonderful, but he was worried. He was already in his mid-thirties, and didn't see any prospect of having a family on the horizon. He wanted to be a father.

During his visits to Israel, Arik followed the local developments regarding the LGBTQ community. There were several appeals to the Supreme Court for recognition of the rights of partners, regarding discrimination at the workplace, and the right to parenthood. Most of the petitioners won, and discriminatory laws against the community were changed. But one event, which could have been insignificant, changed the attitude of society in general toward the community. In 1998, Dana International, an Israeli transgender singer, was selected to represent Israel in the Eurovision competition (an European singing competition) that was hosted in England. The ultra-Orthodox and religious Knesset members opposed the decision, calling it an abomination and an embarrassment, but to no avail.

That Saturday night, before hundreds of millions of viewers all over the world, Israel won first place. Dana went on stage with the Israeli flag and excitedly invited everyone to Jerusalem the following year. That Shabbat, the Beitar Jerusalem football team won the state cup.

Beitar fans are often known for their use of racist and homophobic language. That night, after both victories, members of the LGBTQ community came to Rabin Square in central Tel Aviv bearing pride flags, in order to jump into the fountains and celebrate the historic win. A few minutes later, the Beitar Jerusalem fans arrived. The night could have ended with violence or even a murder, but instead, there was just immense joy, straights and gays linking arms and singing "Diva" (Dana International's song) and "Hatikvah" together. This was the big social ice breaker toward the community.

Afterward, more and more artists and public figures started to come out of the closet, and various LGBTQ organizations were founded, including a few religious organizations that attracted adolescents and adults from religious homes, some of whom had come out of the closet. The dialogue was hesitant at first, but sustainable with liberal Orthodox rabbis regarding accepting those in their communities who are different. Pride parades spread from the limited area of a few Tel Aviv streets to the center of town, and to additional cities. The Jerusalem pride parade was initiated, which aroused so much opposition from the ultra-Orthodox community in the city that the police had to recruit large numbers of officers to guard it. A few years later, a heterosexual teenage girl, Shira Banki, of blessed memory, who was at the parade in solidarity with her LGBTQ friends, was murdered by a religious fanatic.

Arik, who was visiting Israel to support the parade, witnessed the murder and was deeply shocked. The murder of the teen, who was straight, was another breaking point between the institution and the proud community, who felt that their blood was cheap. The Orthodox community, on the liberal side of the spectrum, organized discussion groups between the religious community and the proud community, with the religious members of the proud community standing in the center and shouting, "This is the limit."

Arik felt that it was time to come back to Israel and try to advance the rights of LGBTQ people in the religious community. He parted with the American community that had been so supportive and came back to Israel. Since conversion therapy was still taking place in Israel, he worked on establishing an organization that would promote dialogue between the religious educational institutions and the proud religious community, in order to convince educators not to send their students for these terrible treatments, and instead view them as religious people who are able to bridge between the worlds.

Arik didn't feel whole; he had no community, and more than that, he wanted to be a father. As a religious, conventional person, he wanted his children to have a mother and a father, so he chose shared parenting. This is a pretty common family arrangement among members of the LGBTQ community in Israel: a gay man establishes a family with a straight woman, without getting married and without living together, and they conduct family life like an amicably divorced couple. Arik met Shira, a childhood friend, and together, they built a family of three children.

As more religious adolescents come out of the closet, and more religious LGBTQ families are established, a demand developed for a synagogue with the capacity to serve this community, both in terms of its numbers and its style. Arik connected with a childhood friend, a straight man married to one of the first female authorities on Jewish law in the Orthodox world, and together with a few other friends, they established the Yachad community in Tel Aviv. It has adopted the verse "The Lord is near to all who call Him, to all who call Him with sincerity" as its slogan, and has hundreds of members, less than half of whom belong to the LGBTQ community.

When you ask Arik how he reconciles his identities as a religious person and a gay person, he answers with a story that he heard from his father. When Arik told his parents that he was planning on becoming a father through a shared parenting arrangement, his father went to consult with a well-known rabbi and returned with a broad smile on his face. "The rabbi reminded me that there are 613 commandments in the Torah, and it is impossible to observe them all. You, Arik, who had everything going against you, are choosing and trying to observe them all, and for that, you deserve our blessing and support in your desire to become a parent."

Becoming a parent wasn't the only thing that Arik attempted against all odds; the fact that he is the head of a family, a senior member of his synagogue, and a member of a community is too. He chose to be part of the Chosen People, but in his own way.

This is the story of Arik, which could also be the story of many Orthodox people who are attracted to members of their own gender. Despite the advancement in the world of Jewish law in a range of areas, the subject of accepting the gay, the lesbian, and the transgender into the Orthodox community is still in its early stages. Although documents have been written and declarations made by rabbis on the liberal side of religious Zionism calling for their acceptance, in Israel, same-sex marriages or civil marriages are still not possible, mostly due to pressure from the ultra-Orthodox parties in the Knesset. Despite the opposition to conversion therapy from Knesset members and ministers on the right and the left, senior military officials and economists, and the Union of Psychologists in Israel, it is still not illegal, and every year, dozens of teenagers are sent for this dangerous treatment that usually ends with destructive results in the best-case scenarios, or in suicide in the worst cases.

But big changes happen in small steps, and as the radicalism increases, the more moderate groups are increasing too. When Orthodox Judaism had to find solutions in Jewish law for existential issues related to Shabbat or family purity, it found them. More and more synagogues in the liberal Orthodox community are including LGBTQ families, and while there is no "permit" for it in Jewish law, the tolerance and the understanding that gay, lesbian, bisexual, and transgender people are God's creations just like any other human being triumphs over isolationism in the name of Jewish law. As Rabbi Akiva said, "Love your fellow as you love yourself – this is a big rule in the Torah." I sincerely hope that sooner or later, this verse will be what triumphs over all of the prejudices and the fears, and there will be room for inclusion and love.

Childhood Memory, 2020
Oil on canvas
mounted on wood
120X65

25

The Mosaic

A Society of Immigrants

Shari Robins

A country and its society are made up of individuals who belong to various groups of people, similar to stones in a mosaic that form an image. To integrate into a country, immigrants often need to learn a new language. In the case of *olim*, Jewish immigrants to Israel, that means Hebrew. Language is full of nuances, which means that interpretation as well as translation is required. There is an expression in Hebrew, "*Meshaneh makom, meshaneh mazal*," which literally means, "Change [your] place, change [your] luck"; in colloquial terms it means to have a "fresh start." This is the immigrant story.

Most English-speaking Jews will recognize the word *mazal* as part of *mazal tov,* understood as "congratulations." However, *mazal* or "luck" is also associated with astrological signs. An ancient synagogue mosaic floor found in 1928 in the Beit Shean Valley at Kibbutz Heftziba has a zodiac wheel in the center with the twelve *mazalot* written in Hebrew. Mine, for example, is Scorpio. When I see the entire mosaic, a collection of white, black, gray, red, pink, orange, brown, and yellow-colored stones, along with green and purple glass pieces, I think about the story of *olim* in Israel. Each immigrant to Israel is a stone and each country of origin is a color; the image and story created is that of Israeli society. We miss the richness of the contribution of *olim* to Israeli society if we focus only on one color.

Since Israel's founding in 1948, 3.3 million Jews have made aliyah, immigrated to Israel, from the four corners of the earth. Much of the Israel we experience today has been defined and shaped by this ingathering of the exiles, *kibbutz galuyot*, and makes up the mosaic of Israeli society. Being an *oleh/olah* requires an ability to be flexible and adjust to a new environment after leaving behind a familiar culture, language, cuisine, social norms, and family, just as Avram and Sarai, our patriarch and matriarch, the first Jewish "immigrants," did. But it also means maintaining part of your identity and even influencing Israeli society. In short, it means being part of a mosaic, rather than a melting pot, where each stone adds a color and together creates a scene.

Avram and Sarai, whose names later become Avraham and Sarah, take a very long journey from Mesopotamia to Canaan back in the nineteenth century BCE after God says to Avram, "*Lech lecha*... Go out of your country and from your family, and from your father's house" (Genesis 12:1). They don't know what to expect from their new, unfamiliar surroundings and have no way of predicting how this move will shape their lives – much in the same way *olim* today are faced with anxiety and uncertainty when they think about the unknown in Israel. Once in the land, their immigrant story intensifies, as we see in the second panel of the Beit Alpha mosaic: the story of the Binding of Isaac (Genesis 22:1–19).

After finally having a son, Avraham is told to sacrifice him on a hill-top, Mount Moriah. He is holding Isaac in one hand and a long knife in the other. Their names are inscribed above them. To the right is an altar with flames rising from it. Above Avraham's right shoulder is a hand emerging from a cloud, symbolizing the angel of God and the Hebrew inscription "Don't lay your hand on the boy." Avraham then notices the ram caught in the thicket. The tension of the moment is frozen in mosaic time and has been discussed, analyzed, and questioned ever since.

While such drama is not generally part of modern-day aliyah, each wave of aliyah to the land of Israel has been historically analyzed, having its own general character and at times viewed with suspicion and criticism by immigrants who came before, depending on the time period, the motivation, and from which country they came. A marvelous entertaining comic skit from 1973, aired as part of the Israeli TV series *Lul,* shows actors Arik Einstein and Uri Zohar playing the roles of two *olim hadashim,* new immigrants, who arrive on the shores of the Mediterranean. They are resentful and suspicious of the next wave of *olim* reaching the shores of Israel, with their strange smells, attire, language, political backgrounds, and expectations.

Indeed, each group has added cultural dimensions to the mosaic of Israeli cuisine, language, music, sense of personal space, and social mores. It is said that within each bit of humor lies some truth. Perhaps that is what makes this skit such a classic, because we are able to laugh at the screen and at ourselves while acknowledging Israeli societal reactions to the smell of Yeminite *hilbe* in the fifties, the preciseness of German *yekkes* in the thirties, or the clash between Ashkenazi, Sephardi, and Mizrahi worldviews in the mid-twentieth century. More recently, years after *Lul,* waves of aliyah from Ethiopia and the former

Soviet Union have ignited religious debate over who is a Jew and raised issues of skin color.

Imagine the following scene. A couple of New York *olim* are standing in line to be seated at a restaurant that serves malawach, Yemenite fried bread. Behind them, perhaps too close for American comfort, is a group speaking Russian. Mizrahi music is heard and before entering, bags are checked by someone from Ethiopia. Once seated, the server is a young student whose parents came from Morocco in 1952. It's a mosaic of Israeli society which brings us to the Beit Alpha zodiac wheel.

Jews have always been influenced by the dominant cultures among which they have lived. Aspects of different cultural elements become stones in the overall mosaic of Jewish culture. During the Byzantine time period, fourth to seventh centuries, it was common to incorporate astrological symbols into synagogues, and the study of the stars was not foreign to Jews. Even the image of the sun god Helios in the center of the Beit Alpha zodiac was not contradictory to the Jewish faith. There are Hebrew names for the symbols and the four seasons in the corners of the panel, like the ingathering of the exiles, are each associated with a Hebrew month where, in the land of Israel, Jewish time rules.

When I bring tourists to the Beit Alpha mosaic, or to Tzippori or Tiberias where there are also mosaic zodiac wheels, people naturally begin to look for their sign, to see where they fit in the picture. I made aliyah in 1984, which makes me an Israeli, right? My first trip to Israel was when I was seventeen years old, on a six-week summer program. I fell in love with the diversity of the landscape, language, history, and yes, the hummus! I returned to Cleveland, Ohio, where I announced to my parents that one day I would live in Israel and be a tour guide. It is a story I share with all my tourists, because guiding and sharing Israel is me living the dream! However, I can also say that after more than thirty-six years of living in this amazingly miraculous yet at times frustrating wonderment called Israel, once an immigrant, always an immigrant.

Finally, the mosaic's top panel has an image of the Ark where the Torah would be housed. Two large seven-branched menorahs and two roaring lions are on each side, all surrounded by Jewish ritual objects such as the lulav, etrog, shofar, and incense shovel. The direction is facing south toward Jerusalem, where Jews have traditionally directed prayer. Those who have chosen, or for whom history perhaps chose for them, to make aliyah left their country of birth, as did Avraham and Sarah, and changed their "luck" for a "fresh start" in Israel. Was it guided by the stars? That is for you to decide.

Understanding now that each immigrant, each mosaic piece, has a story and is part of the mosaic of Israeli society, which site would I take you to in order to explain Israel as an immigrant society? It wouldn't be an archeological site or a hike in Israel's diverse landscape or floating in the Dead Sea. I would suggest that you simply observe your surroundings and interactions, beginning with your airport arrival. Talk to your bus or cab driver! Cab drivers are known in particular for sharing their opinions with passengers. Pay attention to the clerk at the reception desk at your hotel and the server in the dining room. Look around at the people walking down the street, on the beaches, or in the stores. Listen to the variety of languages people chatter in, and read the diverse menu items coming from a multitude of countries. Initiating a conversation with a stranger is not always practical or even easy, but if there is anywhere to do it, Israeli is the place. It is in this way that you will discover the mosaic of an immigrant society.

26

Text and Travel

Muki Jankelowitz

Travel is an opportunity to see and experience different things. Travel to a place like Israel with its rich and long history takes one not only to a different place but frequently also offers the opportunity to travel to a different time. Fortunately, literacy has long been a defining characteristic of the Jewish people and very often their stories and thoughts have been collected in one of many books.

Yet although the Jewish people have long carried the name People of the Book, today's hectic modern reality seldom offers us a chance to glance at the bookshelf. And frequently even when there is time, a lack of familiarity with the texts stops us from opening any of the books on the shelves.

The idea of reading text frequently conjures up images of a boring Sunday school class or an old academic sequestered in the corner of a musty library. But reading a text can be anything but boring or musty and making sense of the words written long ago at the place they were written or looking at something they described can be exhilarating.

> The land of Israel was the birthplace of the Jewish people.
> Here their spiritual, religious and political identity was shaped.
> Here they first attained to statehood, created cultural values of
> national and universal significance and gave to the world the
> eternal Book of Books.

With these words, Israel's Declaration of Independence begins. Reading these words or indeed any part of the declaration always moves me. This opening paragraph was carefully crafted to concisely convey what Israel represents for many Jews. Reading this text in the hall where David Ben-Gurion first read these words only intensifies the experience. It still gives me goosebumps.

In that way, reading a text is also like traveling back in time. Through a text, one gets to hear the voices of the past, be they fictional or historical. Through a text, the personalities of days gone by get to tell us about their world. Sometimes we only catch fleeting glimpses of their reality and have to work at gleaning information from the text, but other times we hear directly that which was important to them. From time to time, the text even allows us to enter directly into their conversations.

For me, the Bible comes alive when I stand at the remains of the Broad Wall in the Old City and read Isaiah's description of the Assyrian siege on Jerusalem. Similarly, when I stand at the Muhraka (church commemorating Elijah's battle with the prophets of Ba'al) atop Mount Carmel looking out to the north over the Kishon River, it is not difficult to immerse myself in the book of Kings' description of Elijah's confrontation with the 450 prophets of Ba'al. Regardless of one's personal understanding of the Bible, reading the text on site ensures that what the biblical writer saw then, we see now.

Even more importantly, a text enables us to participate in the dialogues of the past and to engage with the people and especially with their ideas. A text offers us the opportunity to both connect with them in their time but also to reflect on their thoughts for our time.

In the Babylonian Talmud in *Gittin* 55b, the rabbis record a story that teaches us that the destruction of the Second Temple began when a servant was sent to invite a person called Kamtza to a banquet. However instead the servant mistakenly invited someone else called Bar-Kamtza, his master's enemy. From this simple beginning, things escalate quickly. And when one reads the pithy story, it quickly becomes clear that it's much more complicated. It's a powerful story not only because it shows complexity, but because we can read about events that are set in the Jerusalem of two thousand years ago and cannot but help thinking about today's reality. Moreover, when we read it amongst the ruins of Second Temple Jerusalem, the lessons the rabbis wished to teach are that much clearer to see.

The story of Kamtza and Bar-Kamtza is not unique. The Talmud is filled with vivid tales that tell of the lives of the sages of old, or stories and parables that were used by the rabbis to teach a certain insight. Although the words may be printed in black and white, the stories are colorful, easily accessible, and help bring many sites to life.

But the Talmud is also filled with arcane legal discussions, which often seem daunting and impenetrable to the uninitiated. And yet sitting in pairs just as traditional students do, but under a fig tree in Tzippori close to where Rabbi Yehudah Hanasi (the second-century rabbi recognized as the redactor of the Mishnah, the primary written collection of the Oral Torah) once lived, suddenly even the inexperienced can join the legal discussions. Gradually almost unwittingly they find themselves wanting to be part of the conversation.

The same can be said of engaging with the mystic kabbalistic texts of the medieval rabbis in one of Tzfat's old synagogues, or when reading from the diaries or grappling with the manifestos of the halutzim:

the Zionist pioneers and thinkers at the Kinneret farm or on the streets of Tel Aviv.

Reading Bialik's poetry in the neighborhoods of early Tel Aviv or that of Amichai in Yemin Moshe in Jerusalem, or contemplating the prose of Amos Oz or Yossi Klein Halevi while looking out at the sites they describe, changes the way we experience the places. Texts take us from the outside – from looking in at an event or experience – to the inside of an event. Taking on and taking in a text changes us from being spectators to something else. Not tourists who move through a series of sites but rather seekers for whom the sites move through us.

Vision and Reality

Sabra, 2016
Oil on canvas
mounted on wood
61X54

27

Unified or Uniform

What's Holding Israel Together?

Eran Shlomi

A visit to Israel is a wonderful opportunity to meet Israelis. *Israeli* is a complex term. When you think of your Sabra (native-born israeli) archetype, you may have a vision in your mind based on the Zionist ethos and its myths. On your trip, you will discover that Israeli society is no less diverse than Israel's natural landscapes, which are among the most diverse in the world.

The term *ethos*, as it is commonly used today, refers to the character, values, norms, and ideals of various organizations and societies. The ethos of the nineteenth-century American frontier, for example, glorified ideals such as coarse individualism, independence, and initiative, during a period and place referred to as the "Wild West." At the end of the nineteenth century, Zionists in Eretz Israel (the land of Israel) developed a unique ethos that continued to evolve as the pre-state community grew. This ethos strived to create a "new Jew" in the land of Israel who would live the antithesis of the European Jewish diasporic lifestyle during that period.

At the center of the Zionist ethos stood ideals such as taking personal and collective responsibility for the fate of the Jewish people. Due to this mindset, the Zionist pioneers, who were the heroes of the movement, encouraged waves of immigration to the land of Israel starting from the end of the nineteenth century, while simultaneously building agricultural settlements. At the beginning of the twentieth century, members of the Second Aliyah incorporated socialist ideas with the Zionist pioneering spirit and founded the first kibbutzim. These pioneers' ideals focused on "conquering labor" – transforming the Eastern European Jew into a farmer and a productive person in general – and "conquering security" – transforming the Jew into a guard with a weapon, who will even use it if necessary in order to protect the new settlements and their fields.

Three expressions have come to embody the Zionist ethos over the years. In 1920, following a local, bloody battle at Tel Hai in the north of the country, the expression "It is good to die on behalf of our country" became part of the Zionist ethos. These were allegedly the last words of the battle's hero, Joseph Trumpeldor. In the thirties and forties, the Zionists rediscovered Mount Masada, and added the expression "Masada shall not fall again" to the Zionist ethos. The slogan emphasizes that the land of Israel is the "last stronghold" for the persecuted Jewish nation. During the War of Independence, a new term was coined, "the silver platter," which describes the sacrifice of the fighters of the 1948 generation, a sacrifice upon which the state was given to the Jews. The victory of the War of Independence proved, from a Zionist perspective, that the revolution had succeeded – the Zionist ethos had created a new Jew, a nationalistic Jew, with chutzpah, strength, and ingenuity, who had established a new country with its own hands.

Yet after the war ended in 1949, the accepted Zionist ethos was challenged by the young country's new reality. The small Jewish settlement, with its population of just 600,000, mostly of Eastern European descent, began absorbing millions of new immigrants from all over the world: Holocaust survivors from Eastern Europe and Jews from North Africa, Yemen, and later Ethiopia, Russia, France, among other countries. My mother was born in Paris, the daughter of Holocaust survivors from Poland and France. As an adolescent, she was mesmerized by the idea of the "new Jew" who determined his own faith, fought for his freedom, and protected his country. She joined a Zionist youth movement, and in 1974, at the age of nineteen, immigrated to Israel and joined Kibbutz Ruhama in the Negev.

Every two weeks, my mother would visit relatives living near Tel Aviv. Her visits became more and more frequent when she noticed the tanned, tall young man, the son of the neighbors who were new immigrants from Egypt. The young man, who later became my father, grew up in a home where Arabic, Hebrew, and Ladino (spoken by Jews of Spanish descent) were the spoken languages. The music in his home was Egyptian music, mostly songs by Egyptian singer Umm Kulthum. Every Friday, shortly before Shabbat began, the entire family would sit in front of the television to watch a popular Arab film from Egypt. His mother, my grandmother Karoline, would dish up her culinary specialty: mulukhiyah, a thick, chicken soup-type dish full of herbs that is popular in Egypt. My mother, on the other hand, grew up in a home where they spoke French, Yiddish (the language of Eastern European Jews), and Polish. They mostly listened to French chansons and classical music, and in the kitchen, the specialties of Grandpa Shmuel, originally from Sosnowiec, Poland, were chopped liver, *p'tcha* (calves' foot jelly), and gefilte fish. My father and mother, who were born in two distant worlds and diverse cultures, met in a public housing project for immigrants on a sandy hill a few kilometers south of Tel Aviv – the city that became the symbol of the Zionist ethos.

The different cultures that the immigrants brought from their countries of origin caused the leaders of young Israel to worry that the "new Jew," created by the Zionist ethos of the pre-state community, would become extinct. Many immigrants were asked to change their names, which were perceived as "Diaspora" names, in favor of names that had a Hebrew or biblical ring to them. My father's last name was Salama, and in the atmosphere of the melting pot that was Israel at the time, he changed it to Shlomi.

However, as the years went by, Israelis abandoned the melting pot idea. The Zionist ethos, which had been appropriate in a small and relatively uniform society, was no longer relevant to the Israeli mosaic that was being created. A new, multi-ethos human and cultural diversity emerged in its place. Today, more than seventy years after the state's establishment, it is possible to say that Israeli society celebrates its multiculturalism: Israelis of all descents celebrate holidays such as Mimouna, Novy God, and Sigd, holidays which were once exclusive to immigrants from Morocco, Russia, and Ethiopia, respectively. Popular music in Israel combines distinct elements of Mediterranean and European-American music styles. The "Israeli" kitchen is a winning combination of diverse dishes, such as Iraqi kubbeh, Yemenite jachnun, Eastern European gefilte fish, Egyptian falafel, Turkish bourekas, and more. Each group has its own food, music, stories, and narrative. There is no single Zionist or Israeli ethos today; rather, many different Israeli ethe and narratives.

There are additional developments that testify to the abundance of ethe in Israeli society. In 2015, Israeli president Ruby Rivlin presented, in what has since been referred to as the "Four Tribes" speech, the fact that in Israel, there is no single "tribe" that makes up the clear majority of society. The demographic trends in Israel point to four central "tribes," each with its own ethos – the secular tribe, the religious-Zionist tribe, the Arab tribe, and the ultra-Orthodox tribe.

These "tribes" are inherently different from each other, and they are becoming similar to each other in size. In other words, the old divisions of a Jewish majority and Arab minority, or secular majority and religious minority, are no longer relevant.

My father, for example, grew up in a secular home. While he attended synagogue with his father every Shabbat, kept kosher at home, and fasted on Yom Kippur, if you were to ask his family, they viewed themselves as completely secular. This complex type of identity can be found in almost every Israeli family. In other words, even the division into four tribes does not accurately depict the complexity and colorful nature of Israeli society. Many secular Israelis consider themselves traditional-secular (Jews with a secular approach to most of the commandments, but who observe Shabbat, kosher, and Jewish festivals), or slightly-traditional-secular (for example, only celebrate Jewish festivals). Moreover, an increasing number of ultra-Orthodox Israelis, especially among the younger generation, are being exposed to the Internet and to modernism in general. Some of them have become Zionists, and many voluntarily serve in the IDF, despite the enlistment exemption for the ultra-Orthodox community. There are also many religious-Zionists who have adopted perspectives and customs from the ultra-Orthodox world, and they are referred to as ultra-Orthodox-Zionists. Each "tribe" and "sub-tribe" has its own narrative and own Israeli ethos.

The many ethe in Israel are expressed in other ways as well. Israelis are also diverse in their political-ideological stances, on the spectrum between left and right. Beyond support for specific politicians or political parties, this division reflects their diverse worldviews. There are several ways to explain the differences between right- and left-wing approaches in Israel, but the following way is one of the most characteristic, in my opinion: the expression "Never again," which describes the lesson that the Jewish nation learned from the Holocaust – that such a horrific crime must never be committed again. Many Jews in Israel believe that this expression commands us to ensure that such a crime will never again befall the Jews, and so Jews must rely on no one but themselves, in the spirit of the biblical expression "a nation that will dwell alone" (Numbers 23). These Israelis, who, by rough generalization, are on the conservative right of the political spectrum, attribute great significance to Israel's security needs – military strength, the importance of Israeli deterrence, and the need to hold onto regions such as Judea and Samaria, Gaza, and the Golan Heights, in order to fortify Israeli security. There is also an emotional-religious connection among the Israeli right to the land, the sites, and the Jewish history of these regions.

In contrast, there are those who understand the expression "Never again" as a command to remember what the Nazis did to the Jews, and to actively ensure that such a crime will never happen again to anyone, Jews and non-Jews alike. Israelis with this perspective, who, by rough generalization, belong to the "universal" liberal left, are a bit more involved in concern for "others" in Israel, whether this means asylum seekers from Sudan or Eretria in South Tel Aviv, or Palestinians in East Jerusalem.

Thus, it is clear that from one Zionist ethos, different groups have emerged today in Israel with diverse narratives and varied Zionist ethe. Nevertheless, what unites Israelis today? Is there a common denominator, thin as it may be, between the different ethe? Most Jews in Israel will agree that the State of Israel is a Jewish and democratic state. What is more important, though? Its Jewish character? Democracy? There are many disagreements on that point. Israeli Arabs or the Israeli left will emphasize the importance of Israeli democracy, while religious-Zionists and the ultra-Orthodox will place emphasis on Israel as a Jewish state. However, almost all Jews in Israel will agree that living in a country to which you contribute, whether in a military or civil framework, is a significant component of the Israeli ethos.

Alongside the Israeli majority in Israel lives a large Arab minority that is influenced by the Jewish-Zionist ethos as well. The Arab-Israeli-Palestinian minority, which makes up 20 percent of the total population and numbers about two million today, is integrating into Israeli culture more and more. Arabs in Israel, whose primary call is for integration and equality, are becoming a more significant part of the joint Israeli space: in the media, in politics, in sports, and so on. This phenomenon also reflects a complex reality: on the one hand, the Arab-Israeli ethos views the defeat of 1948, the Nakba, as a central component of the Arab-Palestinian-Israeli identity. On the other hand, there are more and more examples of increasing integration of Arabs into mainstream Israeli society. Among others, I will mention Supreme Court Justice, Salim Joubran, captain of the Israeli football team, Bibras Natkho, and co-host of the Eurovision Song Contest, hosted by Israel in 2019, television presenter Lucy Ayoub. One of the interesting results of the Arab integration trends in Israel are the changes to spoken Arabic in Israel, which has adopted an increasing amount of Hebrew vocabulary and even more significantly, Hebrew syntactic structures and grammar.

One of the important researchers of the Jewish nation today, Shmuel Rosner, believes that despite the multiculturalism, arguments, and rifts, a shared Jewish-Israeli culture has developed (and is still developing) in Israel today, which unites most of the factions of the Jewish nation in Israel. It is possible to say that there is a national consensus that the State of Israel is the sovereign nation state of the Jewish people. Or in the words of the author of the Zionist anthem that became the Israeli national anthem – "Hatikvah": "to be a free nation in our land." This perspective is adopted, perhaps as a default, by non-Jewish citizens as well, and therefore, if we look at developing Israeli culture, there are two prominent trends that complement each other: variety and differences which exist in parallel to the existence of distinct common elements. The result is a colorful mosaic, surrounded by a thick frame – a frame of a fate and future shared by citizens living together in a small country, trying to create a better life for themselves.

28

Between Jerusalem and Tel Aviv

Mike Hollander

I grew up in a Jewish Zionist home in Vancouver, Canada. My Jewish identity was formed around three pillars: home, Orthodox Jewish day school, and Zionist summer camp. Israel always was a central part of my Jewish identity. I first came to Israel for my bar mitzvah and returned for a gap year program on a kibbutz after high school, as well as for another gap year after I finished my BA in Canada. That year, I studied at Tel Aviv University, but my open agenda was to spend an additional year in Israel to make sure that I was certain about making aliyah.

It was clear that there was only one choice as to where to settle in Israel – on a kibbutz. After all, having grown up in a Socialist-Zionist youth movement (Habonim Dror), I knew that Israel's founders were the *halutzim* (pioneers) of the early twentieth century who had created the first kibbutzim and moshavim. Why would I consider living anywhere else? What other choices did I have? Jerusalem? Too old, religious, and conflict-ridden. Tel Aviv? I don't know how many of you visited Tel Aviv in the eighties, but it was a run-down, hot and sticky, ugly urban center that didn't attract me. Besides... ideologically, I could only really become a New Jew if I lived on a kibbutz, and therefore, this was the only place where I could reach my full potential.

I made aliyah in 1988 with a group of thirty-five North Americans, all of us in our mid-twenties, to Kibbutz Ravid, a beautiful community in the north, overlooking the Golan Heights and the Sea of Galilee. After two years, however, my communal ideology began to wane, but my commitment to living in Israel continued unabated. Where should I go? My friends were trying to get me to join them in Tel Aviv, whereas my girlfriend (my wife now for almost thirty years!) wanted to move to Jerusalem, where her sisters lived. I was hesitant because Jerusalem never appealed to me, as it was too Orthodox (traditional) and, in the early nineties, was in the midst of the violent first Palestinian Intifada.

However, we moved to Jerusalem, and like a good wine or whiskey that gets better over time, I grew to love the city. Our children were born there, and we were optimistic in the nineties that the peace process would ensure a better future. Unfortunately, the second Intifada that erupted in 2000 resulted in a steep decline in tourists – and as a tour guide I began to explore alternative employment that would still be in line with my commitment to Israel. I was approached by the Jewish Agency for Israel to work as a *shaliach* (emissary) in London, England, connecting the Jewish community to Israel. I excitedly took the position that would focus on teaching UK youth about Israel and developing Israel programs, and our family spent three years in London.

Upon our return to Israel, we had to figure out where to settle. My wife was adamant about not returning to Jerusalem, and neither of us considered Tel Aviv. So we chose a town exactly in the middle, equidistant from both major cities. I often describe Modi'in as "Middle Israel," essentially because it is! Geographically as well as spiritually. It doesn't have the thousands of years of tradition and history of Jerusalem (although it was the hometown of the Maccabees over two thousand years ago!), nor does it have the hectic pace and congestion of Tel Aviv. It's a suburban, planned community that is over twenty years old.

I've come to realize how Modi'in is the right place for us to live, as it allows us to embrace Jewish tradition, but also be a part of the normalization of the Jewish people. Although I moved to Israel over thirty years ago believing that the only "legitimate" form of aliyah was to settle on a kibbutz, I have evolved together with the young country, and realize that there are many ways to live a fulfilling life in Israel. Our city is "Middle Israel," because it is in many ways a fusion of the two major directional pulls in Israeli society. The planned city of almost 100,000 inhabitants boasts a thriving Reform congregation where our three children had their bnei mitzvah and where our eldest was married, as well as Masorti/Conservative, Conservadox breakaways, and egalitarian Orthodox communities.

The country's first pluralistic K–12 comprehensive school with a school for children with special needs on its campus – Yachad – (meaning "together") is in Modi'in, bringing children from diverse families together along the secular-Orthodox continuum. As we watched our eldest son thrive in this school, from first grade until graduation, I realized how unusual and important this school system is in contrast to the exclusive state secular and state religious streams. Students at Yachad recognize the significance of bringing together children from diverse backgrounds and are inculcated with a healthy dose of Jewish tradition and societal responsibility, as well as an understanding that the future of society depends on a healthy fusion of Jewish past, present, and future. I realize that our hometown of Modi'in is a healthy model for Israeli society, rejecting the polarity between Jerusalem and Tel Aviv.

The location of our home allows us to choose whether to head up the hill to the east to Jerusalem, the repository of Jewish memory over millennia, or to head down to the west to the place that symbolizes the normalization and creativity and success of the Jewish people in the last century, Tel Aviv. The Mediterranean city has changed quite a bit since I lived there in the mid-eighties and has won a number of international accolades in recent years. The first of these was the UNESCO designation of Tel Aviv as a World Heritage site in 2003 because, according to the Bauhaus Center in Tel Aviv, "it is a synthesis of outstanding significance of the various trends of the Modern Movement in architecture and town planning in the early part of the twentieth century." This was then followed by many other awards, including the Lonely Planet travel guide, which in 2010 ranked the city as third in the list of the world's best cities (citing it both on its list for Ultimate Party Cities and the Top Ten Hedonistic City Breaks), American Airlines travel magazine's recognition of Tel Aviv as the "World's Best Gay Travel Destination" in 2012, and Travelers Digest's claim that Tel Aviv is home to the most beautiful people in the world. The city also boasts the largest number of start-ups per capita in the world after Silicon Valley.

I often joke with tourists that one can immediately distinguish between residents of the two cities through their dress codes. Many Jerusalemites – Jews, Christians, and Moslems – look east when they wake up, to see when the sun rises, so that they can know when to recite their morning prayer, whose time is connected to sunrise. Tel Avivians look west – to monitor the weather patterns, to see the new fashion trends coming from Milan and Paris, to follow the musical trends, and to be in sync with our biggest trading partners in Europe and the US. Jerusalemites often dress according to their community's long-standing traditions, regardless of whether it is brutally cold or oppressively hot. As one walks around Jerusalem, one encounters Franciscan monks wearing their heavy wool habit throughout the year, Mulsim women wearing their traditional hijab and full-length clothing, or the ultra-Orthodox in their heavy, dark suits. In contrast, Tel Avivians decide what to wear depending on fashion and weather. In the summer, scantily clad beach-goers are seen miles from the beach, whereas in the winter people are dressed according to contemporary European fashion.

I'm reminded of a family from New York that I guided a few years ago. At the end of a week with them and their young children traveling all over the country, while eating sushi on Rothschild Boulevard in Tel Aviv, I encouraged them to reflect on their trip. I asked them where they would live if they lived in Israel. The woman quickly replied, "Jerusalem!" Why? I asked. "Simply because Jerusalem is the reason that we are here. It is the epicenter of our tradition, the repository of Jewish memory, and I feel a deep connection to my Judaism in Jerusalem."

The husband, of course, answered "Tel Aviv." Why? "This is the place where I feel comfortable. All the high tech, young people, amazing energy, restaurants and coffee shops, culture, the beach, and people out at all times of day. There is no place on the planet where we can feel and behave this way as Jews. I can do what I do in the States here [working in finance] and live a Jewish life amongst Jews."

I almost suggested that I put up our home in Modi'in for sale, so that they could buy it and move to the town between the two major cities. That way, they could live in Israel and sustain their marriage, compromising between the husband and wife's preferences! More importantly, it made me realize what this country is all about. There are many Tel Avivians who never make the short forty-mile journey up to Jerusalem, as they say they don't feel welcome in a city of religious fanatics and Jewish-Arab tension. They may go there if they have to attend their nephew's bar mitzvah, but not for much else. Conversely, there are many Jerusalemites who would never consider "descending" to Tel Aviv, the capital of hedonism, where people walk around scantily dressed.

The late Israeli author Amos Oz explained the difference between Israel's two major cities in his autobiographical book, *A Tale of Love and Darkness.* Here he reminisces about his childhood in a traditional Jerusalem neighborhood:

> Over the hills and far away, the city of Tel Aviv was also an exciting place, from which came the newspapers, rumors of theater, opera, ballet and cabaret, as well as modern art, party politics, echoes of stormy debates, and indistinct snatches of gossip. There were great sportsmen in Tel Aviv. And there was the sea, full of bronzed Jews who could swim. Who in Jerusalem could swim? Who had ever heard of swimming Jews? These were different genes. A mutation. "Like the wondrous birth of a butterfly out of a worm.
>
> Tel Aviv. Sea. Light. Sand, scaffolding, kiosks on the avenues, a brand new white Hebrew city, with simple lines, growing up among the citrus groves and the dunes. Not just a place that you buy a ticket for and travel to on an Egged bus, but a different continent altogether."[1]

After living here for over thirty years, I want visitors to Israel to realize that both major cities are essential to the past, present, and future of the Jewish state. They are two sides of the same coin. Jerusalem is the bastion of Jewish memory and is essential to our connection to this land. There is no place else to have a Jewish state. Tel Aviv is the center of Jewish artistic and technological creativity that symbolizes the normalization of the Jewish people. Israelis must understand our Jewish past, tradition, and memory centered in Jerusalem, as well as embrace the creative urge to ensure our continued growth and development. Israelis who see only one side, and either look east to the past

---

1. Amos Oz, *A Tale of Love and Darkness*, trans. Nicholas deLange (New York: Houghton Mifflin Harcourt, 2004).

to interpret and live in the present, or those who only look west to the future, are missing the point: the future of the Jewish state depends on embracing the unique amalgam of Israel as the past, present, and future of the Jewish people.

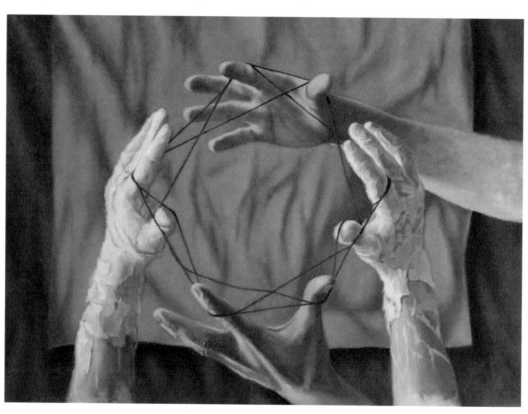

Cat's Cradle 2, 2017
Oil on canvas
mounted on wood
45X65

29

Never Again?

Israel and the Holocaust

Gilad Peled

Jerusalem is built on a series of three hills. To the east is the Temple Mount, the ancient political and religious center of Judea. In the center is Givat Ram, home to Israel's modern national institutions and government agencies. To the west is Mount Herzl, the site of Israel's central military cemetery. For many Israelis, the first hill represents our past, the second represents our future, and the third is dedicated to those who paid with their lives in order to connect between the two. At the edge of the military cemetery and behind it, slightly concealed on the slope of the mountain, lies the central Holocaust memorial site, Yad Vashem. It is no coincidence that Yad Vashem is hidden behind the military cemetery, nor is it a coincidence that the short walk from the cemetery, situated at the top of the hill, is a downhill walk. A lot of thought went into designing the memorial symbols of the young State of Israel, determining their locations, and the connection between them. Yet the Holocaust, whose story the country's founders attempted to conceal behind Israel's young, daring, and revolutionary appearance, eventually crept back in through the cracks of history, enveloping the country.

The change in the attitude of Israelis toward the Holocaust can be ironically seen in the negligible number of people who visit military cemeteries, compared to the number of visitors to the Holocaust museum. Today, the Holocaust has a significant presence in everyday life in Israel, shaping its character and its conduct. Our eyes are focused on the past rather than on the future, and we are more often motivated by fear than by hope.

This was not always the case.

My father was a modest, active man who dedicated his life to making the world a better place. He was born in Budapest two years before the outbreak of World War II, and he was seven years old when the Nazis imprisoned him in the ghetto, took his father to the Mauthausen labor camp, and deported his grandfather to Auschwitz. My father survived, and at the age of twelve, alone, he reached the home of his uncle on a kibbutz. At the time, the Holocaust held no special interest for the new Israelis, who had just established a state and fought for its existence, and all my father wanted was to be one of them. He adopted an Israeli name for himself, enlisted in the army, and worked in the fields of the kibbutz.

Zionism was founded in order to provide an answer for a persecuted Jewish minority – a fact that was borne out by the Holocaust. It was commonly believed in Israel at that time, that Jews in the Holocaust went to their deaths "like sheep to the slaughter" – a mindset that stood in direct opposition to the Zionist ideals of initiative and self-defense. The new Israelis preferred to emphasize those Jews who rebelled in the ghettos, most prominently the Warsaw Ghetto uprising, and they named the national Holocaust Memorial Day "Holocaust and Heroism Remembrance Day." The two elements of this name, "Holocaust" and "heroism," represented contrasting rather than complementing ideas. They were ashamed of the Holocaust, which, as far as they were concerned, was a direct result of the passivity of Jews in the Diaspora. However, they could identify with the heroic fighting of those who rebelled in the ghettos and the camps. The combination of "Holocaust" and "heroism" gave the Zionist movement a powerful educational tool to shape the next generation.

In the fifties, Israeli society was a collectivist, enlisted society challenged by existential problems, which could not address, and was not interested in addressing, the troubles of the individual. The stories of the Holocaust survivors were neither appreciated nor heard. Yet the hundreds of thousands of scarred Holocaust survivors who reached the country in unimaginable ways, including my father, quickly became full partners in the Israeli ethos. They constituted about half (!) of Israel's fighting forces in the War of Independence, and that was also their rate among the fallen. They played a central role in establishing new settlements and developing the fledgling Israeli economy. The Holocaust had no presence in Israeli society during those years, and the survivors were mainly busy developing their "Israeliness" and building their new futures.

The capture of Nazi criminal Adolf Eichmann in a daring operation in 1960, and his subsequent public trial in Israel, changed the Israeli attitude toward the Holocaust for the first time. Firstly, thanks to the trial, Israelis confronted for the first time the personal stories of the Holocaust survivors who lived among them. The pieces of information they had about the Holocaust melded together into one coherent picture and turned into knowledge.

Haim Gouri, a poet and novelist who covered the trial for one of the newspapers, wrote:

We already knew these things, didn't we?! Yes, we knew. We knew even before the Eichmann trial.... But when this material was placed on the prosecution table and became part of the indictment, when these documents broke free of the silence of the archives, it seemed that now, they were speaking for **the first time,** and **this** knowledge was very different from **that** knowledge.... The Holocaust happened **now,** not on any other date between those years and the beginning of the trial.... [Emphases in the source][1]

Secondly, the descriptions of the Holocaust during the Eichmann trial began the process of mythization of the Holocaust – its perception as a mythical event, larger than life, an event that constitutes a yardstick for life itself. Most memorable was the dramatic testimony of author Yehiel De-Nur, at the end of which he fainted on the witness stand. In response to the prosecutor's question as to why he used the pen name K. Tzetnik[2] in his books, which describe the Holocaust in merciless detail, he responded:

This is not a pen name. I do not see myself as a writer who writes literature. This is a chronicle from the planet Auschwitz. I was there for about two years. The time there is not the same as it is here, on Earth. Every split second there moves in a different sphere of time. And the inhabitants of this planet had no names. They had no parents and no children. They did not dress the way they dress here. They were not born there and did not give birth.... They did not live according to the laws of

---

1. *La'Merchav,* September 10, 1961, p. 5. Translated from the Hebrew by Sarah Mageni.

2. The name comes from an abbreviation of the German word *Konzentrationslager* (concentration camp) and was a common nickname among the camp prisoners. It is pronounced Katzetnik and means "a prisoner in a concentration camp."

the world here and did not die. Their name was the number K. Tzetnik.[3]

This shift gained momentum after the trial when the survivors' commitment to making the Holocaust visible to the Israeli public deepened the perception that Israelis are an inseparable part of the Jewish chain of history. This idea dramatically contrasted the classic Zionist philosophy that was dominant in Israel until then – the hope of creating a new beginning in the land of Israel, disconnected from the shackles of the humiliating Jewish past of persecution and wandering. The impact of the Eichmann trial on Israeli society was immense, yet it did not lead to a sense of empathy, understanding, and identification with what had happened in Europe during the war, nor with the helpless reality of Jewish existence during the Holocaust. The final internalization that led to the change of consciousness regarding the Holocaust only occurred a few years later.

In 1967, a series of military incidents and hostilities led to an overall sense of tension and anxiety in Israel. For the first time, it was feared that the tiny, young State of Israel was facing existential danger. It was just nineteen years after the establishment of the state, following a prolonged, difficult war, and just twenty-two years after the Holocaust. Native-born Israelis and Holocaust survivors stood shoulder-to-shoulder to face what appeared to be an impending holocaust. As we know, the war ended with a decisive victory for Israel and a national feeling of control and security, but this was just a short lull before the storm.

In 1973, Israel was attacked completely by surprise, and dragged into an additional war, fighting for its life on all fronts. This war changed the Israeli perception of the Holocaust forever. As the Egyptian and

---

3. Eichmann Trial, session 68, June 7, 1961. Translated from the Hebrew by Tomer Golan.

Syrian armies advanced toward the center of the country uninter-
rupted, the petrifying fear of a loss of control that would end with
another Holocaust engulfed Israel. The soldiers in the war of 1973
were the children of Holocaust survivors. They heard the testimonies
in the Eichmann trial as teenagers and lived with the memories of the
Holocaust in their homes. For them, the feeling that annihilation and
destruction were chasing the Jews even in their independent country
was the realization of all of their personal and collective nightmares.

The war of 1973 completed the process of internalizing the
Holocaust for Israeli society – the information that had become knowledge a decade earlier now became consciousness. During the seventies
and eighties, Israelis gradually adopted the approach that views the
Jewish nation as a special case of a persecuted and threatened nation
that has done no wrong, a nation forced to fight for its right to exist
on a daily basis. The fact that this nation now possessed the strongest
military in the Middle East did not change this feeling of persecution
and danger that Israelis feel to this day.

In 1987, I went on a trip to Poland. I was seventeen, and it was
the first time that I had ever left Israel. I was chosen out of my entire
class to participate in a Holocaust memorial journey, where we met
Jewish teenagers from all over the world. It was a gut-wrenching trip
that gave my world a whole new perspective: no more small, threatened Israel; we were part of an ongoing historical and national story.
On the last day of the journey, we all stood around a large monument
in the middle of an open field dotted with sharp rocks jutting out of
the soil like threatening teeth. It was the site where the extermination
camp Treblinka once stood, the place where about 870,000 Jews were
murdered. My young self stood there, and in stark contrast with what
I was being told had happened at the site, all I heard was the wind
blowing silently through the nearby pines. The futility of the calculated, absolute mass murder, and the pure evil that had enabled all of

this to happen, shocked my young soul more than anything else. It was there that I made the resolute decision that I would fight for the rest of my life to ensure that a Holocaust would never happen again to any human being in the world.

Over the years, teenage trips to Poland became common in Israel, and hundreds of thousands of Israeli adolescents experience them. The impression of my journey never left me and has influenced my decisions at many crossroads in life. In the mid-2000s, I started guiding teenagers on trips to Poland myself, and I noticed that since I was there as a teenager, not only had Poland changed following the fall of the Iron Curtain, but so had Israel. The universal-humanistic lesson that I had learned at the age of seventeen had been replaced by many Israelis with a particular national lesson: never again will the *Jews* experience another Holocaust.

The perception of the Holocaust in Israel today vacillates between these two poles – the universal and the national. Does the Holocaust obligate us to be an ethical light to the nations, or does it obligate us to ensure the security of the State of Israel above any other consideration? Over the past thirty years, the second approach has become increasingly dominant in Israel. Few Israelis are interested today in injustices occurring overseas, and there is fierce opposition to any attempt to compare the Holocaust to other cases of genocide. Most Israelis participate in memorial ceremonies for victims of the Holocaust but do not mention the other victims of Nazi cruelty, such as the Sinti and Roma peoples, the disabled, and homosexuals.

Over the years, the Holocaust became more and more present in everyday Israeli life, and using the Holocaust as the basis of a worldview became more frequent and widespread. The process of mythization of the Holocaust transformed the survivors from "sheep to the slaughter" to "holy sheep." From a group that was ridiculed for its heritage and values, it became a group that is held in esteem above others, an example and symbol of resistance and courage. Their very existence made the Holocaust a palpable part of daily life in Israel. The dream of establishing a state that would ensure a better future for the persecuted Jews was replaced by the fear of another destruction, spurring an armament race and aggressive policies. Looking at the future was replaced by looking back at the past, and instead of hope, an important force in Israel today is fear.

The Holocaust is present in Israeli life today in an infinite number of ways. The more central the Holocaust became in the Israeli definition of self, the more Holocaust research institutions were opened, to the extent that today, there are over a dozen institutes dedicated to Holocaust research and education of Holocaust remembrance. This remembrance focuses today on the personal stories of the victims and survivors, rather than national lessons, as it did in the past. This trend is most clearly visible in the new Yad Vashem museum, which was established as a response to the change of perception in Israeli society – from a collective to a privatized society. The old museum, established in the sixties, presented a national narrative that focused on two main points: emphasizing the armed resistance in the ghettos and the camps, and the establishment of the State of Israel as an answer to the Holocaust, or as it is commonly referred to in Israel: "From Holocaust to Revival." On the other hand, the new museum, which opened in 2005, emphasizing the individual experience in the Holocaust, presents a range of responses by Jews and non-Jews to the terrible dilemmas people had to face during that period.

However, the complex perspective presented in museums does not reflect the public understanding of the Holocaust as a founding national event. In the public sphere, the personal stories emphasize and even reinforce the narrative of national persecution. The stories of Holocaust survivors connect, in the collective memory, to the sequence of historical stories of Jewish persecution throughout the generations.

They thus prove that the Holocaust was not a one-time occurrence, but rather another peak in the trend – that continues even today – of baseless persecution and discrimination against the Jews.

Yet there is a group, mostly young in age, who are not willing to submit to the shadow that the Holocaust casts over our lives. These young people choose to concentrate on both the future and the past. My maternal grandfather immigrated from Germany to Israel in the thirties. His mother, who didn't want to leave behind her comfortable lifestyle, was taken from her home and sent, along with all of the Jews in the city, to her death. For the past few years, my cousin has been living in Germany. The German citizenship that she received for our grandfather's cancelled citizenship allows her to enjoy the social benefits of the German welfare state. She feels no guilt about living in Germany.

While it is impossible to ignore the memory of the Holocaust in Israel today, the choice whether to live by the light of the Holocaust or in its shadow is still a personal decision that each of us makes for ourselves.

Flavor, 2020
Oil on canvas
mounted on wood
63X63

30

Daring to Dream

The Story of the Kibbutz

Doron Wilfand

Every time I find myself at that sharp decline toward the Sea of Galilee, when the dark stretch of green surrounding the sparkling blue of the water becomes visible to the eye, my heart is flooded by a sensation of coming home, to a home that is no longer there but remains deep in my memory.

About twenty-seven miles away is the kibbutz where I grew up – Kibbutz Ein Hashofet. Two images instantly come to mind: it's right before Passover, and eighteen first-grade children are shaking with excitement, wearing white and bending over in a field of wheat. The last rays of delicate sunlight caress and color the green and golden in a soft light. When they hear the first notes from the trumpet, they step out together from among the stalks, holding hands and dancing with the harvesters.

The second image is of a little girl with blonde hair who ran away from the house where the children slept, standing opposite her parents' room in a two-story building, crying silently. She doesn't dare cross paths with the huge dog blocking the entrance so that she can hug her parents, who are already asleep.

These images encapsulate the constant tension that existed in the unique, ambitious human creation called the kibbutz, the cooperative agricultural communities that were unique to Israel and played a central role in realizing the Zionist dream. The tension was between the almost-total togetherness that was required in order to create a home that is also a way of life, and the danger that this togetherness would erase and crush the individual.

The girl, who was my sister Yael, and the boy, who was me, didn't know then that here, on the west bank of the Sea of Galilee, between 1908 and the thirties, within a radius of just over a mile, the triangle that shaped the future state, Israeli society until the eighties, and the fate of the kibbutzim, perhaps more than any other source, was created.

Almost all of the central figures of the Second and Third Aliyah passed through the gates of the agricultural training farm at Kinneret Courtyard. Together, they transformed a dream which seemed completely disconnected from reality into institutions such as the Haganah (the main paramilitary organization of the Jewish population between 1920 and 1948), the kibbutz movement, and the Histadrut (Israel's national trade union center). This was also the site from where eleven women and men set out to cultivate a plot of land called Umm Juni where they shared whatever meager means they had and founded Degania, the first collaborative group, which was the example and inspiration for what would be called a "kibbutz" twelve years later. Above them, in the eagle's nest of Bitania Illit overlooking the Sea of Galilee, twenty-four of the first immigrants of Hashomer Hatzair gathered together. They were even more radical in their attempt to achieve cooperation and intimacy, while erasing their Jewish Diaspora past and blurring the borders that separate people from each other.

At its essence, the kibbutz was an attempt to bridge between a series of values that are almost impossible to fuse. It was a voluntary society, but after a person joined it, they almost completely lost their ability to make personal choices. It believed in the sanctity of physical agricultural labor but also wanted these cultivators of the soil to love and be familiar with poetry, art, and philosophy. It attempted to create a renewed connection between the Jewish people and their land, while almost completely erasing its heritage and the Jewish culture that was created in the Diaspora, from where the founders had come. The members espoused peace and fraternity between nations, while many of the kibbutzim were founded on the ruins of Palestinian villages and raised generations of fighters to volunteer to serve in the most elite IDF units. This was a rebellion that was meant to be pursued not only by the founding generation, but also by its children and grandchildren. At their highest point, the kibbutzim succeeded in achieving synthesis, at least partially, between the contrasting points, but in most cases, time, as well as ideological and economic crises, dissolved the stitches holding it all together, to the point that the classic kibbutz collapsed.

Despite the many differences between the various kibbutzim, it is possible to name a few foundations upon which most of them were built. First, almost all of the kibbutzim believed in utopian socialism, which, in contrast with Marxism, did not strive for change via violent revolutions, coercion, and the use of force, but rather by creating communities that would serve as a perfect example of a model society based on sharing and equality that the rest of the residents of the country, and later the entire world, would adopt as a way of life.

The kibbutzim operated according to the principle that every person contributes according to their ability and receives according to their needs. For example, the man who created, established, and managed the factory which brought in millions for the kibbutz over the years, but who only had two children, received a lower monthly stipend than his neighbor, who washed the dishes in the dining room (and wasn't so good at it either) but who had six children. The difficulty lay in the fact that the abilities and needs of each individual member were determined by all of the kibbutz members together. As a result, the lofty principles of cooperation and equality often turned into a petty, calculated verdict regarding all aspects of one's life, such as the fateful decision regarding how much toilet paper the members needed every month, what to study in university, or whether spouses of the members who weren't suited to a collaborative lifestyle would be allowed to stay on the kibbutz.

Giving up some of your freedom to choose your occupation or what to spend your bit of personal money on, which was always challenging, became unbearably difficult when many of the second-generation members of the kibbutz, who were born into the dream of the founding generation and hadn't chosen it for themselves, became the leaders of the kibbutz. It is much harder to give up on your personal and professional aspirations for a dream that isn't yours, all while your friends from the army and from school who aren't members of a kibbutz are living comfortable and even wealthy lifestyles, managing some of the largest businesses in the country without needing to give up anything on behalf of the greater good.

Another fundamental principle was labor, not just as a means of making a living, but as the essence and center of life. Many of my childhood and adolescent memories are connected to working: in the winter of 1978, in second grade, in the pouring rain, I remember dipping moldy bread into green water to feed the ducks in the children's farm, which was a little zoo for the children of the kibbutz. My hands are freezing, and I am shaking from the cold, but Iris tells us funny stories and Chagit occasionally sings, and we're together. I remember the summer vacation of eighth grade, walking around with yellow, forty-pound spray tanks on my back, their thin straps digging into my shoulders. Standing between the long, scorching rows of the patch, with the spray tank on my back, everything around me was silent aside from the humming of all sorts of bugs that I couldn't identify. My thoughts and feelings skipped from the beauty of the sunrise over our mountain, which was in fact a flat hill that wasn't that tall, to a sense of longing for our house and friends in Chicago.

The centrality of labor in kibbutz life was one of the reasons for the exceptional success of its agriculture, and afterward, of the kibbutz industries and the survival of kibbutzim under the most difficult conditions. On the other hand, this veneration of physical labor also took a serious toll on people who left advanced studies or a job that they loved in favor of the needs of the kibbutz. At Ein Hashofet, there was an older Holocaust survivor who was completely bald and a bit hunchbacked. He would set the tables in utter silence: napkins, salt and pepper, small dishes for garbage, and the sugar. He organized it all symmetrically, perfectly, and the tables were all identical. As children, although we saw him in the dining room every day, we didn't know his name and barely noticed his presence. Only years later, when a friend from a different kibbutz struck up a conversation with him, did I discover that he was a genius in physics and mathematics, who could also analyze works by Dostoevsky and Tolstoy.

Although most of the kibbutzim supported coexistence and peace, and the need to give up parts of the land of Israel on behalf of these principles, a love of the homeland and the need to protect it at all costs were a central part of the kibbutz ethos. From a very young age, we knew the heroic legacy of Shalom Cholawski, a partisan, by heart. We knew about Shimon Avidan, who strangled Nazi officers with his bare hands while serving in the German division of the Palmach, and then founded the Givati Brigade, which is named after him, during the War of Independence. We heard from Assaf Ziv and Menachem Shiloni, who served in the Paratroopers Brigade, a detailed description of the battles in Jerusalem's Old City during the Six-Day War.

We retold the story of how Dan Avidan was taken captive and Elisha Shapira was wounded in the Yom Kippur War. During every trip to the Golan Heights or the Negev, with heavy backpacks on our backs, after climbing up another mountain, we would imagine that we were Palmach fighters, or in one of the elite units, and recall the relevant battle stories. For me, the strongest connection I felt to these heroic stories was actually evoked by memorial and war songs which I always associate with walks with my father, the two of us walking down the dark path on Saturday night on the way to the children's house. My small hand grasps his big one, and we sing together.

Being completely prepared to give your all to protect the country meshed well with the fact that Ben-Gurion created the future borders of the state through the kibbutzim, leading to an exceptional percentage of kibbutz members who served in the Paratroopers Brigade, the IAF flight course, the elite Shayetet navy unit, Sayeret Matkal (elite reconnaissance unit), and as generals and chiefs of staff. However, the glorification of military service and the willingness to use force did not always mesh with the ideal of basing human relationships on the utopian philosophy of Buber, Landauer, and Fromm, who espoused fraternity between nations and pacifism. In addition, most of those who chose military careers found it difficult to incorporate with the kibbutz lifestyle and ended up leaving the kibbutz.

The most radical aspect of kibbutz life was education, especially the communal sleeping arrangements. It is unclear whether this sleeping arrangement started out of a need to protect the first babies of the kibbutzim in the Jordan and Jezreel Valleys from malaria and the terrible heat by putting them all in the best living quarters, to be cared for by the most skilled women. Or perhaps, it was borne out of the belief that growing up in the cooperative, equal environment of the children's house would create the ideal kibbutz member. Regardless of the reason, for over sixty years, this method was applied in the vast majority of kibbutzim.

In some kibbutzim, the communal sleeping arrangements began the moment that a new mother came home from the hospital, when she was met by the caregivers of the babies' house at the entrance. With us, they waited until the age of three weeks, and then I was moved to the babies' house, where there were always two caregivers on staff who, until the baby reached a certain age, would run to wake up the mother every time the baby woke up and wanted to nurse. At a slightly older age, we moved up to nursery and kindergarten. Until two in the afternoon, we would play, work, or study, and at four, after the midday rest time and shower, we would put on our nicer clothes and go to our parents' house, where we would stay until seven. Then we would return to the children's house for bedtime. From the age of four, we were alone at night, with an intercom on the wall that was called the "babysitter." We could cry into it if we woke up from a bad dream or if one of the children couldn't fall asleep. Within a few minutes, one of the women would come from the nearby babies' house.

My happiest, funniest, and saddest childhood memories are bound to the communal sleeping arrangements. The evening ritual in our room when I was in second and third grade was that each child in turn would tell a story to the others until we all fell asleep. I also remember sneaking out together at night to listen to broadcasts of basketball games on the radio, to watch movies that were playing in the hall for the adults, and especially to peek at the Purim parties. One of the most vivid memories is from kindergarten, when Yochai woke up Zohar and me to look at a giant in the window; to this day, it has never been determined whether it was a tree shaking in the wind or a real giant.

Beginning in seventh grade, we moved to a school that served four kibbutzim, where we learned, slept, and managed our lives with almost complete independence, which included organizing and guiding our hikes, cultural events, and ideological and political seminar days. From the days at that school, I remember red-orange sunsets from the summits of the Negev and Eilat mountains, followed by nighttime conversations during which we discussed anything and everything next to the bonfire. Hitchhiking all over the country to reach parties at the Kinneret and at other schools. Night time conversations at the beach, when the wind is blowing and the water is dark, holding hands and jumping in. The warm sea water that seems to caress, as it touches the body and raises small sparks of soft, broken light. This is the special light of the Mediterranean Sea, not too strong, not blinding, not actually real. A second goes by, it passes, then returns.

There are also sad memories, of quiet suppressed sobs so that no one would notice. The feeling of not knowing whether to approach, try to calm, hug, or maybe call the adult in charge for the night. The grunting and heavy breaths of the asthmatic children, and the fear of a sudden asthma attack. The deep sadness of Saturday night, when we would come back from a wonderful Shabbat with our grandparents in Kibbutz Ein Dor, realizing that we wouldn't be sleeping with our parents again tonight, but rather in the children's house.

Many years later, I am in Bitania standing with a group of students from all over the world and attempting to summarize everything that I feel about the kibbutz into just a few minutes. How do you bind together all of the hopes for a different world, for a better humanity, even if only slightly better, some of which were realized? The very central role that they played in establishing the state and in its existence, in reviving the Hebrew language; the courage to be happy. How do you reconcile the loud, breathing green landscape – which unravels and connects the threads that run deep like drops of water seeping into the ground – with the mundanity and tediousness of our daily routine and surroundings? How do you mend the schism between the passion of the kibbutz dream with the reality that some kibbutz members became disillusioned and alienated by this very dream?

The dream was not burst in a sweeping tragedy of blood, screams, and destruction; it gradually decomposed, dissolved in a barely noticeable way, slowly slipping off of the foundations that were never fully entrenched.

Those foundations – built upon truly lofty principles such as equality and sharing, practical Zionism of cultivating the land through agriculture, shared living and education, and the renewal of the Hebrew language – also led to phenomena such as a small hand abandoned in the dark, even before falling asleep, BBQ bonfires on Yom Kippur, productions of holiday-ceremonies and festivities filled with jokes and riddles, beautiful songs and a lot of content, but with barely any true joy or tradition.

In the end, the economic crisis of the eighties merged with the ideological crisis of the second generation, that had to continue what they had not chosen: the dream of the founders, who had left everything behind or had run toward something that did not yet exist. The second generation didn't know how to create this sacred secularism. The sanctity dissipated and with it, over the years, went the sense of belonging and desire to continue on the long road toward the dream of getting up each morning to build a new world of refined humanity within the ongoing reality of the old world.

Yet it has not all disappeared. Aside from the cultural, social, technological, and economic industries that still exist, there are about thirty cooperative country-style kibbutzim, as well as hundreds of kibbutz-like communities in development towns, underprivileged neighborhoods, and within privatized kibbutzim, who believe that the old kibbutz failed because its level of sharing and equality was not sufficient. Due to the geographic distance from the large concentrations of the population and the exaggerated focus on creating an ideal cooperative society – the kibbutz itself lost its central role in Israeli society. Therefore, these cooperative communities focus on education and social activism in places where the biggest challenges exist today. Even if it sometimes seems that these groups are too radical in their attitudes toward higher education, sharing, and even the nature of the family unit, it is possible that like the young dreamers of those days, on the shores of the Sea of Galilee, they are creating the basis for a new kibbutz, and perhaps even for a more just, equal Israeli society.

31

From Prophets to Profits

A Changed Vision

Jeremy Aron

I often ask people who visit Israel for the first time what they expected to see, hear, feel, and discover on their trip. The answers and expectations vary, but amongst the assortment of responses, they are all almost certainly going to mention "ancient" places and "religious" people.

I have clear recollections of my family vacations to Israel during the eighties. The country looked very different back then (albeit not that long ago!). I remember the selection at the neighborhood *makolet* (mini-mart) was very limited, certainly in comparison to the supermarkets "back home" in Manchester, England, so my parents would stuff "luxuries" into their suitcases, gifts for their Israeli friends, such as Palmolive creamy soap bars and tubes of Colgate toothpaste.

I also remember traveling around the country on public transportation and thinking that there was no experience that could be more Israeli. Spontaneous conversations with random individuals on the bus and train. In my mind, these interactions were a product of the historic relationship of our people – a deep feeling of common unity and camaraderie embedded in our collective Jewish consciousness. I guess it fed into my own image of Israel being a congregation of my extended family following centuries of being apart. This picture in my head was a utopian fantasy of "ideological perfection." For me, the State of Israel exhibited the realization of the return of *Am Yisrael* (literally "The People of Israel") to their ancestral homeland, and the successful fulfillment of the Zionist dream and biblical prophecy. I moved to Israel because I wanted to be a part of fashioning a country that would embody Isaiah's "light unto the nations."

Many trips to Israel start in Tel Aviv, "the city that never sleeps," where your first impressions might feature beaches with bronzed scantily-clad people, joggers running by the sea, muscular athletes aggressively exchanging a bat and ball, and couples relaxing on the sand or sipping drinks at a beachside coffee shop. Was this what you expected to see? It's not exactly ancient or religious!

Let's swiftly transport you to Jaffa, one of the oldest seaports in the world. The call to prayer of the muezzin in the mosque echoes across the ancient stones, and the church bells toll religiously every hour. Now you have seen a different side of Israel, we can begin to unravel more layers of this country.

Prophets

The view from Jaffa could be seen as a microcosm of the land and State of Israel. From the crest of the hill, under the Statue of Faith, we can gaze down onto the Church of St. Peter and the minarets of the mosques, Andromeda's Rocks, and the sky-scraping towers of Tel Aviv. Culturally, religiously, historically, and emotionally, the story of this region is laid out in front of you. These views represent the three monotheistic faiths that lay a historical and spiritual claim to the immediate region, in contrast with the appeal of Hellenism as an alternative temptation. Having said that, throughout two millennia of historical episodes, bloody conquests, and religious wrangling that this land has witnessed and endured, it has constantly been central to Jewish collective memory.

The Jaffa marina was a major entry and exit point to the land of Israel. It is from here that according to the Bible the prophet Jonah set sail before being swallowed by a big fish, and it is also the arrival point for the cedars of Lebanon that were then transported to Jerusalem to build Solomon's Temple. Throughout history, the port continued to be used by pilgrims, travelers, and conquerors. Eventually, by the nineteenth century, this is where many immigrants disembarked their boats, and subsequently chose to settle. Jewish immigration to Israel through this port was, simply put, a fulfilment of a biblical, rabbinical, and Zionist prophecy. In fact, it could be said that this port is the primary witness of the migration influx over the centuries – the "ingathering of the exiles."

Throughout the generations, the return to Zion has been foretold by biblical figures such as Isaiah, Ezekiel, and Jeremiah, as well as Jewish philosophers, pensive poets, and committed ideologues, all who refused to give up on dreams of Jewish destiny.

In 1906, Zionist activist, architect, and city planner Akiva Aryeh Weiss, who became known as the primary founder of Tel Aviv, declared it in his manifesto that just as New York is the "gateway to America," so, in time, they would build the "New York of the land of Israel." As the twentieth century began, so did the vision of building "the first Hebrew city in two thousand years" – Tel Aviv.

Profits

Looking to the north from Jaffa, one can see the construction cranes of the city. Positioned amid the tower blocks is the Tel Aviv Stock Exchange, sitting in close proximity to what was once the house of Akiva Aryeh Weiss. I have seen considerable development and change since I packed up my life and moved to the Promised Land. In the early twenty-first century, Israel has proven itself to be a heavyweight in the export of knowledge. The economy is strong and the currency is stable. Tel Aviv emanates an air of wealth and prosperity.

Having become a substantial contributor to the international food revolution, with new fancy restaurants and chef boutiques opening almost every week, Tel Aviv has become a popular travel destination. The TLV Fashion Mall implies the city's ostentatious intentions for the future. Grander five-star hotels are opening, luxury apartment buildings are developing, and the cost of living is rapidly accelerating to challenge that of London, Paris, and New York.

Tel Aviv has put Israel on the map of the corporate, fresh, cosmopolitan West. Israelis ambitiously drive global technological advancement. It's an amazing achievement. Nevertheless, I still affectionately remember a simpler Israel, when the emphasis was placed heavily on all those emotions and values I had experienced as a child on those Egged (Israel's main public transportation company) bus journeys. If not for the Hebrew on road signs, shop fronts, and even graffiti, you can almost forget today that you're in Israel and not some European city.

The daily hustle and bustle races past me, each person fixated on their own little bubble. Dri-fit clad speedwalkers purposefully march past in step to their music, determined to get to the juice bar at the end of their exercise before their workday begins. An abundance of lavish European V8 engines chokes the transport system, hoping to be rescued by the impending Chinese-built tram network. I, meanwhile, negotiate the sidewalks, precariously avoiding construction sites and machinery, as electric bicycles hurtle along, perilously veering around pedestrians that gallingly slow them down.

Prophets or Profits?

Back to our hill in Jaffa, we are left questioning: Which way should we face?

On a clear day, if you look to the East, to the hills in the distance, you can see the ancient land of the Bible – the hills of Judea and Samaria. Around thirty-five miles away, as the crow flies, is the Temple Mount in Jerusalem. Jews the world over pray in this direction three times a day. Christians and Muslims flock to their holy sites. It is the central destination of the spiritually and religiously offered prophesies.

Meanwhile, the beach-goers relaxing on the sands below you, nonchalantly worshiping the sun, are facing the Mediterranean Sea. They're looking to the West, fantasizing about making their fortune and spending their future days surfing the waves. They sit with their backs to Jerusalem. Across the sea, in the far distance ahead of them, are the popstars, sports idols, fashion labels, and fast-food chains of Europe and North America.

Tel Aviv-Jaffa is where East and West grapple; the crucible of monotheism challenged by the enticement of hedonism; Judaism, Christianity, Islam, and paganism jostle for our attention, and all this presented through this magnificent vista.

Israel continues to struggle between the East and the West, the old and the new, the religious and the secular. Has the prophecy of the return to Zion and the ingathering of the exiles been completed, thus reaching the finishing-line for Zionism?

Alternatively, has there been a change in ideological direction, in that the vision of biblical prophets has been calculatedly converted to focus on developing a shrine for making huge financial profits?

Hayim Nahman Bialik, the famed Hebrew poet, stated during the twenties that the Jews would know that their dream of a nation state had been fulfilled when there were Jewish prostitutes, Jewish thieves, and a Jewish police force. As a dedicated and staunch Zionist, is Bialik suggesting that the essential contributions to the Jewish national enterprise would be with the intention to create a "normal" country?

Maybe the answer is in the name of the city in which we are standing. Tel Aviv symbolizes both ancient legacy and rebirth. A "Tel" is a manufactured hill that bygone civilizations once inhabited. Through its layers, it tells life stories of former inhabitants from a period long before the Zionist era. "Aviv" is the season of spring, the season of renewal. It's about redeveloping anew for the future generations. Perhaps it doesn't need to be either/or, as this fusion of the old and the new is simply presenting a microcosm of a land and state where prophets and profits can live out their destinies in parallel.

Epilogue

We Parted, Then Met Again

Ya'acov Fried

It's Saturday afternoon, a Jerusalem summer in the sixties. I'm eleven years old, and my family is gathered on the porch at my grandparents' home in Jerusalem's Meah Shearim neighborhood. This is an ultra-Orthodox neighborhood that has retained the lifestyle and atmosphere of a nineteenth-century Eastern European Jewish town. Yeshivas, study halls, Hassidim, Litvaks, and lives that revolve entirely around observance of the commandments. A lively, loving conversation is underway on the porch between my grandfather, grandmother, mother, and father. I, the curious child, listen attentively to the adults' conversation as they reminisce and share their opinions and thoughts.

I am captivated by the conversation, as if it were one of the films that my mother often took me to see. I listen as if it was one of the stories about the exodus from Egypt, or the fall of the walls of Jericho, or the war between David and Goliath, which my father often told me.

Next to the porch is a huge fig tree heavy with ripe fruit. My grandfather stretches a long arm toward the tree and picks a large fig. He splits it into two, bites into one half, and hands me the other. My grandmother chastises him, saying, "It's the holy Shabbat today and you, aside from desecrating it, are showing the child a bad example."

My grandfather replies, "He should enjoy the taste of the fig, and for me, you've known this since the day we met, there is no connection between picking the fig on Shabbat and the Jewish soul of our grandson." He doesn't relent and continues, "The most important thing is for him to be familiar with the Seven Species." My mother intervenes and says, "Please stop confusing the child with so many conflicting opinions." My father hurries to join the conversation and adds, "The most important thing is for the child to remember the words of the Zionist thinker Ahad Ha'am: 'More than the Jews kept the Shabbat – the Shabbat kept them.'"

Throughout my childhood, ethical and ideological conversations like this one were part of the regular ritual at my grandparents' house, where we celebrated Shabbat and Jewish holidays together. Years later, I had similar conversations as part of my educational work in North America with Jewish communities and synagogues of different affiliations. In response to their attempts to understand my complex Jewish identity, that of my family, and of Israelis in general, I would often explain: "Israel, the Jewish state, is a young state of immigrants. In order to understand our complex Jewish identity, and how different it is to the Jewish identity in North America, it is important that you hear as many personal stories from Israelis as possible. The components of our identity, as Israeli Jews, is so different than yours, and yet our identities are so intertwined and connected."

I continued, "I chose to pursue educational work in the Jewish world out of a sense of common destiny. The way I see it, we all left Egypt together, we were all at Mount Sinai, we all went into exile together. At some point, a few generations ago, our grandparents or their parents made the decision to immigrate from Europe to the United States, to other countries, or to Israel. In order to understand what is going on between us today, where the secret of Jewish partnership lies, and the source of the feeling that we are one family, I think it is important to check what happened to our families over the past generations, and then we'll also ask what is going on today in our common space."

In the spirit of "doing as I say," I will share with you my colorful family. I will share the conversations, the "dramas" between my ultra-Orthodox grandmother, my Bundist (secular-socialist) grandfather, my traditional father, and my secular mother. I will tell you about the curious child who was captivated by the conversations of the adults, attempting to decipher and understand what each of them believed. I will add that I never got over this childhood passion of mine – trying to understand the root of the similarities and differences between the members of my nuclear family and the members of the entire Jewish tribe.

To illustrate, I will go back to my grandparents and share how they immigrated to Palestine in the midst of the third wave of immigration in 1923, from Bialystok, Poland. They moved to Palestine due to a lack of political and social security in their country rather than for Zionist reasons. When I was a child, my grandfather would often sit me on a chair and rock me back and forth meditatively. He told me the story of his family before they reached Palestine, when it was still under the British Mandate. His younger brother was killed in a pogrom at the beginning of World War I, and his older brother immigrated to Milwaukee, in the United States. His brother integrated into the local community, taught and wrote for a Yiddish newspaper, and I later learned that he and his family lost all connection to the rest of the family and the Jewish tribe. My grandfather's family broke assimilation records during the first and second generations after their immigration.

For hours, I would listen to the stories of my grandfather's journeys as a glove merchant, and how he became a full-fledged Bund enthusiast. He told me that in Russia, he was an active member of the Bund, a Jewish movement that called for justice, social and economic equality, and sought political rights for Jews, as individuals and also as a national minority on European soil.

My grandfather was dedicated to Yiddish culture his whole life. He spoke Yiddish with those around him and taught me the intricacies of the language. He played me songs in the unfamiliar tongue. I never forgot the sentence that he would say every time he handed me a piece of chocolate, "Yiddish is the spearhead of our culture, and it needs to stay that way." He told countless stories from World War I and would always say that "we should continue to fight for worldwide socialism." I later realized that he would have preferred to continue to live in Europe as a Jew, as part of the socialist world, but my grandmother's dominant personality was what motivated the family's decision to immigrate. As an adolescent, I understood that while my grandfather was disappointed at what happened in the socialist world, and the direction in which it had been led by communism, socialism deeply remained part of his values.

In contrast, my grandmother – a born leader who was free of ideological ties – worked on obtaining immigration visas to both the United States and Palestine simultaneously. "I worked on all fronts so that we could escape the anti-Semitism in Europe, where we would never be accepted as members of a different religion," I remember her saying. My grandmother's brothers and sister, their spouses, and their children, had immigrated to the United States a year earlier and joined the Orthodox and ultra-Orthodox communities in New York and Philadelphia. A month before the visa to the United States arrived, they received the "certificates" from the British Mandate government, allowing them to immigrant to Palestine/the land of Israel.

My grandmother was not ideologically Zionist; she simply wanted a "safe place" to raise her young children, where she could promise them a free, safe Jewish life. She was a very religious woman who carefully observed all of the commandments. In today's world, she would be considered ultra-Orthodox (in the Litvak sect). I don't remember her ever preaching to her children to follow her religious lifestyle. She mainly served as an example through her own actions. She was pleasant and respected the worldview of her husband, despite the different lifestyle and significant discrepancy between their worldviews. Both my grandmother and grandfather came from culturally open and pluralistic backgrounds that allowed the two to cross paths and marry – despite their religious differences.

To support the family, my grandmother made wigs. Her small workshop was in their house, and I remember the ultra-Orthodox women who would come to try on the wigs she had made for them. I remember her asking my grandfather, "Please put a kippah on your head when they come, to respect them." He obliged. Another request that she made of him was, "Please go to synagogue on Friday, for me. Judaism without practical observance of the commandments will not last, and you won't have anything to pass on to the next generation." My grandfather obliged this request as well, which served as a good excuse for him to take me with him on a long walk.

Friday night in Meah Shearim, everyone is rushing to the synagogue to pray, wearing their best Shabbat clothes, their shtreimels crowning their heads. We exited the neighborhood, walked a few hundred meters, and ascended Strauss Street, passing by a local synagogue. Walking with my grandfather, we never entered this synagogue, or any other synagogue for that matter. My grandfather, who liked the songs in the prayer service, convinced me to stand for a few minutes outside of the synagogue so that we could listen to the cantor and the congregation singing together, from the street. After that musical interlude on our trip, he took me to the real attraction. Edison Theater, Jerusalem's first movie theater, named after one of the inventors of cinema – Thomas Edison.

We often took this walk to the announcement boards at the front of this enchanting theater. I remember how we would stand in awe and look at all of the different pictures of the movies currently being shown and those that would be coming to the theater soon.

My grandfather would tell me, at length and with endless patience, all of the plotlines of the different movies being shown, as he visited the theater every week. He shared the names of the actors that appeared on the silver screen, as well as his own thoughts and insights about each film. A few times, he even took me with him to the cinema. I remember the first time I saw Paul Newman, in *Exodus*, which tells the story of the immigrant ship SS Exodus and the story of the War of Independence. I remember my grandfather saying, "We could have continued to be Jews in Europe. While socialism was a disappointment after communism mercilessly took over, I still believe that as Jews, the best and most appropriate solution for our existence didn't need to be in the State of Israel. Look how much suffering we went through during this struggle for illegal immigration and in the War of Independence."

I also remember the advertisements on the announcement board for the film, *Ben Hur*, the image of Jesus, which I encountered for the first time, and my grandfather's comment on these images: "Religions and religious zealousness is the mother of all sin." I especially remember the announcements advertising the upcoming performance of the pair of Jewish comics from the United States, Dzigan and Shumacher. I never saw my grandfather so excited. For years, I heard him quoting their comedy routines, which were in Yiddish, of course – the light of his life.

I distinctly remember the mantra that he would constantly repeat to me, "We must protect Yiddish culture and Jewish culture. Socialism hasn't died, and it will prove itself again one day." As a socialist, he made sure to add, "Forget about God, Yankele; he's not in the picture. Being a Jew has nothing to do with God. Judaism means being a member of the Jewish culture," he would conclude.

But in their home, my grandmother would lead me to the end of the long hallway, far from his room, and whisper, "Without observing the commandments, there is no Jewish existence." She encouraged me to make the blessing over bread, to recite the Shema before I went to sleep, and of course, to make sure to cover my head.

A few steps away from the enchanting Edison Theater, there was an orphanage and the Anglican School, planned by the architect Conrad Schick. My mother, the daughter of a Bundist and an Orthodox mother, studied in a religious school. But her dreams centered around what was happening in the missionary school. I remember how much she admired the design and aesthetics of the impressive building, which looked like an English castle to her, and the cleanliness and order of the school. She appreciated the opportunity that it gave its students to study English and French from a young age, to learn math and science, to study poems in foreign languages, and to become a "worldly person," as she put it.

I later met one of her friends, a graduate of the Anglican School, and then I understood what my mother had meant when she said, "The Anglican School enabled its students to stop living in the old, fossilized world and break the boundaries to the modern world." She also tried to keep in touch with her cousins in the United States, but with no success. I remember her describing to me the vast differences that developed between the ultra-Orthodox world of her cousins and the free world in which she had chosen to live.

My father integrated into this world when he married my mother, and he built his own complex world. He was born in Romania, the son of an ultra-Orthodox family who were anti-Zionists and belonged to the Hassidic sect of Vizhnitz. The family lived a separate life within the Jewish town, disconnected from their non-Jewish surroundings. Some of the family immigrated to Argentina and to Chile prior to World War II. There, the family abandoned their ultra-Orthodox lifestyle and joined the modern traditional communities. In my childhood, my father shared with me the saga that occurred in his family when they sat shiva (mourned) for his older sister, who immigrated to Israel for Zionist reasons and decided to "stop waiting for the Messiah."

I will never forget the sentence that my father often repeated: "The Zionist movement is a secular movement at its core. It puts an end to the apathetic world in which you aren't required to do anything in order to change the painful reality of Jewish life replete with suffering. Zionism means taking your fate into your own hands and working to find a national solution for the Jewish people, just like the French have a solution in France."

Years later, almost the entire family perished in the Holocaust, and my father, who survived, immigrated to Israel with his sister. Once he immigrated, my father removed his ultra-Orthodox garb, cut off his sidelocks, joined the religious brigade of the Haganah and partially continued to observe the commandments with great openness. Visiting the United States with him, I introduced him to the Conservative and Reform movements. It wasn't an easy experience for him. The equality between men and women during the prayer services and driving to synagogue by car seemed foreign to him. He was impressed, however, that in North America, there is separation of church and state, and that there are an infinite number of ways to express one's Jewish identity.

I remember our long conversations about the fact that, in contrast with Israel, the Rabbinate does not have a monolithic hold over Jewish life, and because religion and state are separate, different sects can develop. This increases the sense of personal responsibility and involvement in a diverse range of Jewish lifestyles, not just among Jews who observe the 613 commandments. Over the years, I often wondered that if in Israel, in the fifties and sixties, there were traditional or Reform Jewish movements, like those that developed in the United States, my father would probably have felt less torn and more "whole."

A few weeks before my bar mitzvah, my father told my grandfather, "I know that on Fridays, when we come to your house, you don't take the boy to synagogue, but rather to the movie announcement board. Tomorrow on Shabbat, I will take my son to my synagogue, so that he can understand the chain of Jewish generations. Both things are important to the child – the movies that you take him to and entering the walls of the synagogue." He sarcastically added, "It's my obligation as a father to open the Jewish bookcase to him." He didn't relent, saying, "There are bookcases in the center of your home and in the center of our home. As an immigrant to Israel, who arrived just over twenty years ago, I must improve my Hebrew, so that new works in Hebrew will also be part of my bookcase. In yours, the Gemara and the Mishnah are on the shelf collecting dust, while Sholem Aleichem and I. L. Peretz in Yiddish are the only books that don't collect dust. I hope that for my children, *all* of the Jewish books will be in use, including modern Israeli literature in Hebrew, the language in which I try to improve every day…"

Because my father was not observant in all of the commandments, he would say to my grandmother, "I will continue to attend synagogue, despite the accounting that I have with God after the Holocaust. That's my internal accounting. I will continue to attend synagogue so that my children will feel that they belong to the Jewish nation. Upholding our traditions is a central element in the existence of our nation. Without Hebrew, prayer, studying the Jewish sources, and creating a new Israeli culture that incorporates and is rooted in Jewish culture, there will be no foundation for a state with a Jewish character."

My father occasionally took me to pray with the Hassidim in the shtiebels (very small synagogues) in Meah Shearim, hugging me and whispering in my ear, "Prayer is a song from the heart, not from the head. Prayer and song are a soul connection to your Jewish essence, and a connection to every Jew in the world." If he were alive today, I would tell him – it's a pity that you were unable to see how prayer and song have become the heart of Jewish identity even in the pluralist communities of North America, South America, and many communities worldwide. In order to feel that soul connection, an infinite number of vibrant, relevant opportunities have been created around the world, in contrast with the reality in Israel.

The year that my father passed away, I kept one central mourning custom in his memory: I attended synagogue every Friday night, though I don't usually pray, in order to recite the Kaddish prayer for him. During the year, on my trips through Israel and the world, I found my way to prayer services on Friday night at the Reform synagogue Kol Haneshama in Jerusalem, the traditional Kehillat Sinai synagogue in Tel Aviv, the Stephen Wise Free Synagogue in New York, the Conservative synagogue Park Avenue in New York, the Rambam synagogue in Maadi, Cairo, the Slat Al Azama Synagogue in Marrakesh, and Altneuschul in Prague.

In all of them, there was singing from the heart.

In this travel guide, the authors shared insights that they collected on their journeys within Israeli society, with all of its complexities. We did this in order to provide you, the future tourist, a window to see alternative perspectives on your visit, including the perspectives of the authors, who opened their hearts to you.

On this journey, you will meet a diverse country. Every trip to every location in the world invites an encounter with moving landscapes, a range of cultural experiences, and perhaps the chance at spiritual depth. We, the writers, believe that in Israel, we have the gift of a unique mixture of all of these elements. The magic that can happen is an opportunity for personal and internal discovery on intellectual, emotional, and hopefully spiritual dimensions.

Because Israel is the Holy Land, I believe that it has a unique, deeply rooted cultural "genetic" code, carried by every person that comes from a Western culture, even if they do not have religious tendencies. This is expressed by the historical events that took place in this half of the world, and in the holy texts to the three religions, especially Judaism and Christianity, which gave rise to Western culture. In addition, the huge, unique human mosaic of people who have gathered here from every corner of the world provides an opportunity to glean relevant insights into our world as we know it today.

My hope is that this book will help arouse the intellect and emotions, facilitate study, and sometimes even dissolve prejudices or preconceptions, in order to open the heart and mind to new insights. The authors of this book believe in the Jewish perception that the spirit is not a separate entity from the mind and emotion, and every deep learning experience touches the spirit and is changed by it.

From my own experiences, I would like to share two pieces of advice that will help turn your trip into a chance for discovery. The first – try to talk with older members of your family and hear where they lived before they came to North America. Where did they come from? What was their lifestyle like before they came? What motivated them to immigrate? How did they deal with the cultural and religious openness in the United States?

My second tip – try to create as many opportunities as possible for personal encounters. These are opportunities for challenging contact with people whose identities are different and similar to yours. Try to find what you both share, and what makes you feel that you belong to the same nation. Try to understand the Israelis that you meet, and you may even end up with a deeper understanding of yourself.

Remember! You could have been me, and I could have been you, had our families made a different decision prior to their immigration from Europe. In this spirit, I believe that you may discover a new family. There's no "they" – there is "you," there is "me," and there is "us."

Scent of the Field, 2019
Oil on canvas
mounted on wood
55X65

Our Contributors

Ya'acov Fried

Ya'acov Fried became a resident of Jaffa in the last decade, after being a Jerusalemite all his life. A graduate of Hebrew University, Ya'acov devoted his career to informal Jewish education in the following roles: educational officer in the IDF (reserves), director of Melitz Institute in Jerusalem (a seminar center for Israeli Jewish identity), senior analyst at the Van Leer Institute (leading Israeli thinktank), community shliach (emissary) in the Midwest.

Ya'acov's immersion in the North American Jewish community – together with his involvement in the world of culture, art, music, and consciousness studies in Israel and around the world – inspired him to become a pioneer in Jewish educational travel. Ya'acov founded Da'at Educational Expeditions, a pioneering educational travel company which creates Jewish educational journeys for north American clientele to Israel and to other destinations. With the creation of Da'at, Ya'acov has led the revolution in transforming the classic touring style to a multifaceted journey.

Ya'acov is involved in a variety of voluntary roles in nonprofit organizations that are attempting to impact Israel to be a society of social justice. He is a father of two, and a grandfather of four and a half.

Ya'acov has partnered with Gilad Peled and Yishay Shavit to create this book.

Gilad Peled

Gilad grew up on a kibbutz and served for four years as a combat offi-cer in the IDF. Gilad's home taught him that education is the best way to shape our future, which is why he has invested the last thirty years working in informal education. Since 1998, Gilad has been traveling around Israel with a wide range of groups. As a licensed tour guide, he's been teaching about the country. As a tour educator, he's explored personal experiences. Specializing in Holocaust education, Gilad has worked as a guide for Yad Vashem and leads groups on tours to Jewish Eastern Europe. For the past ten years, Gilad has worked with Jewish communities from around the world. For five years, he lived with his family in Rome, Italy, where he worked as an Israeli emissary with the Jewish community.

Gilad holds a bachelor's degree in archaeology and Jewish thought from the Hebrew University, and a master's degree in Jewish history from the University of Haifa. Gilad is married to Inbar and is a father of two.

Yishay Shavit

Yishay was born on a kibbutz in the northern part of Israel. In 2000, he moved to Jerusalem, fell in love with the city, and hasn't looked back. Yishay, a history and hiking lover, was first introduced to the world of guiding at the age of fifteen, in his youth movement. After high school, he served in a tank unit of the IDF for three years. Yishay holds a bach-elor's degree in history, focusing on Indian Jewry and contemporary Jewry. Yishay is a political and social activist who is devoted to mak-ing Israel an equal and just society for all. When not guiding, he enjoys spending time with his wife Noa and their two sons, Yotam and Assaf.

Erez Aharon

A realistic painting of the delicate metaphors of Israeli life. An olive leaf hanging by a thread. A flower with no roots attached to a wall. These are some of the identifying trademarks of the artist, Erez Aharon. A graduate of Beit Berl College and a student of Israel Hershberg, one of Israel's most accomplished artists, Erez combines in his work the concept of art as a meditative contemplation and down-to-earth art that reflects reality. Erez Aharon is definitely not a classic landscape artist but attempts to capture elements of his surroundings. The fragments of the reality that he captures in his work teach us about the big picture. His work is similar to that of an archeologist who tries to recreate an entire world from a handful of fragments. In this respect, his work is perfect for a book that deals with different perspectives on Israeli society.

Jeremy Aron

Jeremy grew up in Manchester, England. After completing his bachelor's degree in geography and sociology from Sheffield University (UK), he made aliyah in January 2002. In 2007, Jeremy became a tour educator and has since guided Jewish Federations, Reform and Conservative congregational groups, Birthright, Christian and interfaith groups, multigenerational families, teens, and adults.

Jeremy was one of the founders of a new urban kibbutz in northern Israel, where he established and coordinated a nonprofit organization bringing volunteers and professionals to work in socioeconomically deprived communities, focusing on informal education, social action, and coexistence.

Jeremy enjoys listening to and playing music. As well as being a loyal and devoted fan of Manchester United, he is an Israeli National Ultimate Frisbee Team coach and a senior coach of an international organization promoting Arab and Jewish Arab youth coexistence through sport. Jeremy lives in Herzliya with his wife, Rona, and their two boys, Lior and Mikey.

Hana Bendcowsky

Hana is Director of the Jerusalem Center for Jewish-Christian Relations at the Rossing Center for Education and Dialogue. She has a master's degree in comparative religion from Hebrew University and twenty years of practical experience in interfaith activities in Israel and abroad. She coordinates and teaches in the center's various educational programs, as well as producing educational materials, consulting, and doing advocacy work. Hana is a professional tour educator in Jerusalem, leading study tours in the Christian Quarter.

Rivka Brama

Rivka has worked as content developer at Da'at for over ten years after working for various educational organizations, such as The Israel Experience and The Nesiya Institute. Rivka was born in the UK but grew up travelling the world. During her youth and childhood Rivka lived in Israel, the United States, England, and France. Rivka is married to Oded, and they have four children. They live in Jerusalem, are very involved in local city life, and are fans of the local Hapoel basketball team.

Koren Eisner

Koren Eisner grew up in Jerusalem, and after completing his military service, lived for a while in Kibbutz Ze'elim in the Negev and then returned to Jerusalem to study and raise a family. In 2005, Koren became a licensed tour guide and joined Da'at, guiding federations, interfaith groups, families, adult tours, Christian groups, journalists, and hiking tours. His favorite place to guide is his childhood home – Jerusalem. In his guiding, Koren incorporates his knowledge of archaeology and history and challenges his travelers to ask the tough questions, analyzing narratives while appreciating the beauty and truth of the story. Koren now lives in Kibbutz Hukuk in the Galilee by Lake Kinneret, a young community dedicated to improving society through education and adapting kibbutz life to the twenty-first century. When Koren is not guiding, he dedicates as much time as possible to his family and community life.

Uri Feinberg

Uri Feinberg has been a Jewish educator for twenty-five years. Born in the United States, Uri immigrated to Israel when he was ten, grew up in Jerusalem, served in the IDF, and then traveled the world. Uri has a master's degree in contemporary Jewish studies from Hebrew University and was for many years a Jewish history teacher for North American teens in semester programs in Israel. Uri spent three years in the US with his wife and three daughters where he served as the Interim Director of Education of Temple Israel of Boston. A licensed tour guide since 1999, Uri has worked as a tour educator for a wide range of groups including synagogue, Federation, URJ, and CCAR leadership, and interfaith. He has guided Jewish heritage trips throughout

Europe and has lectured on Israel and Jewish identity across North America. Uri and his family live in the city of Modiin and are active members of their Reform congregation, YOZMA.

Michal Granot

Michal's romance with guiding started at the age of sixteen, as a guide in a youth hiking movement. During her IDF service, she helped develop and teach computer programs in Arabic that were aimed at changing Israeli children's perceptions of Arabs. She then became an officer who dealt with logistics on Mount Hermon. At age twenty-four, Michal started guiding jeep trips in the mountains of Turkey, and after guiding in several countries, she decided to get a proper guiding education in the most fascinating country she knew – Israel.

Educating people in Israel and leading adventure trips around the world became her lifestyle. Michal holds a bachelor's degree in Islam and Middle East history from Hebrew University and a master's degree in the Land of Israel from Haifa University. Michal's favorite place to guide is Masada, Herod's mountain palace, and the site of the Jewish Zealots' last stand against the Roman Legionnaires. She loves telling its story and showing how it is still relevant today. When Michal is not guiding, she enjoys life in the most fascinating city in the world, Jerusalem, and introduces her son Yonatan to the wonders of this world.

Mike Hollander

Mike Hollander grew up in Canada, where he earned a bachelor's degree in history from York University. Upon the completion of his degree, he enrolled in a master's program for Middle Eastern studies at Tel Aviv

University for overseas students. He made aliyah in 1988 to a kibbutz in the Galilee, and in 1990, Mike moved to Jerusalem, where he worked in fundraising, after which time he became a licensed tour guide in 1994. For over twenty-five years, he has worked full-time, lecturing, teaching courses to teenagers on long-term programs in Israel, as well as taking visitors of all ages around Israel. As a Jewish educator outside of Israel, Mike has led many groups on Jewish travel journeys throughout Eastern and Central Europe. He has also lectured and taught as a scholar-in-residence at Jewish communities throughout North America. He completed his master's degree in Jewish-Christian relations from the Cambridge Centre for Jewish-Christian Relations in 2008. Mike is married to Michele, and they have three children, Tal (twenty-seven), Adi (twenty-four), and Matan (twenty-one).

Muki Jankelowitz

Muki emigrated to Israel from Johannesburg, South Africa, where he was very involved in the local Jewish community. Muki holds a bachelor's degree in sociology from Wits University and an honors degree in biblical archeology from UNISA. Muki's first and only career has been Jewish education; he has filled a wide range of educational roles – from senior teacher specializing in history and leadership at the Institute for Youth Leaders from Abroad (Machon LeMadrichim) to senior educator of the JDC Buncher Community Leadership Program, training Jewish community leaders in the FSU and India.

Of all of Muki's educational experiences and work, he views guiding as the most significant. Muki is most interested in the Jewish journey of the individual, believing that working with text allows for grappling with the big questions. In addition to enjoying nature, reading, and studying Jewish text, Muki enjoys spending time with his wife, Mandy, and their two sons, Shaked and Niv.

Yona Leshets

Yona was born and raised in Haifa, where he also earned his BSc (summa cum laude) and MSc degrees in electrical engineering from the Technion – Israel Institute of Technology. For almost thirty years, Yona was fully engaged in the world of technology, serving in the 8200 intelligence unit of the IDF, and later as part of the seed team of a successful start-up company that was acquired by Intel. During his technology career, Yona filed eight patents and was honored twice by presidents of Israel for his security and technological achievements.

As of 2010, after two years of college studies, Yona channeled his passion for open fields, history, geopolitics, culture, and technology into his second career as a tour educator. He focuses on guiding tourist in Israel, and occasionally he leads groups to Greece and Japan.

Yona lives in Kohav Yair, a small suburb outside of Tel Aviv, and is married with four children and a newborn granddaughter.

Nadia Mahmood Giol

Nadia Mahmood Giol was born in the early seventies in the Galilee. As a daughter of Palestinian refugees with Israeli citizenship, Nadia encountered firsthand, from early childhood, the Israeli-Palestinian conflict. Nadia studied special education, alternative medicine, and nonviolent communication. She is the manager and chief guide of the visitor's center of Sindyanna of Galilee, a female-led nonprofit that actively promotes the concepts of "business for peace" and fair trade in Israel.

Nadia strongly believes in coexistence between Jews and Arabs and promotes the idea of nonviolent conflict solutions. She is fluent in Arabic, Hebrew, English, Spanish, and the Catalan language.

She is a happily married mother of two and lives in the northern city of Nof Hagalil near Nazareth.

Ronen Malik

Although born in South Africa while his parents were on *shlichut* (emissaries) for the Jewish Agency, Ronen Malik is a seventh-generation Jerusalemite. Following his army service in a paratrooper unit as a combat soldier, he worked as a tour guide with Egged, the national bus company. Ronen earned his bachelor's degree in engineering at the College of Engineering in Jerusalem, but ultimately chose to become a professional tour educator. Recognizing the daily dilemmas and challenges Israel is facing, Ronen encourages his travelers to ask the tough questions, showing them where history and modernity meet. Ronen is a father of two, and he lives in a small mixed religious and secular community of families next to Jerusalem. Ronen enjoys spending quality time with his family, hiking, biking, traveling, and running (he has completed five full marathons!).

Hillel Meyer

Born in Montreal ,Canada ,Hillel moved with his family to Israel as a child. After obtaining his bachelor's degree in Jewish Studies from Hebrew University, Hillel worked as an educator, both in Israel and in the US, and became a licensed tour educator in 2011. He has since guided families, federations, synagogues, Birthright groups, and inter-faith groups in Europe and Israel.

Hillel is Da'at's in-house educator and international guide. He plays a major role in the process of program and content development for all Da'at and ARZA World groups by inspecting new sites, meeting with potential speakers, and crafting customized itineraries.

Hillel lives in Tel Aviv and is a proud father to Yair and Nadav. He is also a cross-fit enthusiast and enjoys playing the piano.

Shari Robins

Shari Robins grew up in Cleveland, and during her first visit to Israel at age seventeen, decided she would make aliyah and become a tour guide. Her dream became reality when she made aliyah at age twenty-five, but she was too old to serve in the IDF, so Shari volunteered for a program to train women to become bus drivers in case of national emergency. While teaching English at Hebrew University, she studied for her tour guide license and has been guiding ever since. Shari passionately shares her love for Israel through storytelling, texts, and songs with the goal of building a Jewish connection to Israel. Shari lives in Jerusalem with her wife and two daughters, all avid hikers and foodies. Shari's oldest daughter is in the Israeli Air Force, and her younger daughter is in her senior year of high school. Shari hiked the entire six-hundred-mile Israel Trail from north to south to experience the quote from Genesis (13:17): "Walk the land, the length and breadth of it."

Nimrod Shafran

Nimrod is an example of Israel's melting pot. Born to parents who made aliyah from Romania and Iran, he grew up in a Zionist and non-religious home, and ended up marrying Deborah, who grew up in a Conservative family in upstate New York and made aliyah in 2006. He spent seven years in Montreal and New York and integrated into Jewish life in North America. Nimrod holds a bachelor's degree in hotel management and tourism and is a licensed tour guide. He has been working in the educational travel industry for the last twenty years and has had the pleasure of planning hundreds of trips to Israel and the Jewish world. Nimrod currently serves as Da'at's Senior Vice President.

Eran Shlomi

Eran Shlomi grew up in Azur, just outside Tel Aviv. After graduating from high school, he served the IDF in a combat intelligence unit and afterwards moved to Be'er Sheva in the Negev for his bachelor's and master's degree studies. While still working on his master's degree, focusing on medieval Europe, Christianity, and the Crusades, he took a guiding course and has been guiding groups in Israel and Morocco ever since. Eran is currently completing his PhD in Zionist history at Tel Aviv university while working as an educational director in Birthright Israel's department of education. He is a strong believer in encouraging his travelers to challenge their preconceptions and worldviews. To that end, he uses visual aids, music, and a lot of group engagement. Eran is happiest when guiding in the Judean and Negev Deserts, where there is a bit of everything – nature, landscapes, history, holy sites, archaeology, beaches, and tranquility. When not guiding, he enjoys playing the piano, touring Israel on his motorcycle, and eating good food.

Raz Shmilovich

Raz is forty-four years old, married to Moran, and is the proud father of four boys. He lives in Moshav Netiv Ha'asara by Israel's border with the Gaza Strip. Raz was born in Sinai when it was still a part of Israel, and in 1979, as the Egypt-Israel peace treaty was signed and Israel withdrew from the peninsula's territory, Raz's family along with the entire moshav moved to its current location. Raz holds a bachelor's degree in geography and environmental studies from Ben-Gurion University. His favorite place to guide is the desert, where nature and genesis meet. Becoming a tour guide was an easy choice for Raz. It combines three of his loves – Israel, people, and the outdoors. Raz volunteers at the moshav and at Hashomer Hahadash, a grassroots organization helping farmers and ranchers in the Negev and the Galilee safeguard their land through education and social action.

Netanel Zelicovich

Netanel Zelicovich is a Jerusalemite social entrepreneur and a member of the Haredi community. Growing up in the small town of Pardes Hana, Netanel became familiar with the non-Haredi world. After moving to Jerusalem, he noticed a real gap between the Haredi community and the rest of Israeli society. To bridge the chasm, Netanel spearheaded several educational activities in Jerusalem, chief among them "meetings outside of the box," an organization that brings groups from Israel and all over the world to Haredi neighborhoods. During those visits, the groups experience firsthand what Haredi life looks like: they spend time with local families, eat Haredi food, learn about Haredi fashion, tradition, and everything else that makes Haredi life so distinctive. Netanel is happily married and a father of four.

Lana Zilberman Soloway

Lana was born in Moscow and made aliyah with her family at the age of eight. After serving in the IDF as an intelligence officer, Lana obtained a dual bachelor's degree in East Asian studies from Hebrew University and a master's degree in professional Jewish studies from Spertus Institute for Jewish Learning and Leadership in Chicago. For the past three years, Lana has served as a research fellow in the field of Jewish Peoplehood at the Hartman Institute in Jerusalem, where she is also studying toward becoming a rabbi. She will be ordained in September 2021.

Lana began her career as a tour educator in 2008 and has since guided Federation missions, congregational trips, Birthright, Honeymoon Israel, families, and interfaith groups. She also leads Jewish heritage tours in Eastern and Central Europe, including a refugee relief mission to Greece and Berlin.

Lana is a part of the Reform movement in Israel and is dedicated to social justice causes and peacemaking as well as religious pluralism. Lana lives in Mevasseret Zion with her husband Daniel and three children, Talya Doron, Shalev Yehonatan, and Yael Shoshana.

Doron Wilfand

Doron was born and raised on Kibbutz Ein-Hashofet .He received a PhD in religious studies from Duke University and has been working for over 20 years as a licensed tour guide for Reform and Conservative Synagogue trips ,interfaith journeys ,Christian and Jewish pilgrimages, various Federation Missions ,JCRC study tours ,specialty tours with an emphasis on social and religious issues ,family tours ,business and law school tours ,and Birthright trips .Recently Doron is dedicating most of his spare time to trail running) including a-100 mile race (and song writing .Doron lives in Jerusalem with his wife Yael and their four children.

Acknowledgments

This book would not have been possible if not for the goodwill of many who gave of themselves to write these thoughtful essays. We thank these tour educators who happily contributed their valuable time, experience, and energy. If they hadn't agreed to open their hearts and share their personal experiences, you wouldn't be holding this book in your hands.

We owe special thanks to our gifted editor, Amnon Jackont, who throughout the process was there for us providing good advice and guidance, and who taught us the art of telling a personal story. To Sorelle Weinstein who helped "translate" our Israeli way of thinking into something comprehensible for English readers. Special thanks go to Sarah Mageni who further assisted in this important endeavor. Also, to Muki Jankelowitz who took upon himself the Sisyphean task of the final proofreading of the entire manuscript.

From the outset, we knew the artistic aspect of the book was very important to us. We would not have come this far without the generous help of Amon Yariv, the owner of the Gordon Gallery, the leading gallery of Israeli art. Thanks to him, we became acquainted with the extraordinary art of the painter Erez Aharon, who contributed his work to this book. We are grateful to Erez, who happily helped us explore the art he created, so we could choose the pictures best suited to us. On the artistic side, we would also like to thank Tal Hefner, Lior Gulsad and Avi Chai, who photographed Erez's work which was included in this book.

Many people have contributed helpful advice along the way and for that, special thanks to Rabbi Hara Person, Guy Millo, and Nimrod Shafran.

Creating a book is no simple task, but sharing it between the three of us made it a unique experience. For the past few months we've had a common dream. It took shape in long exhilarating conversations into the night, endless correspondence and a whole lot of team-spirit, arguing and laughing at the same time. We hope you enjoy reading this book as much as we enjoyed putting it together.